HISTORY OF BROADCASTING: RADIO TO TELEVISION

HISTORY OF BROADCASTING: Radio to Television

Economics
of the
Radio Industry

HIRAM L. JOME

ARNO PRESS and THE NEW YORK TIMES

New York • 1971

Reprint Edition 1971 by Arno Press Inc.

Reprinted from a copy in The Newark Public Library

LC# 75-161149
ISBN 0-405-03568-3

HISTORY OF BROADCASTING: RADIO TO TELEVISION
ISBN for complete set: 0-405-03555-1
See last pages of this volume for titles.

Manufactured in the United States of America

ECONOMICS OF THE RADIO INDUSTRY

BY

HIRAM L. JOME, Ph.D.

PROFESSOR OF ECONOMICS, DENISON UNIVERSITY

CHICAGO & NEW YORK
A. W. SHAW COMPANY
LONDON, A. W. SHAW AND COMPANY, LIMITED
1925

PREFACE

THE art and the science of wireless were more than 25 years old before the general public began to take much thought of the legal and economic problems which this development caused. This is characteristic of a constantly changing society. The time comes, however, when technical developments give rise to social problems of such magnitude that it would be folly to ignore them. Wireless communication has reached this stage. Scientists have so perfected this new agency of communication that its future organization and uses have become a matter of public concern. If the radio deserves a place alongside our other recognized social agencies and means of communication, then it behooves us to mold this instrument of service according to our desires. To accomplish this purpose, however, knowledge of the economic problems raised by wireless communication is a prerequisite.

The following chapters constitute a brief study of these problems. It is hoped that the presentation of this book to the public will stimulate further investigation of the many interesting problems in the radio field. Subjects which limitations of space have made it impossible to develop in this book but which afford fertile fields for further investigation include: labor policies in the radio industry, the radio in time of war, the radio and the aeroplane in international relations, the problem of property and sovereignty in the air, radio securities and their position in the investment field, the nature of the radio audience, financial histories of the important radio corporations, economic effects of the introduction of the short wave-length and the beam system, problems in the distribution and the selling of radio, processes in radio manufacturing, and many others.

In the perusal of this book the reader is earnestly requested to bear in mind that radio is much older than popularly supposed and that the telephone, which has done the most to popuuarize radio, is, from the social point of view, little, if any, more important than the radio telegraph. Both the telephone and the telegraph are used for two kinds of service; namely, broadcasting and point-to-point communication. We have thus four types of wireless communication and different principles apply to all.

The reader is also asked to keep in mind the central trend running throughout the discussion; otherwise the book will seem more of a labyrinth of details than a completed story. The writer has attempted to emphasize the principle of service throughout. The function of the radio is to render a more or less distinctive service of communication. From this point of view of service to the community the radio should be judged in comparison with other agencies of like character. The legal and economic problems of radio operation and regulation are fundamentally problems of social significance and it is appropriate to look upon these as service problems and to analyze them from the social point of view. This approach is indicated by the main divisions of the subject. In Part I the writer takes up the development and present extent of the radio industry. Part II is devoted to a consideration of the most effective ways of making this service available to the people. Part III considers the problems facing the organizations rendering radio service. Part IV is devoted to the future of the radio service and its relation to the other social agencies and means of communication.

In the preparation of this book the writer has secured aid from many sources. He has drawn freely from magazine articles, government reports, and books and investigations of others, as the numerous footnotes will indicate. Radio business men have been very cordial to him in his search for information and requests for interviews. Foreign governments, especially those of Canada and Great Britain, have turned over to him official documents in regard to the radio situation in their respective countries; W. E. Downey, radio supervisor of the Bureau of Navigation, and R. A. Lundquist, chief of the Electrical Division of the Bureau of Foreign and Domestic Commerce, granted several interviews. Of the people to whom the author is indebted none are responsible in any way for any of the opinions herein expressed. The writer also wishes to acknowledge aid from his colleagues at Denison University: Professor F. G. Detweiler of the Department of Economics and Sociology and Professor E. L. Jacobs of the Department of English (now at New Mexico State Teachers College) for reading and criticizing the book in manuscript, and Professor Richard H. Howe of the Department of Physics for preparing the first two sections in Chapter VIII.   Joseph L. Speicher, senior at Denison University, has prepared some of the tables and most of the charts, besides helping in the collection and the classification of the data involved.   Professor Harry R. Tosdal of the Graduate School of Business Administration at Harvard University and E. W. Morehouse of the Institute for Research in Land Economics and Public Utilities, have also criticized parts of the manuscript in detail.   The writer's wife has been very helpful during the course of the work. Miss Julia Rogers has aided with bits of constructive criticism.

Finally, the author has the great privilege of dedicating these efforts to Dr. Richard T. Ely, the eminent economist, who has carefully perused the manuscript and during the course of its preparation has always, in his beloved and characteristic manner, been ready with helpful suggestions and words of encouragement.

H. L. J.

Granville, Ohio, August 18, 1925.

CONTENTS

CONTENTS

Corporation and the future. World wireless by and for Americans. The "Big Four" and broadcasting. Service plans of the Marconi Company. Radio and the future.

APPENDIX

TABLES

FORMS

ECONOMICS OF THE RADIO INDUSTRY

PART I

DEVELOPMENT AND EXTENT OF THE
RADIO SERVICE

I

BEGINNINGS OF WIRELESS

The advent of Marconi. Predecessors of Marconi. Conduction. Induction. Electromagnetic waves. Marconi, the commercializer of radio. Wireless early brought to the service of man. Early use of radio for life-saving purposes. Use of radio for transmitting news. Marconi spans Atlantic. Appearance of DeForest. Importance of the vacuum tube. Development of wireless telephony. Effect of World War. Adaptation of wireless to aerial use. Practical services performed by aeroplane radio. Recent appeal of radio to popular imagination.

WE live in an age of rapid and miraculous mechanical achievement. Fifty years ago the man who ventured to prophesy that the sky-line of New York City would soon be broken by 40- and 50-story buildings was thought an idle dreamer. Today the development of structural steel construction has made this a common sight. Almost a century ago when Andrew Jackson was inaugurated, Nashville, Tennessee, was several days' ride by stage from Washington; today New York and Chicago are only 20 hours apart. The aeroplane will decrease this time by possibly 60%.

Viewed from the perspective of history, these achievements in building construction and transportation pale beside the developments in the field of electricity. When the commercial telegraph made its appearance in the forties, the most sanguine believer in the invention would hardly have supposed that wires could be dispensed with or that the human voice could be transmitted across a continent. Yet in 1925 the voice of Chief Justice Taft administering the oath of office to President Coolidge could be heard by millions of American citizens without leaving their homes. What is more, by the time a radio fan had listened to the inaugural address he might leave his home and see an actual photograph of the scene he had just heard. Similarly, in

3

1921, when President Harding officially opened the Radio Central on Long Island, 19 countries—including Japan, Australia, and New Zealand—acknowledged the President's message, four of them within 15 seconds. Again in 1921, David Sarnoff, vice-president and general manager of the Radio Corporation of America, in the course of a lecture in Boston, communicated with 16 ships at sea and with Great Britain, France, Germany, Norway, and Poland, received replies, and read them to his audience. The elapsed time for sending and receiving these messages ranged from 5 minutes to a half-hour.

Thus within the span of a single lifetime human standards of space and time have been revolutionized by man's ingenuity. These striking accomplishments are apparent and visible to every one. Back of the seen is the unseen, which in the future may prove yet more significant. Such mechanical improvements leave their mark on the social and economic structure. While we marvel at the perfection of radio, we tend to lose sight of the effects upon habits of living, upon popular judgments of men and affairs, upon economic organization and processes. The contraction of space and time may easily, but less obviously, even subconsciously, lead to an enlargement of mental horizons.

Such considerations as these give value to an economic and social study of radio as an agency of communication. An analysis of this kind cannot be restricted to the private aspects of the radio industry, but must necessarily include the discussion of economic and legal problems from the public point of view. Throughout it will be well for the reader to bear in mind that we are dealing with a new medium of communication that is just beginning to take its place alongside other and well-established agencies rendering similar service. Consequently, the public aspects of radio may be expected to gain increasing prominence as the industry develops on both its technical and economic sides.

Finally, it is evident that any economic analysis of the radio industry must start from a brief summary of its technical development. This is necessitated not only by the fact that the radio is still undergoing rapid improvements in technique, but also by the fact that the economic aspects of the industry have unfolded hand in hand with the advance in technique. In truth, remarkable technical accomplishments are part of the unseen progress which has brought the radio to its present position. We see today what seems to be a comparatively perfect instrument, but behind this present-day state of comparative perfection lie the struggles and accomplishments of scores of inventors and investigators. Let us first analyze the work of some of the more important of these pioneers.

THE ADVENT OF MARCONI

In the spring of 1896, a modest Irish-Italian youth of 22 arrived in London from his Italian home and applied for the first British patent for wireless telegraphy. Sir William H. Preece, the chief electrical engineer of the Post-Office, who had done some experimenting in wireless himself, was very courteous and helpful to the youth, asking him to set up his apparatus in the General Post-Office in London.

The young inventor was Guglielmo Marconi. After his arrival in England, he carried on further experiments under the observation of the postal authorities.[1] In September, 1896, he succeeded in transmitting a message over a distance of 100 yards. Mr. Preece was so greatly impressed with Marconi's success that he referred to his devices as "highly novel and very beautiful." In June of the next year he summarized other steps of progress in these words:

"The distance to which signals have been sent is remarkable. On Salisbury Plain Marconi covered a distance of four miles. In the Bristol Channel this has been extended to over eight miles, and we have by no means reached the limit. It is interesting to read the surmises of others. Half

---

[1] In Great Britain the Postmaster-General exercises control over matters of communication.

a mile was the wildest dream."[1] The "surmise" referred to
was probably that of Sir Oliver Lodge, who said concerning
some of the earlier experiments in wireless: "I mention 40
yards because that was one of the first out-of-door experiments, but I should think something more like half a mile
was nearer the limit of sensibility. However, this is a rash
statement not at present verified."[2]

Thus, from humble beginnings has radio communication
developed into a potent reality.

PREDECESSORS OF MARCONI

Guglielmo Marconi was not, however, the originator of
the idea and theory of radio. For many years men had
worked on the problem of wireless communication. Their
efforts may be summarized under the following three heads:
(1) conduction, (2) induction, (3) electromagnetic waves.

CONDUCTION

The essential characteristic of the principle of conduction
is the use of some sort of material substance for the transmission of sound waves or electrical energy. The old custom of the Indians who placed the ear close to the ground
in order to detect the presence of enemies is familiar to us.
The material early used for electrical conduction was either
the earth or water. By this method wires were stretched
along opposite banks of a body of water—for example, a
river. These wires were grounded at both ends, so that
when a current of electricity was sent through the one circuit, some of it passed by means of the water as a conductor
to the circuit on the opposite side. Thus, by the breaking
and connecting of the circuit into a system of dots and
dashes, a message could be transmitted. Morse is given

---

[1]Speech June 11, 1897, before the Royal Institute of Great Britain,
reprinted in the *Report of the Smithsonian Institute*, 1898, p. 256. See also
213 Fed. Rep. 815 at 830.

[2]*The Work of Hertz*, p. 18.

the credit for the discovery of this principle in 1842.[1] The weakness of the method was the great length of the wire circuits needed in proportion to the distance covered, which was never more than three miles.[2]

INDUCTION

The method of induction may be subdivided into electromagnetic and electrostatic. The essential characteristic of the former is the running of a current through a wire circuit, which sets up an electromagnetic field cutting the wires of a second circuit, thus inducing a current therein. Electrostatic induction, on the other hand, depends upon the existence of a variation of potential in two circuits. Faraday discovered the latter phenomenon in the year 1831. Thomas A. Edison developed a system of communication between railway stations and moving trains without the use of connecting wires. In 1891 he took out a United States patent (465,971) for "a signaling system having elevated induction plates, supported on masts and connected with the earth."[3] Concerning this invention Mr. Edison stated: "If sufficient elevation be obtained to overcome the curvature of the earth's surface and to reduce to the minimum the earth's absorption, electric telegraphing or signaling between distant points can be carried on by induction without the use of wires connecting such distant points."[4] But as a means of communication without wires, induction, like conduction, is today of only historical importance.

---

[1]For the names and achievements of others who proceeded on this principle, see Chronology in the Appendix.

[2]An English scientist stated that in 1888 the dynamo at one of the electric lighting plants in London through some derangement became connected to the earth. The railway telegraphs in South London were temporarily put out of order, while the currents flowing in the earth were received as far north as Leicester and as far south as Paris. Speech of Professor Silvanus P. Thompson, F. R. S., in 1898, published in *Smithsonian Institute Report* for 1898, p. 235. Professor Thompson here gives a very good description of early attempts at wireless.

[3]213 Fed. 815 at 818.

[4]*Ibid.*

ELECTROMAGNETIC WAVES

The next and the successful method attempted was the employment of electromagnetic waves. Maxwell, in 1867, saw the possibility of the existence of electrical waves. He did not, however, prove it except by mathematical deduction. It remained for Heinrich Hertz, professor of physics at Bonn University, to prove the physical being of such waves. Hertz experimented with a wire circuit which contained a spark gap. When a current was sent through this coil, the pressure finally became so great that the air between the balls became highly conductive, producing a spark in the ether which resulted in the radiation of a wave. These waves, Hertz concluded, are radiated through space in all directions by means of the ether.

The real contribution which Hertz made was the discovery of a means of detecting the presence of such radiation. He invented a simple device consisting of a turn of wire provided with a small spark gap between two metallic knobs. As this loop was held near an oscillator, described in the preceding paragraph, the waves struck it and set up impulses which revealed themselves by minute sparks at the gaps. This apparatus is called the resonator.[1]

While Hertz did not make any practical use of his discovery, his experiments and disclosures aroused wide-spread interest. Other scientists took up the development of wireless. Sir Oliver Lodge was one of Hertz's disciples, and he, together with Edouard Branly, devised the coherer for the detection of electromagnetic waves.[2] Sir William Crookes in 1892 predicted the commercial use of radio through the propagation and reception of electromagnetic waves, reveal-

---

[1] The description of Hertz's apparatus is taken freely from the opinion of Federal Judge Veeder in 213 Fed. 815 at 821. For accounts of Hertz, see *Reports of the Smithsonian Institute*, 1889 and 1894.

[2] The coherer consists essentially of a glass tube filled with filings, in either end of which are sealed terminal wires. When an electric current is passed through this device, the filings are arranged so as to serve as a conductor. When it is slightly tapped by an automatic device, the circuit is broken.

ing a "new and astonishing world—which is almost within the grasp of daily life."

MARCONI, THE COMMERCIALIZER OF RADIO

This was the condition of radio when Marconi began his experiments. Men had dreamed and experimented in wireless for 60 years. "Keen intellects and indomitable wills—one after another—never ceased to be turned to the solution of the problem [of communication without wires]. First, they sought the answer in one direction, then in another. Ever there was a reply sufficient to keep the ball rolling—to keep the ranks of the investigators full; and the achievement of one generation of workers after another served as the stepping-stones over which their successors moved to more assured success, until finally the goal was won."[1]

Into this state of scientific knowledge appeared Marconi, the commercializer of radio. His forerunners had predicted and speculated; Marconi acted. "I believe," he said in his claims, "that I am the first to discover and use any practical means for effective telegraphic transmission and intelligible reception of signals produced by artificially formed Hertz oscillations." He used or improved the oscillator of Hertz and the coherer of Lodge. He, however, inserted a Morse key in the sending apparatus and thus cut the current into a definite system of dots and dashes. All these devices are at the present time out of date in wireless communication, but in addition Marconi contributed the grounded vertical antenna attached to both the transmitting and the receiving apparatus, which his predecessors had not developed.[2]

We must admit that Marconi was not a pioneer like Morse in wire telegraphy or like Bell in wire telephony. He did not discover the principles of radio. In his original

---

[1]Story, A. T., *The Story of Wireless Telegraphy*, 1904, p. 10.

[2]There is some evidence, however, that certain predecessors of Marconi had also conceived the idea of the vertical antenna.

application for a patent he claimed only to have made *"improvements* in transmitting electrical impulses and signals and apparatus therefor" by means of Hertzian waves.[1] Marconi coordinated the principles of others, improving their operation by additional devices of his own invention, and thus made radio a commercial possibility.

Like Bell in the wire telephone field, Morse in the wire telegraph, and Fulton and Stephenson in water and land transport, Marconi at first met with skepticism and criticism. Wise men denied the practical value of the invention. It was a mere plaything, a toy to engage the attention of theorists.[2] But Marconi continued his efforts in his chosen field. In November, 1897, the first Marconi station was constructed on the Isle of Wight off the south coast of England, from which experiments were conducted covering a range of 14½ miles. On December 6, of the same year, signals were transmitted from shore to a ship at sea 18 miles distant.[3]

WIRELESS EARLY BROUGHT TO THE SERVICE OF MAN

With the growing success of his apparatus, Marconi early looked about for methods of making it of practical value. Armies had made use of the land telegraph and telephone, but up to the invention of the wireless, the navies of the world were forced to depend upon wigwagging and other primitive methods of signaling. It was, therefore, to be expected that wireless would find its first extensive use for communication at sea. The year 1897 saw the Marconi system adopted by the Italian navy. In 1899 tests were made on a large scale by the British Admiralty, resulting in the subsequent installation of wireless on 32 warships

---

[1] 213 Fed. 815 at 833. Italics the writer's.

[2] See, for example, Marconi's complaint of the attitude of cable companies in an interview in *Technical World Magazine*, October, 1912, pp. 145-150 at 149; and *Investors' Review*, December 21, 1901, p. 776.

[3] An enumeration of the record distances reached would be superfluous. The reader has only to consult the Chronology in the Appendix, and note that the progress of Marconi in conquering distance was very rapid.

and shore stations.[1]   W. K. Towers cites a British "sham battle in which all the orders were sent by radio, and communication was constantly maintained both between the flagships and the vessels of their fleets and between the flagships and the shore."[2]   On April 22, 1899, the first French gunboat was fitted with wireless telegraph apparatus; in 1899 tests were made by the United States navy; and in the year 1900 Belgian and German shipping companies installed radio.

EARLY USE OF RADIO FOR LIFE-SAVING PURPOSES

Likewise, radio stations were very early installed on lightships, and wireless was introduced for life-saving purposes. In 1899 the East Godwin Lightship was damaged by collision with a steamer, and the accident was reported by wireless.   On January 19, 1901, the SS Princesse Clementine ran ashore, and news of the accident was flashed through the ether to Ostend.   The momentous aid given by wireless in saving passengers in the collision between the SS Republic and SS Florida impressed upon the governments of the world the necessity of having radio on ships as a life-saving device.   In rapid succession several nations passed acts requiring radio equipment and operators on certain vessels carrying more than a specified number of people.   At present radio is widely used for reporting distress signals, positions of icebergs, storm and time signals, direction finding, and many other things needful for the safeguarding of life and property.[3]

---

[1] 213 Fed. 815 at 830-831.

[2] *Masters of Space*, 1917, p. 215.   In this book the author gives a very interesting description of the development of wireless as well as cable, wire telegraph, and wire telephonic communication.

[3] In January, 1924, because of the breakdown of wire communication, radio was used during a blizzard in the region of the Great Lakes for dispatching trains.   For several days wireless was the only means of communication between Chicago and the outside world.   Pacific cables were broken during the terrific Japan earthquake of 1923.   Full details of the disaster were given to the world by radio.

USE OF RADIO FOR TRANSMITTING NEWS

Concurrently with the scientific development of radio came its ever-increasing use as a means of transmitting news. The events of the Kingstown regatta, July 20-22, 1898, were reported by wireless from the steamer Flying Huntress for the *Dublin Daily Express*. The news was sent from the Marconi-equipped vessel to a specially erected land station, whence a telephone wire carried it to the newspaper office. Only two weeks later, at the request of Queen Victoria, wireless communication was established between the Royal Yacht Obsorne and Ladywood Cottage, Osborne, in order that her Majesty might communicate with her son, the Prince of Wales, who lay ill on his yacht. One hundred and fifty messages passed by wireless between the two during the 16 days the system was in use.[1]

The international yacht races of September and October, 1899, were reported by wireless for the New York *Herald*. Newspapers began to be published aboard ship, the first known being the *Transatlantic Times* printed on the SS St. Paul in the fall of 1899. A wireless message informed the world of the surrender of Port Arthur. In 1904 the first press message was transmitted across the Atlantic. Numerous passenger and even freight steamers now publish newspapers for distribution to passengers or crew. High-power stations daily send news messages among all the nations of the world. It is needless to mention the fact that during this stupendous development, the use of radio for commercial purposes was being enlarged. June 3, 1898, was the date of the transmission of the first paid radiogram.[2]

MARCONI SPANS ATLANTIC

After seeing the early practical application of his inventions and improvements, Marconi sought to perfect his

---

[1] Towers, *Masters of Space*, p. 213.

[2] Sent by Lord Kelvin (William Thompson) from the Wight station.

methods. He attempted to increase the range and sensitiveness of his apparatus. After conquering Western Europe, he attacked the problem of transatlantic communication. For this purpose he constructed a powerful station at Poldhu, England. The aerials were, after difficulties in erection, finally supported by four wooden towers, each 210 feet high. This was to serve as the transmitting end of his transatlantic experiment. The receiving apparatus was installed in Newfoundland.

Let Marconi tell the story: "I landed quietly, on December 9, 1901, at St. Johns in Newfoundland, with my two assistants . . . and set my instruments in a low room in the old barracks of Signal Hall, which stands about half a mile from the town of St. Johns. . . .

"I had cabled my assistants to begin sending signals on December 12 at 3:00 p.m. in England and continue until about 6 p.m., which hours correspond to about 11:30 to 2:30 in St. Johns."

On the morning of December 12 Marconi filled a balloon and sent it with the aerial through a thick fog—about 400 feet in the air. "I remained waiting an hour without a sound, except the roaring sea, to break the silence. Then suddenly I heard the tapper as it struck against the coherer. I listened, my hand trembling with excitement. A few minutes' pause, and again I heard, faintly yet distinctly, the three low clicks, signifying the letter 'S.' My assistants were in the other room, and unable to control myself, I exclaimed: 'Gentlemen, did you hear it?' The question was solved and I experienced a feeling of the greatest joy. . . ."[1] In another connection in the same account Marconi said: "The mere memory of it makes me shudder. It may seem a simple story to the world, but to me it was a question of the life and death of my future."

Thus was the Atlantic spanned—a distance of 1,800 miles. Marconi was then only 27 years old.

[1] Quoted in an interview in the *Technical World Magazine* for October, 1912, p. 145.

APPEARANCE OF DE FOREST

Here we take leave of Marconi the inventor. In Chapter
II we shall see him as the business man, the exploiter of his
patents. This Irish-Italian youth had, however, by no
means a monopoly of the radio imagination. While he was
making application for his patent in London, another young
enthusiast, Lee DeForest, of Iowa, was graduating from
Yale University. After receiving his Doctor of Philosophy
degree at Yale in 1899, DeForest obtained employment with
the Western Electric Company in Chicago, testing and
assembling at $8 a week. He had followed the work of
Marconi and his predecessors, and now he set about improving their methods.[1]

Marconi had used the coherer invented by Lodge and
Branly. Instead of this device DeForest attempted to use
the gas flame as a rectifier of radio currents, but with little
success. In the meantime an English scientist, Dr. J.
Ambrose Fleming, had taken the Edison hot and cold electrode incandescent lamp and used it for the rectification of
wireless waves. (Edison in his search for the principle of
the electric light had, in the course of his "trial and error"
experiments, devised a two-electrode lamp Not knowing
that he had constructed a rough vacuum tube, Edison
abandoned this device.) This was the so-called two-electrode audion. A patent was granted Fleming on November 7, 1905.[2] Some time in this interval DeForest began
a series of experiments upon the same principle. He added
another element, the grid—making three in all, the filament,

---

[1] For stories of DeForest's life, see an article entitled "The Man Who
Made Broadcasting Possible," by Owen MacLean in the *American Magazine*
for February, 1924; a serial article on the life of DeForest in *Radio News*,
beginning October, 1924; and "Making Wireless History with DeForest"; a
series of articles in *Radio Broadcast*, beginning December, 1924.

Professor E. A. Dolbear, of Tufts College, had been issued a United
States patent for a radiotelegraph system in 1881. See Newark, Ohio,
Advocate, December 5, 1924.

[2] Not till 1906 were the rectifying qualities of carborundum and silicon
crystals discovered by Dunwoody and Pickard, respectively. These discoveries form the basis of the widely used crystal detectors.

the plate and the grid—and from 1906 to 1908 was granted several patents based on this method of reception.[1]

IMPORTANCE OF THE VACUUM TUBE

The discovery of the audion, the "magic lamp of radio," is probably the most important milestone in the history of the wireless art since the original invention of Marconi. This device has multiplied the sensitivity of radio receiving apparatus, and in its later use in transmitting sets has greatly increased the range and lowered the cost of operation.

DEVELOPMENT OF WIRELESS TELEPHONY

Just as the discovery of the wire telegraph led to the search for the means and methods of wire telephony, so the development of radio telegraphy was followed by the advance of radio telephony. Important progress had been made by Armstrong, Fessenden, Branly, Hazeltine, and many others; but it remained for the American Telephone and Telegraph Company to make radio telephony a commercial possibility.

The work was in charge of John J. Carty, chief engineer of the Bell System, who associated with himself some of the foremost men in the field. After a number of successful short-distance tests, Mr. Carty, in the latter part of 1915, conducted an experiment which showed that wireless telephony was no longer a dream but an accomplished fact. The words of President Theodore Vail, spoken into the telephone of his New York office, were carried by wire to the Arlington Naval Station near Washington, whence they were broadcast by wireless. Mr. Carty, in Mare Island, California, carried on a free and easy conversation with his president. It is interesting to note that a few hours later, words sent on the air at Arlington were heard not only at Mare Island, but were also intercepted in Hawaii and

[1] For litigation between the assignees of these patents, see Chapter XI.

Panama. In the same year wireless telephonic communication was established between Arlington and Paris.[1] In 1924 wireless telephone conversation on a short wave length was carried on between Australia and England.

Some idea of the comparatively rapid development of the radio telephone is conveyed by the fact that though the wire telephone had been successfully demonstrated by Bell at the Philadelphia Centennial in 1876, the continent had not been spanned by wire telephone until January, 1915, only eight months before the Vail-Carty demonstration.

EFFECT OF WORLD WAR

The World War and the years following saw a rapid growth in both wireless telephony and telegraphy. Very early in the war the cables to Germany were cut, and the United States communicated with the Central Powers by means of wireless.[2] The year 1918 witnessed great progress toward continuous-wave communication. This development derived impetus from the steady evolution of the electron tube as an efficient receiver and generator of undamped oscillations. Aircraft were equipped with both telephonic and telegraphic apparatus. The United States army and navy maintained schools for instruction and research in the art. During the war the government undertook the operation of practically all land and ship stations. Progress was made in direction-finding and submarine-detection.

ADAPTATION OF WIRELESS TO AERIAL USE

One of the outstanding wireless achievements shortly before and during the World War was its adaptation to aerial use. Even earlier than 1914 France and Great Britain had developed "one way sets," which were capable of send-

[1]Towers, *Masters of Space*, chap. xx, and 1915 *Report* of Bell System.
[2]The Sayville, Long Island, and Nauen, Germany, circuit had been put in operation in 1914.

ing messages to the ground, but provided no means of receiving signals by wireless. The first successful American attempt at radio transmission from aeroplane to ground was made August 27, 1910, at Sheepshead Bay, Long Island. One year later, at an aviation meet on Long Island, a wireless message was transmitted from aeroplane to ground over a distance of 2 miles. In the summer of 1912 radio communication was established from an army aeroplane over Laurel, Maryland, to Washington, a distance of 25 miles. In the fall of the same year at Fort Riley, Kansas, this distance was increased to 50 miles.

Partly because of the difficulty of excluding the noise of the motor and the propeller, the receiving of wireless messages on an aeroplane was a later development. The reception of signals amid the noise of the powerful aeroplane engine presents more difficulties than their interception in a quiet sound-proof chamber. In December, 1914, however, telegraphic messages were received over a distance of 6 miles.

PRACTICAL SERVICES PERFORMED BY AEROPLANE RADIO

In the field of telephony, the progress of aeroplane radio was even slower. It is always more difficult to understand the human voice than it is to follow a system of dots and dashes. In fact, this phase was developed in the United States almost entirely between April, 1917, and the signing of the armistice.[1]

The radio telephone and telegraph as applied to aircraft are already proving of great value in commercial aviation. Just as a seagoing vessel needs constant communication, especially with the shore, so does the aeroplane need to be in touch with the various stations and aerodromes along the route. In foggy and dark weather, direction-finding and

---

[1] *United States Army Aircraft Production Facts* compiled January, 1919, at the request of the Assistant Secretary of War, by Colonel G. W. Mixter and Lieutenant H. H. Emmons of the Bureau of Aircraft Production, pp. 86-92.

position-locating apparatus is necessary; as the number of planes increases, the ground stations must maintain a system of traffic control through dispatching officers; the pilots must be cognizant of weather forecasts and storm signals. All these functions can be performed only by the use of radio. The United States is utilizing a chain of radio stations in connection with its transcontinental air mail. England is maintaining a regular radio service for its London Continental airways.[1]

RECENT APPEAL OF RADIO TO THE POPULAR IMAGINATION

Only comparatively recently, however, has wireless attracted much popular attention. The general public associates radio with telephonic broadcasting, which has of late received increasing publicity. The first United States licenses for broadcasting stations were issued in September, 1921. Out of this fact has come the impression that wireless broadcasting has been a spontaneous and instantaneous growth. For example, *The Outlook* recently remarked editorially: "It has all come about from the development of broadcasting, a lusty child *not yet three years of age*, who, nurtured on the rich milk of free publicity, has cut its teeth and now craves the strong meat of profit. Here *in a moment*[2] has sprung up a device by which an idea, a suggestion, an impulse, may be communicated to an innumerable number of people at one and the same time, a possibility *heretofore undreamed of.*"[3]

On the contrary, however, broadcasting did not spring up

[1] Germany, France, Italy, Holland, and Belgium are also maintaining such service.

The reader who is interested in following out the methods and technique of aviation radio will find valuable material in the article on "Signaling on Our Airways," by Duncan Sinclair, of the Department of Communication, British Air Ministry; and in the regulations and procedure for aeroplane signaling. These may be found in the aviation section of the 1922 *Year Book of Wireless Telegraphy and Telephony.*

[2] Italics the present writer's.

[3] Italics the present writer's. March 29, 1924, article entitled "Broadcasting and the Public Interest."

in a moment. June 2, 1917, had marked the "coming of age" of wireless telegraphy. More than 80 years ago scientists were dreaming of world-wide wireless. Broadcasting is the result of 30 years of steady technical evolution, of hard and tedious study, of early public antipathy and antagonism, of gruesome patent litigation, and of heartrending struggles with poverty. The United States naval radio stations have for many years been broadcasting weather and time signals, instructions to vessels, and news reports. During the writer's war service in the United States Navy, he had many occasions to copy broadcast messages from American, English, French, and German stations. The inventor DeForest broadcast a program by Caruso in the Metropolitan Opera House in the winter of 1908-1909, 13 years before the first broadcasting station was licensed in the United States.

It is true, however, that the last three years have witnessed an unprecedented development of telephonic broadcasting for entertainment. If Caruso were able today to sing in the radiophone, he would have an audience not of a hundred nearby amateurs, but of millions of scattered radio enthusiasts both in the United States and abroad. The songs could be received and rebroadcast in other nations. His program could be heard by the millionaire in his mansion, by the king in his palace, by the farmer in his farmhouse, by the laborer in his cottage, by the explorer in the arctic zone, by the sailor on the bosom of the sea, by the passenger on the train. Not only those who can patronize grand opera, but also multitudes of people in all walks of life, from diverse parts of the earth, would be within the range of the famous Italian voice. The social and political significance of being able to reach such great audiences depends in large measure upon the future use of this agency of communication.

II

EARLY ORGANIZATION FOR SERVICE

Need of organization. Early financial difficulties. Beginnings of world system. Early strife. Marconi and the radiotelegraph conventions. Continued growth of Marconi system. The "imperial chain." Prosperity. Compulsory installation of ship radio. Charges of corruption. Continued extension of control. Fall in price of stock. Post-war developments. Other early wireless companies. The United Fruit Company. The Federal Telegraph Company. The DeForest Company.

MARCONI is a business man as well as an inventor and a scientist. Hardly had he applied for his original patent from the British Post-Office before he had taken steps for the exploitation of his invention and its enlistment in the service of man. The public had to be educated to the use of radio for such purposes as naval, life-saving, and general marine communication, for sending press dispatches and commercial messages. Apparatus had to be manufactured, wireless stations installed and operated, and arrangements made with foreign countries and companies for the handling of their end of international communication. Marconi understood all this. Instead of selling his rights to existing companies, he undertook the establishment of a new corporation, which later he hoped to make the center and nucleus of a world-wide organization.

The Wireless Telegraph and Signal Company was incorporated in England on July 20, 1897. It acquired the title to all of Marconi's patents in every country in the world except Italy and its dependencies. The capital was originally fixed at £100,000, but it was increased in 1898 to £200,000. Mr. Marconi himself became one of the first six directors and has remained a director of the company ever since.

Of the original capitalization of £100,000, £75,000 was

devoted to the payment for patents and patent rights.[1] This fact, as well as the lack of earnings from the very beginning, led the *Investors' Review* to remark rather caustically:

From all we can gather the public will be well advised to keep clear of this concern.... Signor Marconi's ingenious ideas do not seem to have made much headway, and it would be interesting to learn what the government officials reported about them.[2]

In March, 1900, the name of this corporation was changed to Marconi's Wireless Telegraph Company, Limited. This has been, and is today, the chief Marconi Company, and will sometimes be referred to as the British Marconi Company.

EARLY FINANCIAL DIFFICULTIES

During the first two years of its existence this corporation apparently made no financial headway. It did very little remunerative business; its profit and loss statements showed a continuous deficit, for the wireless business was still in the experimental stage. Marconi did not, however, give up hope. Several ships were fitted with the new apparatus, and the results of these experiments were such that the company expected to see its system adopted for the use of the British navy.

In spite of the fact that the income statements of the company showed an excess of expenditures over receipts, the common stock of the corporation was selling, in 1899, at £4½,[3] the par value being only £1. To justify this high price a return of at least 30% would appear to be necessary, but no dividend on this stock was paid by the British company until 1911. It is apparent, therefore, that the attitude of the public toward this new industry and company was one of optimistic speculation. When the corporation issued new shares, they were always snapped up at a premium.

---

[1]Vendor received £60,000 in shares, £15,000 in cash.

[2]Issue of October 7, 1898, p. 484.

[3]Figure from *Investors Monthly Manual.*

BEGINNINGS OF WORLD SYSTEM

But Marconi saw that expansion was necessary. Wireless was proving itself especially adaptable for the use of ships at sea; foreign territory was coming into sight as a fair field for the development of radio. Within a period of 10 years he organized subsidiaries to carry on the work in a half-dozen countries and on the high seas, retaining for himself and associated directors of the original company an interest in the new companies (as well as in those still later organized) both in the form of stock ownership and also of representation on the boards of directors.[1]

EARLY STRIFE

The British Marconi Company and its various subsidiaries became what appeared to certain interests to be a

[1] The Marconi Wireless Telegraph Company of America was chartered in 1899 by the state of New Jersey. This company built stations on both the Atlantic and the Pacific coasts of the United States. The Marconi International Marine Communication Company was organized one year later under the laws of Great Britain for the purpose of carrying on the operation of wireless aboard ships. Corporations were also early organized in Belgium (1901), in France (1903), in Canada (1903), in Argentina (1906), in Russia (1908), and in Spain (1910).

The holdings of the British company in the various associates have been of a more or less shifting nature. The following table from the 1917 *Moody's Manual, Public Utilities Section*, gives the holdings of the Marconi parent on December 31, 1912.

STOCK HELD BY BRITISH MARCONI COMPANY, DECEMBER 31, 1912

Shares (Number)	Company	Amount Par Value
198,790	Marconi International Marine..........................	£198,790
	Cia Marconi de Teleg. sin Hilos del Rio de la Plata.	
157,740	Series AA...................................	157,740
78,250	Series BB...................................	27,387
566,826	Marconi Wireless Teleg. Co. of America................	566,826
414,855	Marconi Wireless Teleg. Co. of Canada................	414,855
250	Marconi Press Agency...........................	50
240	Cia Nacional de Teleg. sin Hilos (Pfd.)	4,444
11,560	Societe Russe de Tel et Tel sans Fil....................	122,340
100,750	Spanish and General Wireless Trust....................	100,750
	Cie Francaise Maritime et Coloniale de Teleg. sans Fil	
175	Ordinary....................................	700
90	Parts. benefic.................................	......
100	Founders' shares...............................	700

monopoly. The International Marine was rapidly installing apparatus on ships of many nations. Shore stations
were being established to carry on transoceanic, as well as
ship to ship, and ship to shore, traffic. The parent company
and its subsidiaries were buying up the patent rights of a
large number of inventors, including those of Fleming and
Sir Oliver Lodge. The American Marconi Company erected
eight high-power stations in the United States and Hawaii.
Other subsidiaries were increasing their facilities. Marconi
dreamed of world-wide wireless.

Foreign nations beheld this development and began to
show signs of fear. In 1897 the German Professor Slaby
had come to London to witness Marconi's experiments. He
had then gone back to Germany and had caused wireless
apparatus to be manufactured by a German company—Die
Allgemeine Electricitäts-Gesellschaft. We have no proof of
infringement, for Professor Slaby had for many years been
working on the idea of wireless telegraphy. On his return
from England, however, he admitted that his efforts had
been in vain and that Marconi had apparently solved the
problem of radio communication.

The competition between this new German enterprise and
the Marconi Company was not on an equal basis. Wireless
apparatus is valuable only so long as there are messages to
be heard and receiving stations to hear them. A radio set
on board ship is useless unless there are shore stations with
which it may communicate. The Marconi companies had
very early recognized this fact, and while the International
Marine was installing ship stations, the parent company or
its associates were erecting shore stations. So the growth
in the number of ships installing the apparatus was commensurate with the increase in the number of land stations.
The German company, however, adopted a different policy.
It installed radio apparatus on board vessels but failed
to erect the necessary number of coastal stations. The
German-equipped ships were thus forced to rely on the Marconi stations for the shore end of the communication circuit.

The British company and its subsidiaries immediately objected. Why should they feed their competitors? If I manage to tap a telephone wire with my own apparatus, could I force the telephone company to accept my message? Would not the telephone company be justified in refusing to listen until I had installed the apparatus which it required? Would I not be encroaching upon the telephone company's prerogative of using its inventions as it sees fit? Thus the Marconi interests argued. So they forbade their coastal and ship stations to communicate with any vessel equipped with German sets. The Marconi operators were not even permitted to relay for any station using a different type of apparatus. This attitude naturally placed the German-equipped ships in a dilemma. With no one with whom to communicate, the sets became practically worthless. The result was that the German apparatus was being dropped and replaced with Marconi.

MARCONI AND THE RADIOTELEGRAPH CONVENTIONS

The German Imperial Government now took action, and sent official notes to a number of foreign nations, including the United States. These notes declared that England was attempting to obtain a monopoly in the field of wireless just as she had done in submarine cable communication. Germany requested the foreign powers to help overthrow this threatened monopoly. She invited the nations of the world to convene at Berlin in 1903 for the purpose of drawing up an international agreement for the regulation of wireless.

This conference met as planned, but accomplished little. Three years later, however, another similar convention, held in the same city, reached an important agreement.[1] The clause (Art. IV) which interests us in this connection stipulates that with certain exceptions, intercommunication among companies and countries must not be refused on account of differences in the system of wireless telegraphy

[1] See Chapter XII.

used. It provides for the exchange of radio messages without regard to whether any business or commercial arrangement for the interchange of traffic has been made or not.

The Marconi companies were up in arms against this international agreement. Strong pressure was brought against its adoption and ratification in both England and the United States. Magazine articles were written; interviews were given out; speeches were delivered; and representatives of the companies appeared at legislative hearings to argue against this unfair and enforced "partnership in which one partner furnished all."

The British Government faced a serious issue. If they refused to ratify the convention, and if Marconi maintained his attitude of non-intercommunication, the result would necessarily be that Marconi apparatus would have to be removed from all ships and stations belonging to the assenting countries. This would seriously retard British wireless development and would "diminish the scope and effectiveness of the Marconi organization."

On the other hand, if Great Britain ratified the convention, and if Marconi maintained his avowed purpose of non-intercommunication, then the government and the company would possibly end their hitherto friendly and cooperative relations. The two had always maintained a spirit of friendliness and good-will. The prosperity of the Marconi interests and of the English Government seemed to be closely interlinked. Furthermore, if the government ratified this convention, the Marconi interests might cause legal trouble under an earlier agreement between them and the government, whereby it was agreed that in case the Berlin convention were ratified, the patent rights of the company should be kept intact. The company might refuse to obey the International Convention on this ground.[1]

---

[1] For a detailed statement of the objections of the American Marconi Company to the ratification of the Berlin Convention of 1906, see Hearings before the House Committee on Merchant Marine and Fisheries on bill H. R. 15357 to regulate radio communication, 1912, pp. 114 ff; and article by H. Cuthbert Hall in *Empire Review* for 1908, p. 548.

The British committee appointed to investigate this difficult problem recommended the adoption of the convention. But it stipulated that if the company could show a loss, then the government would compensate it for a period of three years, the computation of the loss to be based upon a comparison with the average annual net traffic receipts from British stations during the three years preceding the ratification.

CONTINUED GROWTH OF MARCONI SYSTEM

In spite of the early charges of monopoly, the Marconi system continued its steady growth. Magazines which at first had derided the company as the dream of an impractical theorist, were so impressed by its accomplishments that they eventually became out-and-out Marconi partisans. Nations were beginning to see the benefits of marine wire-

TABLE I

INCREASE IN AUTHORIZED STOCK OF BRITISH MARCONI COMPANY

Year
1897 capital was £100,000
1898 capital was increased from £ 100,000 to £ 200,000
1903 capital was increased from 200,000 to 300,000
1905 capital was increased from 300,000 to 500,000
1908 capital was increased from 500,000 to 750,000
1911 capital was increased from 750,000 to 1,000,000
1913 capital was increased from 1,000,000 to 1,500,000
1919 capital was increased from 1,500,000 to 3,000,000
1922 capital was increased from 3,000,000 to 4,000,000*

*Computed from data in *Stock Exchange Official Intelligence* (London). In February, 1925, the directors announced the offering to stockholders of an additional 500,000 one-pound shares at 27½ shillings per share. This is, however, included in the authorized stock of 1922.

less and were either urging the installation of apparatus or were enacting laws providing for the compulsory use of a radio system on ships of certain types. Striking examples of the use of wireless for the saving of life at sea were multiplying and were creating a favorable public sentiment[1]

[1]See Chronology in Appendix.

To accommodate the growing business the Marconi Company and its subsidiaries from time to time increased their capitalization. The parent needed more capital in order to hold its interest in the subsidiaries, which were constantly growing and increasing in number. Table I will illustrate the capital stock increase of the British Marconi Company.

The common stock of the British Marconi Company paid its first dividends in the year 1911, and has passed no dividends since that year. The annual dividend disbursements of the company from 1911 to 1924 have averaged about 18%.

THE "IMPERIAL CHAIN"

The British Marconi Company, like the Radio Corporation of America, has looked with longing eyes toward the formation of a system of world-wide wireless. In the case of England it has been called the "imperial chain." Although several contracts have been entered into with the British Government, the most interesting was the agreement with the Postmaster-General in 1912. Under this contract the Marconi Company was to construct all the long-distance wireless stations necessary for the imperial wireless chain. The stations were to be used for commercial purposes. The company was to begin immediately the construction of stations in England, Cyprus or Egypt, Aden, Bangalore, South Africa, Singapore, and others as occasion demanded. The English Government agreed to provide the land and buildings, and was to pay the company £60,000 for equipping each station. The Marconi Company agreed to operate the stations. The company's share was to be 10% of the gross receipts from long-distance traffic. The term of the contract was 18 years. The government had the privilege of canceling the agreement at the end of this term, but in such case it would be deprived of the right to make use of the company's patents.[1] This agreement was characterized by the *Investors' Review* as a "first-rate contract."

[1]See *Investors' Review* for March 9, 1912, p. 333.

PROSPERITY

If the reader will examine Figure 1, below, he will note that the price of Marconi stock rose steadily from the middle of 1911 to the end of the first quarter of 1912. The highest in June, 1911, was £2$^{15}/_{32}$ for each one-pound share of the ordinary stock. In the preceding month of May it was only £1¾. The price steadily rose until in April, 1912, it had reached the record height of £9$^{13}/_{16}$, which in United States terms would be the equivalent of almost $975 for a $100 share. In May, 1912, however, the price began to recede.

In this rapid price fluctuation is found some of the most interesting history in connection with the Marconi Company. The reasons for the tremendous rise in its stock quotations can be summarized as follows:

First, the favorable contract with the English Postmaster-General. It was expected by the stock market that this would redound to the benefit of the corporation, and hence, would tend to cause a bullish movement in Marconi stock.

Second, a number of the important subsidiaries of the

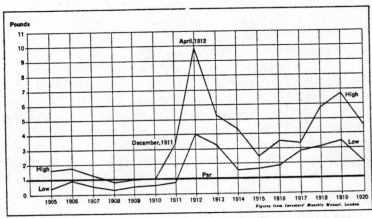

Figure 1: Market prices of common stock of the Marconi Wireless Telegraph Company, Limited.

Marconi Company were beginning to declare dividends. Although the American did not pay its initial dividend (and, incidentally, the only one in its history) until 1913, and although the Canadian Marconi has never paid dividends on its stock, some of the other subsidiaries in which the parent company was holding an interest were paying very liberally. The Marconi International Marine had begun a prosperous period in which its dividend rate never fell below 10%. Its gross earnings increased by £36,159 in the year 1912. The French and Belgian companies had for several years made payments to their owners, the French rate amounting to 5% annually, and the Belgian 10%. The German paid its initial dividend of 4% for the year ended September 30, 1911.[1]

Third, the absorption, either actual or promised, of powerful companies in the wireless field. Especially to be mentioned is the United Wireless Company, which was characterized as "hitherto the most extensive American company in the business."[2] This company was absorbed by the American Marconi Company indirectly through the purchase of the assets by the parent company and subsequent resale to the American company. This amalgamation took place for the following reasons:[3]

1. Decisions in patent cases before United States Federal Courts. The company pleaded guilty to the infringement of certain Marconi patents. The Marconi Company was granted a permanent injunction. This court procedure left the United Company practically helpless with its stations on both Atlantic and Pacific seacoasts and aboard a large number of ships. The existence of these stations was threatened.

2. Internal financial difficulties of the corporation. This was almost cause enough in itself, and the consolidation

[1] See *Investors' Review* for June 15, 1912, p. 847, and June 25, 1910, p. 929.

[2] *Report* of U. S. Commissioner of Navigation, 1912, p. 38.

[3] *Ibid.*, pp. 38-39.

would probably have taken place without the occurrence of the patent suit.

3. In June, 1911, the president and certain other officers of the United Company were convicted of selling stock under false pretenses, and receiverships were appointed for the company in four American states.[1]

The absorption of the assets of this company gave the American Marconi Company a practical monopoly of the supply of apparatus and operators for radio communication in the United States.[2] This relief from a powerful source of competition added to the business prestige of the American Marconi Company and indirectly to the earning capacity of the parent British company. Partly in order to finance this consolidation and partly to take care of normal growth, the authorized and issued capital of the American company was increased in 1912. A traffic agreement was also made with the Western Union.

COMPULSORY INSTALLATION OF SHIP RADIO

Fourth, the second decade of this century witnessed a strong wave of sentiment in favor of wireless as a means of safeguarding and saving life at sea. On January 23, 1909, the White Star passenger steamer "Republic" was rammed by the Italian steamship "Florida," off the Nantucket coast. The distress signal was sent out by the radio operator, John R. Binns, who "demonstrated to the whole world the value of radio in such a case by bravely standing by his instruments in the dark on a sinking ship and summoning aid, which arrived in time to save all hands."[3] On this occasion, Jack Irwin and other operators at the Marconi shore station at Siasconset made their names immortal by staying at their posts for many hours at a stretch without

---

[1] Moody's *Manual*, issue of 1911.

[2] *Report* of U. S. Commissioner of Navigation, 1912, p. 39.

[3] *Amrad Radio Products*, 1923, published by American Radio and Research Corporation, p. 8B-4.

sleep, relaying the messages and notifying an anxious world of the success of the life-saving efforts.[1]

The effect of this incident upon an awed world was stupendous. What would have happened had not the ill-fated ship been equipped with wireless? The world shuddered. Two years later, April 15, 1912, the passenger steamship Titanic, on her maiden voyage, struck an iceberg and sank, but, owing to the radio call for assistance, the lives of more than 700 of her passengers were saved. The chief radio operator, Jack Phillips, died at his post, having refused to desert the radio "shack." Again the world shuddered—and praised.

The nations of the world acted. On June 24, 1910, and July 23, 1912, the United States put into effect laws which provided that "From and after October 1, 1912, it shall be unlawful for any steamer of the United States or of any foreign country navigating the ocean or the Great Lakes and licensed to carry, or carrying, 50 or more persons, including passengers or crew or both, to leave or attempt to leave any port of the United States unless such steamer shall be equipped with an efficient apparatus for radio communication, in good working order, capable of transmitting and receiving messages over a distance of at least 100 miles, day or night."[2]

These laws also provided for the installation of auxiliary apparatus and contained regulations for the number and duties of the radio operators. The act of 1910 also contained this significant provision: "For the purpose of this act apparatus for radio communication shall not be deemed to be efficient unless the company installing it shall contract in writing to exchange, and shall in fact exchange, as far as may be physically practicable, to be determined by the master of the vessel, messages with shore or ship stations using other systems of radio communication."

---

[1] Other examples of the early use of wireless for such purposes will occur to the reader.

[2] Barnes, *Federal Code*, 1919, pp. 1784-1785.

The Third International Radiotelegraph Conference met in London on June 4, 1912, and its convention containing provisions for the safeguarding of lives at sea was signed on July 5. In June, 1913, Canada passed its Radiotelegraph Act, which, among other things, provided for the compulsory installation of wireless apparatus on Canadian and foreign ships leaving Canadian ports. In November, 1913, the Safety at Sea Conference was held at London.

Naturally other nations followed the Canadian and American examples.[1] Furthermore, if neither a foreign nor a domestic ship can leave an American or a Canadian port without being equipped with wireless, plainly the ships of other nations will rapidly of necessity be supplied with such apparatus. Ships of all nations of the world enter these harbors.

The effect of this legislation on the number of radio installations is apparent. For example, while in 1912 there were 367 American private ships equipped with radio, in 1913 this number had increased to 483, and in 1914 to 555. The number of British ships carrying wireless increased in the period 1910-1913 by nearly 300%.

CHARGES OF CORRUPTION

As can be noted from Figure 1 on page 28, the price of the Marconi stock receded in May, 1912. We have just completed a sketch of the causes of the prosperity of the Marconi interests at this time. What, then, was the reason for this decline? It will be remembered that one of the things that made for the Marconi progress was the consummation of a favorable contract with the British Government, providing for the construction of a British wireless chain. But almost immediately charges and countercharges of corruption clouded the atmosphere. Lloyd George and other public officials, it was pointed out, had bought stock

---

[1] The laws were passed to give effect to the London convention.

in the British Marconi Company when the quotations were comparatively low and had unloaded them when the prices were high. The motive behind the contract was not difficult to find, said the critics. The agreement had been made in order to bolster up the price of the stock and thus to permit these public servants to take advantage of the increase.

These were serious and ugly charges. An official investigation was necessary. So a parliamentary committee was appointed in 1912 to inquire into the motives and effects of the Marconi-Government agreement, and to report on the desirability of continuing or breaking the provisions of this contract. The committee reported favorably to the carrying out of the agreement, thus exonerating the public, and the company, officials from the charges which had been brought against them.

CONTINUED EXTENSION OF CONTROL

Now began another period of expansion, which took not only the form of increased number of installations of radio apparatus, but also of the absorption of old companies and the formation of new subsidiaries. It is this latter phase which will be taken up in this connection. In 1913 the Marconi companies had either secured or were negotiating for concessions in more than 20 foreign countries.[1] The Marconi system promised to assume colossal proportions.

The British Marconi Company, in 1913, acquired a majority of the shares of the Compagnie Universelle de Telegraphie et Telephonie sans Fil, of France, which owned the world-wide rights (outside of Germany) of Professor Goldschmidt's inventions. To finance this expansion 500,000 new one-pound ordinary shares of the British Marconi Company were floated in 1913.[2] In the same year the British

[1] *Investors' Review*, September 27, 1913, p. 409.

[2] From the *Stock Exchange Year-Book*, 1924, p. 1270. See Table 1, on page 26, showing the increases in the Marconi stock.

TABLE 2

LIST OF. DIRECTORATES HELD BY THE DIRECTORS OF MARCONI
COMPANY, LIMITED, OF ENGLAND*

SENATORE GUGLIELMO MARCONI

Compania Nacional de Telegraphia sin Hilos (Madrid)
Marconi's International Marine Communication Co., Ltd.
Marconi Wireless Telegraph Co. of Canada
Nederlandsche Telegraaf Maatschappij Dario-Holland (Amsterdam)
Nederlandsche Seintoestellen Fabriek (Hilversum)
Russian Company of Wireless Telegraph and Telephones (Petrograd)
Societa Anonima Fiumina per le Radio Comunicazione
Societa Italiana dei Servizi Radiotelegrafici Radiotelephonici (Rome)
Societe Anonyme Internationale de -Telegraphie sans Fil (Brussels)

ALFONSO MARCONI

Marconi's International Marine Communication Co.
Spanish and General Corp.

GODFREY CHARLES ISAACS (Retired November 13, 1924)

Marconi's International Marine Communication Co.
Spanish and General Corp.
Aircraft Disposal Co.
British Broadcasting Co.
British Danubian Trading Corp.
Carreg-e-Llam Quarries
Federation of British Industries
Marconi Wireless Telegraph Co. of Canada
Sterling Telephone and Electric Co.

CAPTAIN HENRY RIALL SANKEY

British Klip River Colliery Co.
British Niclausse Boiler Co.
Carreg-e-Llam Quarries
Eastwoods, Ltd.
English Oilfields, Ltd.
Hamonite, Ltd.
Light Steelwork, Ltd.
Marconi International Code Co.
Marconi's International Marine Communication Co.
Never-Stop Transit, Ltd.
Relay Automatic Telephone Co.
Silver Lockstitch Sewing Machine Co.
Societe Anonyme Internationale de Telegraphie sans Fil
Spanish and General Corp.
Still Engine Co.
Transoceanic Wireless Telegraph Co.
Wallerawang Collieries, Ltd.
Wireless Press, Ltd.

*Source, *Directory of Directors*, England.

Marconi Company acquired a majority of the shares of the
Goldschmidt Company.[1]

The Amalgamated Wireless, Limited, of Australia, was
formed in 1913. In this company the International Marine
secured the controlling interest.[2] In 1922 the Amalgamated
Company made an agreement with the Australian Govern-

[1] *Investors' Review*, September, 1913, p. 409.
[2] Moody's *Manual, Public Utility Section*, 1918, p. 915.

TABLE 2 *(Continued)*

LIST OF DIRECTORATES HELD BY THE DIRECTORS OF
MARCONI COMPANY, LIMITED, OF ENGLAND

HENRY WILLIAM ALLEN
: Marconi's International Marine Communication Co.
: M-O Valve Co.
: Marconi Wireless Telegraph Co. of Canada
: Relay Automatic Telephone Co.
: Sterling Telephone and Electric Co.

MAURICE A. BRAMSTON
: Householders' Mortgage Society
: Marconi's International Marine Communication Co.
: Underfeed Stoker Co.

SIDNEY F. STJ. STEADMAN
: Adaptable Code Condensers, Ltd.
: African City Properties Trust
: Aircraft Disposal Co.
: Carreg-e-Llam Quarries
: Foldal Copper and Sulphur Co.
: Handley Page, Ltd.
: Marconi International Code Co.
: Marconi's International Marine Communication Co.
: Relay Automatic Telephone Co.
: Reversion Fund and Insurance Co.
: Spanish and General Co.
: Sterling Telephone and Electric Co.

CHARLES JOHN STEWART
: Anglo-Scottish Trust, Ltd.
: Jurgens, Ltd.
: Marconi's International Marine Communication Co.
: Province of Buenos Ayres Waterworks Co.
: Texas Land and Mortgage Co.

LORD HERSCHELL
: Marconi's International Marine Communication Co.

ADRIAN H. F. S. SIMPSON
: Marconi's International Marine Communication Co.
: British and Hungarian Bank
: British Danubian Trading Co.
: M-O Valve Co.
: Marconi Scientific Instrument Co.
: Marconiphone Co.
: Spanish and General Co.

FREDERICK GEORGE KELLAWAY
: Edinburgh Evening News, Ltd.
: United Newspapers, Ltd.

ment for the construction of the necessary stations for a "direct commercial wireless service between Australia and the United Kingdom."

For the exploitation of the Marconi patents in China, the Chinese National Wireless Company was organized. This company is owned in common by the British Marconi Company and the Chinese Government, the British company owning one-half of the stock and electing a majority of the board of directors.

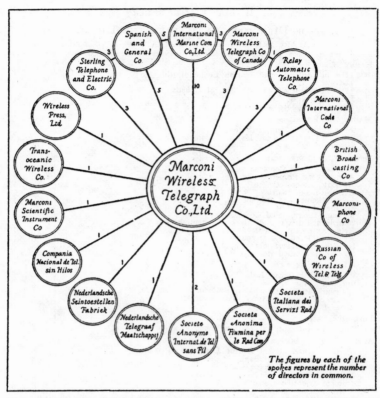

The figures by each of the spokes represent the number of directors in common.

Figure 2: Representation of the directors of Marconi's Wireless Telegraph Company on the boards of other companies.[1]

FALL IN PRICE OF STOCK

A glance at Figure 1, on page 28, will reveal the fact that the price of Marconi stock continued to decline during the years 1913 and 1914.   This fall may in general be attributed to the World War.   More specifically, the causes can be discussed under the following heads:

1. At the end of the year 1914 the British Government

[1]Table 2 gives a complete list of directorates.

repudiated the 1912 contract and took over the stations. This was a war measure, but the effect on the market price of the corporation's stock is apparent. In 1919 the company was finally awarded damages of £590,000.

2. The war disrupted negotiations for concessions in foreign countries. The normal relations between the parent company and its associates were dislocated. Wireless stations in belligerent territory were, as a rule, commandeered for war purposes.

3. On account of the fall in the value of most foreign money in comparison with sterling exchange, the Marconi Company, holding a considerable amount of foreign securities valued in terms of foreign currencies, was forced by bankers to deposit large sums in order to compensate for the depreciation of such securities.

4. Payments of money from nations and individuals were deferred by the course of the war. For example, Turkey owed the Marconi Company £4,347, but failed to pay.[1] The moratorium also indirectly retarded dividend payments.

5. Finally, and in summary, the following statement from Mr. Marconi may be quoted.

We all realize that we are passing through most exceptional and serious times, and everybody, I am sure, will appreciate that the outbreak of hostilities.... must have caused considerable disturbance to a world-wide[2] business such as ours. As was to be expected, wireless apparatus was promptly declared to be contraband of war, and for the time being, therefore, our work in many parts of the world practically came to a standstill.[3]

[1] *Investors' Review*, July 17, 1915, p. 69.

[2] The company letter-head lists the following offices of affiliated companies and representations: Alexandria, Amsterdam, Antwerp, Athens, Bangkok, Belgrade, Berlin, Berne, Bogota, Bombay, Brussels, Bucharest, Budapest, Buenos Aires, Calcutta, Callao, Cape Town, Christiania, Constantinople, Copenhagen, Durban, Genoa, Guayaquil, Helsingfors, Hilversum, Hong Kong, Johannesburg, LaPaz, Lima, Lisbon, Madrid, Melbourne, Mexico City, Montreal, New York, Paris, Peking, Petrograd, Riga, Rio de Janeiro, Rome, San Jose, San Salvador, Shanghai, Sofia, Stockholm, Sydney, Trinidad, Warsaw, and Wellington.

[3] *The Economist*, July 31, 1915, p. 188. Later on the company received large war orders and many associated companies prospered, but these facts did not influence stock prices until 1915 and 1916.

POST-WAR DEVELOPMENTS

The year 1923 showed an enormous decrease in the surplus available for dividends. Besides serious losses in operating income due to the failure to reach a satisfactory agreement with the British Government regarding certain phases of the broadcasting situation and regarding the continuance of the plans for the building up of an imperial wireless chain, and besides the serious loss of wireless traffic due to the destruction of the important Clifden station in Ireland, this year witnessed a drastic and well-considered house-cleaning in regard to some of the uncertain and dubious assets of the company. The period from 1915 to the present day has been one of violent and unprecedented economic and political changes. As already indicated, the assets of the Marconi Company abroad were naturally valued in terms of foreign money. If the securities held were those of Russian, French, or German companies, their values were stated in terms of rubles, francs, or marks, respectively. The political conditions were very unstable in certain nations, and the value of a number of foreign currencies had depreciated much more proportionally than the English pound. Therefore, the directors of the British company decided, in 1923, to convert the whole of certain foreign assets into sterling value. This was done by the creation of reserves to the amount of these uncertain values. This procedure represented an immense loss to the company.[1]

---

[1]See Annual Report for year ending December 31, 1923. See also speech of Mr. Marconi before the stockholders at the annual meeting August 15, 1924. This is reproduced in the London *Times* of August 16, 1924. He thus described the procedure and the amounts involved:

In order that you may have a better appreciation of the way in which we have proceeded, I propose to give to you the amount which we have dealt with under each of the headings set out in the report.

Under (a): To reserve for the whole of the Russian shares, debts, and securities, £370,293. This amount represents cost only and is substantially less than was the value at the time we lost possession.

Under (b): To reserve for overdue debts from foreign governments, £182,345.

Under (c): £648,815, to reserve for depreciation of shares in foreign companies after converting the foreign currencies into sterling at the rate of exchange ruling on June 30 last, so that they now stand in the balance-sheet at sterling values.

Under (d): To write off the amount which represented the Clifden and other sta-

The condition of the British Marconi Company during and after the Great War may be seen from the comparative profit and loss statements in Table 3:

TABLE 3

BRITISH MARCONI COMPANY—PROFIT AND LOSS ACCOUNT*

Year	Balance of Contracts, Sales, and Trading Accounts	Misc. Income	Total Income	Rents, Rates, Taxes, etc.	Depreciation	Station Expense	Surplus for Dividends, etc.
1915	£581,125	£ 540	£581,665	£111,856	£72,540	£19,452	£377,818
1916	485,995	676	486,671	116,478	18,412	33,348	318,433
1917	539,856	329	540,185	109,950	18,413	27,987	383,835
1918	765,700	563	766,263	147,695	18,461	2,169	597,938
1919	946,997	591,043	1,583,040	204,618	19,948	92,734	1,220,740
1920	563,314	1,524	564,838	171,649	23,229	72,278	297,682
1921	553,729	786	554,515	169,556	27,476	82,122	275,361
1922	556,290	1,129	577,419	151,276	29,906	73,289	302,948
1923	552,113	811	552,924	35,361	37,028	66,924	172,543

*Moody's *Manual, Public Utilities Section.*

Several facts may be gleaned from a study of these figures:

1. The total income for the year 1919 was double that of the preceding year and thrice that of 1920. A few reasons for this variation may be advanced.

(*a*) In the year 1919 the company was awarded damages from the British Government amounting to about £590,000. (For breach of contract in 1914.) This sum is entered in the books as "miscellaneous income."

(*b*) The year 1919 also witnessed a spurt of additional business. By 1920 the depression had set in. The net earnings of the International Marine also showed the effects of

tions damaged and thrown out of commission during the Irish troubles, £85,019.

Under (*e*): To write off all obsolescent plant and stock, £218,620.

(*f*) To write off all losses during the year in consequence of further depreciation of foreign currencies in money accumulated abroad or temporarily invested in foreign government securities, which amounted to £151,358; from this amount there is deducted the value of debentures and shares unrealized but which we are satisfied are of their full value, amounting to £120,000, leaving a balance written off to £31,358.

(*g*) To provide reserves in respect of depreciation of shares in associated and other companies in proportion to our shareholding in those companies, £767,635. As we have informed you in the report, there is no obligation on the company to write off such losses, but we feel that in so doing we are presenting to you a more conservative balance-sheet.

Finally, we have written off £31,523 in respect of sundry debts and debit balances unclassified as not coming under any of the above headings, and which we have thought it sound to dispose of in so far as our balance-sheet is concerned.

the hard times. A large number of ships were laid up and many are to this day idle. The company followed the policy of maintaining the oldest telegraph operators in point of service on the pay list; it also granted rebates in the rentals paid by the ships carrying the Marconi apparatus when these ships were idle.

2. The net earnings of the company are, as a rule, equal to about one-half of the gross income. This fact indicates that the Marconi Company is apparently operating very efficiently, and that a substantial reduction in costs of telegraphy may be possible.

The 1923 balance-sheet of the corporation reveals the fact that associated companies owed the parent £1,949,462, and that the parent held shares and debentures in associated and other companies to the amount of £2,346,574. Thus, more than one-half of the British Marconi assets consisted of holdings in other companies. This indicates at once the extent of the Marconi interests abroad. The item "amounts due from associated companies" in the balance-sheet reveals considerable variation from year to year, depending on general business conditions and the financial successes of these concerns. Thus, this account was almost two million pounds in 1923. In 1921 it was only a little more than a million and a half (£1,584,777). The Marconi Company has shown itself to be very willing to come to the financial aid of its associates. For example, the Canadian company announced, late in 1924, that it was to float new stock issues and that subject to the capital being reduced the directors had arranged for the sale to Marconi's Wireless Telegraph Company of sufficient new shares at par to fund the excess of current liabilities, furnish more working capital, and pay for the construction of the first beam station.

OTHER EARLY WIRELESS COMPANIES

While the Marconi organization was progressing and prospering, other interests were also exploiting the field of wireless.[1] Some of these, such as the United Fruit Company, intended the radio to serve as an auxiliary to their regular business; others, such as the Federal Telegraph Company and the DeForest Radio Telephone and Telegraph Company, made wireless their main line and built commercial stations, as well as factories to supply the apparatus; still others, such as the Radio Corporation of America, made radio dealing and communication their main lines of endeavor and relied upon other concerns to manufacture and supply the wireless apparatus.

THE UNITED FRUIT COMPANY

The outstanding example of the first group is the United Fruit Company. This corporation was organized in 1899, and owns fruit and sugar plantations in Central and South America, Cuba, and a number of nearby islands. For the transportation of these products to the northern markets, the company operates the famous "White Fleet." These vessels are equipped not only for the carrying of bananas, the principal product, but for general freight and mail, and also contain comfortable first-class passenger cabins.

It is evident that in the fruit business a rapid and reliable method of transportation and communication is necessary. The plantation managers must be notified of movements of the steamers so that the fruit can be ready for loading immediately, so that loss through spoiling of the fruit or waste of time can be avoided. Since the numerous swamps and rivers very often precluded the use of wire, it was but natural that this company should very early develop a system of wireless, establishing stations at Boston, New Orleans (Burwood), and points in Central America, near the plantations in the tropics, as well as aboard its vessels.

But it is difficult for the same company to carry on both a fruit and a wireless business. So in 1913 the Tropical

---

[1] It will, of course, be impossible to discuss all of the numerous companies which have entered this relatively new business. The writer will briefly describe a few of those he considers the most important.

Radio Telegraph Company was organized to carry on the radio communication field. To manufacture and sell apparatus, the Wireless Specialty Apparatus Company was formed. The parent owns a controlling interest in both companies. The Tropical Radio Company has developed a number of its own radio patents, and has also procured rights from the American Marconi Company and later from the Radio Corporation of America.[1]

THE FEDERAL TELEGRAPH COMPANY

The Federal Telegraph Company was incorporated February, 1911, in California under the original name of the Wireless Development Company. This company owns stations on the Pacific Coast, having recently completed four new high-powered stations in San Francisco, Los Angeles, San Diego, and Portland, Oregon. The company owns the patents of the Danish inventors, Poulsen and Pederson, together with the free and exclusive right to make use of and sell all of such inventions. The Federal Company manufactures and sells high-powered apparatus, and also conducts radio communication between ships at sea and between the United States and the Orient.[2]

THE DE FOREST RADIO TELEPHONE AND TELEGRAPH COMPANY

This company was incorporated under the laws of Delaware, in 1913, as a successor of the Radio Telegraph Company of New Jersey. It owns several audion patents. Under these patents the DeForest Company for a time

---

[1] The Tropical Radio Company also handles radiograms for the United Fruit Company passengers.

For a very interesting and instructive account of the wireless system of the United Fruit Company, see an article entitled "The History of the Development of the United Fruit Company's Radio Telegraph System," by Roy Mason in *The Radio Broadcast*, September, 1922.

[2] For a discussion of the Federal Telegraph Company of Deleware, see Chapter III.

Material on Federal Telegraph Company was taken from Poors' and Moody's *Manual, Consolidated, Public Utility Section*, 1923, p. 2397.

manufactured tubes, but was restrained by a United States District Court. (See Chapter X.) Subsequently, the DeForest Company assigned its patents to the American Telephone and Telegraph Company, retaining for itself a personal, non-transferable right to manufacture and sell. It confined its own business to the manufacture and sale of parts used by amateurs and experimenters in assembling sets. With the expiration of the Fleming patent in 1922, the DeForest Company resumed the manufacture and sale of vacuum tubes.[1]

[1]See Poors' and Moody's *Manual, Consolidated, Public Utility Section,* 1923, p. 69, and *Report of the Federal Trade Commission on Radio Industry,* p. 13.

III

THE RADIO CORPORATION OF AMERICA

Condition of post-war communication. Inadequate service rendered by cables. Great Britain predominant in cable ownership. The vacuum tube situation. Desire of Marconi for Alexanderson alternator. Naval intercession in interest of service to Americans. Organization of Radio Corporation of America. Radio by and for Americans. Confused patent situation. Cross-licensing agreements for the protection of public. Provisions of cross-licensing contracts. Ownership of Radio Corporation stock. The South-American situation. Grant of rights to board of trustees. A new "Monroe Doctrine." Advantages of trusteeship arrangement. The Chinese situation. Agreement with the Federal Telegraph Company. Nature of Radio Corporation service. Growing importance of broadcasting.

THOUGH the Marconi organization was the earliest extensive wireless system, the period during and immediately following the World War saw a number of important and fundamental conditions which were destined to greatly influence the position of the United States in the radio field. The steady development of wireless had convinced people of its reliability and practicability as a medium for long-distance communication. Though for several years the Marconi interests had been carrying on a transatlantic service, their efforts had not been regarded as satisfactory. The World War, far from making for a cosmopolitan sentiment, had apparently accentuated nationalism and international rivalries, one of which manifested itself in the slogan "America for the Americans." Furthermore, the tendency of foreign countries to favor private or public monopolies of radio communication was brought forcibly to the attention of the American people. The desire of American capital to expand in all directions was a direct concomitant of our increased interest in foreign trade, especially exports. This desire for expansion necessitated the extension of our foreign communication facilities. In the wireless field the American Marconi Company, which had been organized to exploit the Marconi patents in the United States, was limited in its license to American territory only. This company, therefore, was not free to expand in other directions.

INADEQUATE SERVICE RENDERED BY CABLES

Moreover, the existing cable facilities (a large number of which were transatlantic and only one transpacific) were being strained to the limit in order to accommodate the vast war and post-war demand. This was especially the case with transpacific communication. When the United States Government, for example, made public the famous Zimmerman note, showing the attempt by the German Foreign Minister to involve Japan and Mexico in a conspiracy against the United States, New York newspapers ordered their correspondents in Japan to interview the government officials as to the matter. The news had not even reached Japan, and it was necessary for one of the newspapers to inform the Japanese Government directly as to the contents of the note.[1]

President MacKay, of the Commercial Pacific Cable Company, stated, in a telegram to the Senate Committee on Naval Affairs, that "Every day brings more messages to the Commercial Cable Company than it can possibly carry. The result is a constantly increasing accumulation of unsent messages and a corresponding accumulating delay, so that the cable has fallen eight days behind and messages are only accepted subject to delay. . . ." This congestion was due to the fact that the war had closed certain eastward cable lines so that the Commercial Cable across the Pacific became the only open route to the Orient. Relief could not

---

[1]"Regarding a New Pacific Cable," by Silas Bent in *Asia*, March, 1919, p. 252. The writer also points out that during the war there were times when the "confirmation sent by mail" outstripped its fellow filed for electrical transmission. The only transpacific cable was so overburdened that often it was 10 days behind with its work.

be immediately obtained owing to the great length of time (at least two years) required for the laying of a new cable.

Most of the existing cables were foreign owned. Captain Samuel W. Bryant,[1] of the United States navy, estimated that in 1919 England controlled 51% of the cable facilities, the United States 26½%, France 9%, Germany 7½%, Denmark 3%, Spain, Japan, and Italy each 1%.[2] In the summer of 1919 the British Post-Office Department informed the public that messages for the Continent of Europe were liable to delay and should be accepted entirely at the senders' risk; and that no inquiry could be made as to their disposal nor could claims for refund be considered. This ruling aroused the apprehension of American officials. It meant that foreign messages would be under the control of the British when they were sent via British cables. As a result, the Navy Department recommended that the naval radio stations be authorized to handle commercial traffic. This incident illustrates the recognized need for a system of American transoceanic communication.[3]

THE VACUUM TUBE SITUATION

The radio patent situation was another constituting factor in the rise of the Radio Corporation of America. The Ameri-

---

[1]Before United States Senate Committee on Naval Affairs, August 14, 1919, p. 28.

[2]The reasons for Great Britain's eminence in the cable field may be summarized: (1) Advantages of an early start; (2) Necessity of an adequate communication system to hold together the Empire on which the "sun never sets"; (3) The possession of an adequate supply of cable materials, especially gutta percha, which is used for insulation; (4) The exercise of wise foresight and planning by the government. For example, though England was in the lead, the Report of the Interdepartmental Committee (1902) had recommended a large number of new cables. This policy has also been followed in the case of wireless. Government boards and committees have from time to time studied the needs and made recommendations as to the location and number of stations.

[3]See letter from Franklin D. Roosevelt to the Senate Committee on Naval Affairs, August 5, 1919.

can Marconi Company, under a patent assigned to it by Fleming, was manufacturing the so-called two-element vacuum tube. DeForest had added a third element. For a short time the DeForest Company manufactured tubes under DeForest's patent, but the Marconi Company of America brought suit for infringement. The court held that the Fleming patent controlled the use of the vacuum tube. DeForest may have improved upon it, but the patent for the vacuum tube as a detector belonged to Fleming.[1] As a result of this decision, DeForest was forced to discontinue the making of this device, but at the same time the Marconi Company of America was obliged to confine itself to the manufacture and use of the two-element tube. Later the DeForest Company assigned whatever rights it had to the American Telephone and Telegraphy Company, retaining for itself a personal, non-transferable license to manufacture and sell these tubes.

Thus the situation stood. Marconi controlled the two-element tube. DeForest could not manufacture the three-element; neither could Marconi. And the three-element tube, with a few improvements, was generally admitted to be the better device.

DESIRE OF MARCONI FOR ALEXANDERSON ALTERNATOR

Marconi had always relied on the spark type of transmitting apparatus, which was rather costly and inefficient. With the development of the radio art, especially the vacuum tube as a transmitter, it became necessary to devise a high-speed alternator to be used instead of the spark apparatus. The General Electric Company had assigned one of its engineers, Dr. E. F. W. Alexanderson (now with the Radio Corporation of America), to the task of designing such a machine. Dr. Alexanderson had, before the opening of the war, succeeded in his purpose, producing what is now known as the Alexanderson alternator.

---

[1]See Chapter XI.

This was exactly the machine which the Marconi interests wanted. So in 1915 the British Marconi Company sent two representatives, Mr. Marconi, the chairman of the board of directors, and Mr. Steadman, the company's lawyer, to the United States to attempt, if possible, to secure the exclusive rights in this machine. Nothing but a tentative agreement was drawn up contemplating the purchase by the Marconi Company of about three millions of dollars worth of these alternators annually. Before the agreement was put into final form, Marconi was compelled to report to the colors in Italy. Subsequently, these arrangements were canceled, but both sides agreed to keep the matter open.

During the war the General Electric Company installed an Alexanderson generator at the New Brunswick station of the American Marconi Company. Later the United States Government assumed the operation of this station. The Navy Department found that the Alexanderson system was very successful, and requested the Marconi Company to install a more powerful machine which the General Electric was then completing. The Marconi Company refused, and then the General Electric installed the machine at its own expense. The United States Government made extensive use of this station during the war.

After the signing of the armistice, the Marconi representatives again came to the United States to negotiate for the purchase of the rights in this machine. The negotiations were practically complete when the officers of the General Electric received a request from the United States navy to postpone closing the contract until the naval representatives had had the opportunity for an informal discussion with them concerning the matter. The officers agreed, and on April 5, 1919, a conference took place in New York between representatives of the United States navy and the General Electric Company.[1]

---

[1] The Federal Trade Commission in its *Report on the Radio Industry*, pp. 1-22, gives a detailed discussion of the events leading up to the organization of the Radio Corporation of America.

NAVAL INTERCESSION IN INTEREST OF SERVICE TO
AMERICANS

The two naval officers were Admiral Bullard, director of
communications, and Commander S. C. Hooper, of the
Bureau of Engineering. They argued against the sale of the
machine to Marconi on the following grounds:

1. The Alexanderson alternator, which proved itself to be
the best in existence, was capable of rendering a reliable
transoceanic service.

2. The United States had never played an important part
in cable communication. Most of the cables running to and
from the United States are foreign owned and controlled.
There should be in wireless a policy similar to the Monroe
Doctrine, by which the control of radio on the American
Continent would remain in American hands.

3. The Alexanderson alternator was such a strategic
device that if the General Electric Company were to sell it
to any British interests, the result would be a practical
monopoly by the British in the field of world communication—wireless as well as cable.

In answer to the arguments of the navy officials, the General Electric asked: If their company did not sell to the
Marconi interests, to whom should it sell? The Marconi
Companies were the largest purchasers of radio apparatus
in the world. The General Electric had spent a considerable
sum of money developing this device, and if it did not sell
to the Marconi interests, the value of the investment would
be jeopardized. These were practical arguments.

To whom should the General Electric sell? To the Marconi Company? That, said the navy men, would not be
desirable. To a new company organized to engage in radio
communication? This again would not be fair to the
American Marconi Company, many of whose stockholders
were American citizens. Or should the General Electric
go into the wireless communication business itself and make

use of its own alternator? This would not be feasible, as the normal business of the company is the building and sale of electrical apparatus. Furthermore, in this way the General Electric would be entering into competition with one of its normal customers.

ORGANIZATION OF RADIO CORPORATION OF AMERICA

It was finally decided to form a new corporation, which (in order to prevent duplication of services and to protect the present investment) should attempt to have transferred to itself the assets of the American Marconi Company. In this manner the idea of the Radio Corporation of America was conceived.[1]

The General Electric then began negotiations with the American Marconi Company for the transfer of the Marconi assets to the Radio Corporation of America. On November 20, 1919, the main agreement between the Radio Corporation of America and the Marconi Company of America was signed. According to this contract, the Radio Corporation of America secured an unencumbered title to all the property of the American Marconi Company except certain "reserved assets." The compensation took the form of stock in the Radio Corporation of America. It was also stipulated that if the Radio Corporation of America is ever taken over by the government, except in the case of war or national emergency, the title to the transferred assets shall revert to the Marconi Company.[2]

[1] For an account of the events and negotiations preliminary to the formation of the Radio Corporation of America, see testimony of Owen D. Young, chairman of the corporation's board of directors, before a subcommittee of the Senate Committee on Interstate Commerce which conducted hearings on S 4301, a bill to prevent the unauthorized landing of submarine cables in the United States, January 11, 1921, pp. 327 ff.

[2] The "reserved assets" include a claim for patent infringement against the United States, against four private companies, a claim against the United States Alien Property Custodian and the Treasurer of the United States, and finally, a claim against the British Government in regard to compensation for its stations commandeered during the war.

For the full text of this agreement, see Appendix B in the *Report of the Federal Trade Commission on the Radio Industry*, December 1, 1923.

RADIO BY AND FOR AMERICANS

The Radio Corporation was organized on October 17, 1919, under the laws of Delaware for the purpose of conducting a general wireless business in the fields of communication, dealing, and manufacturing. To make it an American-controlled concern, the following provisions were inserted:

No person shall be eligible for election as a director or officer of the corporation who is not at the time of such election a citizen of the United States.

The corporation may, if the board so decide, issue share certificates representing not more than 20% of the total shares of the corporation at the time outstanding (including such issue) in special form which may be owned or held by and the shares represented by which may be voted by foreigners without restriction. These certificates will be a special series known as "foreign share certificates" and each such certificate shall bear the words "foreign certificate" upon its face—the aggregate issue of such shares at any time outstanding shall not exceed the percentage above provided. Holders of "foreign share certificates" shall have in all respects the same corporate status and corporate rights as holders of other share certificates....[1]

The Radio Corporation of America began business on December 1, 1919. Arrangements were made with the Societe Francaise Radio Electrique by which the Radio Corporation bought the Tuckerton, New Jersey, station. It will be remembered that the Marconi and the Tuckerton stations were the only high-powered American radio stations in private hands. All high-powered transoceanic stations had accordingly fallen into the hands of the Radio Corporation.

CONFUSED PATENT SITUATION

The problem next became one of developing the acquired resources as rapidly as possible. The corporation had procured certain patents from the Marconi Company, but

---

[1]The amount and kinds of stock, together with an enumeration of the largest holdings, will be found on pages 56-57.

other companies controlled patent rights which were absolutely essential for successful operation in the radio communication field.

The vacuum tube offers a good illustration. Under its Fleming patent the Marconi Company could have manufactured a two-element tube. This patent the Radio Corporation of America now controlled. The three-element tube had been patented by Lee DeForest, who had, through the corporation bearing his name, assigned it to the American Telephone and Telegraph Company. DeForest had, apparently, never entirely abandoned the heated gas theory. He had supposed that a certain amount of air was necessary in the tube. DeForest's theory was found to be incorrect, and now the question arose as to the proper method of creating a complete vacuum in the tube. Two men worked almost simultaneously on this problem. Dr. Langmuir invented one device which was owned by the General Electric Company. A similar improvement was devised by Arnold, of the Western Electric Company. As a result of the interference proceedings in which both these patents became involved, a finding was made in favor of the Langmuir application, from which an appeal was taken by the Western Electric. This situation can be illustrated thus:

DeForest...... { 3-electrode } assigned to American Telephone and Telegraph Company

Fleming....... { 2-electrode } assigned to American Marconi Company and Radio Corporation of America

Langmuir..... { method of creating vacuum } assigned to General Electric Company

Interference proceeding

Arnold........ { method of creating vacuum } assigned to Western Electric Company

From a study of this controversy the Federal Trade Commission concluded:

It seems, therefore, that the best known form of vacuum tube could not be manufactured by the Marconi Company of America unless it had rights in the DeForest patents, and in the patents on pure electron discharge tubes. The American Telephone and

Telegraph Company could not manufacture such tubes for radio purposes unless it acquired rights in the Fleming patent and cleared up the interferences of the Arnold application with the Langmuir application on pure electron discharge tubes, while the General Electric Company could not manufacture, sell, or use such tubes for radio purposes unless it acquired rights in the Fleming, DeForest, and Arnold inventions.[1]

But that is not all. A number of "construction" or "detail" patents were owned by the American Telephone and Telegraph Company and the General Electric Company. These were all considered necessary for the successful operation of the vacuum tube. Then, again, there were patents owned by different concerns covering the character of the filament used.[2]

CROSS-LICENSING AGREEMENTS FOR THE PROTECTION OF PUBLIC

The situation was so confused that in January, 1920, a high official of the United States Bureau of Steam Engineering wrote a letter to the General Electric Company and American Telephone and Telegraph Company simultaneously, of which the following are a few extracts:

Referring to numerous recent conferences in connection with the radio patent situation and particularly that phase involving vacuum tubes, the bureau has constantly held the view that all interests will be best served through some agreement between the several holders of permanent patents whereby the market can be freely supplied with tubes. . . .

In this connection the bureau wishes to invite your attention to the recent tendency of the merchant marine to adopt continuous wave apparatus in their ship installations, the bureau itself

---

[1]*Report of the Federal Trade Commission on the Radio Industry*, p. 27.

[2]These are only a few of the patent conflicts mentioned by the Federal Trade Commission in Chapters I and II of its *Report on the Radio Industry*. For complete details the reader is referred to this report, the first and second chapters of which are often quoted by the very concerns which the Commission was called upon to investigate. See, for example, pamphlet entitled *"Why America Leads in Radio,"* issued by the Radio Corporation of America.

having arranged for equipping many vessels of the Shipping Board with such sets. Such installations will create a demand for vacuum tubes in receivers, and this bureau believes it particularly desirable, especially from a point of view of safety at sea, that all ships be able to procure without difficulty vacuum tubes, these being the only satisfactory detectors for receiving continuous waves.

Today ships are cruising on the high seas with only (*sic*) continuous wave transmitting equipment, except for short ranges, when interrupted continuous waves are used. Due to the peculiar patent conditions which have prevented the marketing of tubes to the public, such vessels are not able to communicate with greatest efficiency except with the shore and, therefore, in case of distress, it inevitably follows that the lives of crews and passengers are imperiled beyond reasonable necessity.

In the past the reasons for desiring some arrangement have been largely because of monetary considerations. Now the situation has become such that it is a public necessity that such arrangement be made without further delay, and this letter may be considered as an appeal, for the good of the public, for a remedy for the situation.[1]

Thus, it appears that at about the end of the second decade of this century there was a genuine need for some sort of cross-licensing agreements among the various companies interested in radio, whereby they would be able to make use of one another's patent rights. The most important of such contracts are graphically illustrated in Figure 3, the arrows pointing in the direction of the grant.

PROVISIONS OF CROSS-LICENSING CONTRACTS

In most cases, with certain minor limitations, the "Radio Corporation of America, under these agreements, secured an exclusive divisible right to sell and use the radio devices covered by the patents involved or by any patents which the other companies may acquire during the term of the agreement. It, in turn, grants to the other companies the right to make devices under all of its patents, or applica-

[1]Quoted from the *Report of the Federal Trade Commission*, p. 29.

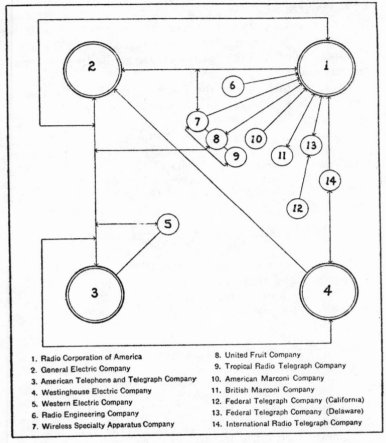

1. Radio Corporation of America
2. General Electric Company
3. American Telephone and Telegraph Company
4. Westinghouse Electric Company
5. Western Electric Company
6. Radio Engineering Company
7. Wireless Specialty Apparatus Company
8. United Fruit Company
9. Tropical Radio Telegraph Company
10. American Marconi Company
11. British Marconi Company
12. Federal Telegraph Company (California)
13. Federal Telegraph Company (Delaware)
14. International Radio Telegraph Company

Figure 3: Cross-licensing of patents.

tions, and so forth, which it then owned or controlled or which it should acquire during the term of the agreement."[1] The ordinary term of the agreements is up to but not including January 1, 1945. The companies usually agree to exchange information regarding radio developments. Most of the agreements contain a clause, or a supplementary contract, stipulating that if the company is ever taken over

[1]*Report of Federal Trade Commission on Radio Industry*, p. 40.

by the government, except during time of war or emergency, the granted rights shall revert to the patentees, or, as in the case of the American Marconi sale of assets to the Radio Corporation of America, to the owner at the time the transfer was made.

Thus, the directors of the Radio Corporation of America could truthfully report to the stockholders on March 21, 1924, that:

The corporation continues to benefit by the engineering and research organizations of the General Electric Company, the Westinghouse Electric and Manufacturing Company, the United Fruit Company, the Wireless Specialty Apparatus Company, the American Telephone and Telegraph Company, and the Western Electric Company.[1]

OWNERSHIP OF RADIO CORPORATION STOCK

In order better to carry out the terms of the cross-licensing agreements, some of the companies bought shares of stock in the Radio Corporation of America, or provision was made for representation on the board of directors. For

TABLE 4

NUMBER OF SHARES AND PERCENTAGE OF TOTAL CAPITAL STOCK
OF RADIO CORPORATION OWNED BY IMPORTANT
HOLDING COMPANIES, 1922

Name of Stockholder	PREFERRED		COMMON	
	No. of Shares	Per Cent	No. of Shares	Per Cent
General Electric Co..	620,800	15.6	1,876,000	32.7
Westinghouse Elect. and Mfg. Co......	1,000,000	25.2	1,000,000	17.4
Am. Tel. and Tel. Co.*	400,000	10.1		
United Fruit Co.....	200,000	5.	160,000	2.7

*The American Telephone and Telegraph Company was for several years the owner of 400,000 shares of the Radio Corporation Preferred Stock, but in 1922 it disposed of these holdings on the ground that "Ownership of stock in the Radio Corporation of America has not proved to be necessary for cooperation. Therefore, in line with our general policy to hold permanently only the stock and securities directly related to a national telephone service, we have disposed of all stock in the Radio Corporation."

[1] *Report for the Year Ended December 31, 1923*, p. 1.

example, on December 31, 1922, the balance-sheet of the
Radio Corporation showed capital stock outstanding:

3,955,974 shares 7% preferred stock,
$5 par value $19,779,870.00
5,734,000 shares common (no par value)... 13,660,163.56

Table 4 shows the number of shares and percentage of
the total owned at the end of 1922 by the important holding
companies.

Since both the common and the preferred stock have
equal voting power, share for share, we can combine the
two.

TABLE 5

TOTAL NUMBER OF SHARES OF CAPITAL STOCK OF RADIO COR-
PORATION OWNED BY IMPORTANT HOLDING COMPANIES, 1922

Held by	No. of Shares	Per Cent
General Electric Co................2,496,800		25.7
Westinghouse Elect. and Mfg. Co.....2,000,000		20.6
American Tel. and Tel. Co.......... 400,000		4.1
United Fruit Co................... 360,000		3.7
Total shares 9,689,974		100.0*

*The other 50% of the stock is either held by former owners of the American
Marconi Company and by other smaller individuals and corporations, or is actively
traded in on the exchanges. See also statements of ownership of *Wireless Age*, which
up to its merger in 1925 with *Popular Radio*, was published by the Wireless Press,
Limited, a subsidiary of the Radio Corporation of America.

THE SOUTH AMERICAN SITUATION

In the year 1920 the South American Radio Corporation
was organized for the purpose of handling the radio overseas business of South America.[1] This corporation was to
be jointly owned by the British Marconi and the Radio
Corporation. Although the capital was to be provided half
and half by the two sponsors, the original contract stipulated that the board of directors was to consist of seven
members, five to be named by the Radio Corporation of
America, and two by the British Marconi Company. The

[1]See *Report of Directors of Radio Corporation of America to Stockholders for Year Ended December 31, 1920*, p. 5.

management and control of the stations were to be in Americans' hands.

This contract was not carried out for the reason that the British Marconi immediately began an agitation to change the provisions as to the representation on the board so as to give the British company the same number of directors as the American company. Finally, toward the end of the year 1920, it was agreed that the South American Company should have nine directors, of whom the British should appoint four and the Radio Corporation five. The management was still to be in the hands of Americans.[1]

But other countries and their companies were getting a foothold in South America. French and German wireless companies had procured concessions and were contemplating the erection of high-power stations in the principal republics of South America. To quote the *Report of the Directors* of the Radio Corporation for the year ending December 31, 1921: "The erection of individual stations by different nationals would have meant duplication of capital in countries where the prospective business was too meager to warrant such duplication, particularly as the construction of stations was very expensive; and the wave lengths suitable for long-distance international radio communications were so few that they should be used at their full capacity; moreover, the national feeling with reference to communications ran too high to permit the successful execution of competitive programs. To have proceeded with individual competitive stations would have been highly wasteful and uneconomic."[2]

GRANT OF RIGHTS TO BOARD OF TRUSTEES

With the purpose of preventing this duplication of sta-

---

[1] See testimony of Owen D. Young before a subcommittee of the Committee on Interstate Commerce of the United States Senate in regard to S 4301—a bill to prevent the unauthorized landing of submarine cables in the United States, January 11, 1921, pp. 343 ff.

[2] Page 5.

tions, a meeting of representatives of the four companies was arranged.[1] The conference took place in Paris, where, on October 14, 1921, an agreement was signed. This unique document resembles so strikingly a "Radio Monroe Doctrine" that it deserves more detail treatment.[2]

The four parties agree to make certain grants to a board of trustees numbering nine in all. These assignments include:

1. All concessions now owned or hereafter acquired by the four parties, or any of them, up to February 26, 1945, relating to communication from South America to external points, but not including ship-to-shore traffic.

2. Exclusive divisible and transferable license to use, but not to make and sell, radio apparatus under all patent rights now owned or hereafter acquired by the four parties.

Each of the parties also agrees that it will not directly or through subsidiary and affiliated companies engage in the business of external radio communication in the South American republics during the period of the trusteeship; and that if any concessions are already held by any company in which either of the four contracting companies is interested, the interested party will use its best endeavors to persuade the subsidiary to grant its external communication and patent rights to the trustees.

A NEW "MONROE DOCTRINE"

As mentioned above, the board of trustees is to consist of nine members. Two are to be appointed by each of the four contracting parties; the ninth, or the chairman, is to be the nominee of the Radio Corporation and is to be an American "of high standing" and not connected with the

---

[1]The four companies were: Radio Corporation of America, British Marconi Company, Compagnie Generale de Telegraphie sans Fil, and Gesellschaft für Drahtlose Telegraphie, m.b.H.

[2]The reader will find a complete copy of the main and supplementary agreement in the Appendix (SS) of the Federal Trade Commission *Report on the Radio Industry*.

American company. The chairman may vote in case of tie. Then comes this peculiar provision, which has been characterized as the "Monroe Doctrine in Radio":

In any case in which the voting of the trustees appointed by the four parties hereto respectively shall so result as to leave the trustees appointed by any one of the four parties in a minority and the said party believes that injustice has been done to it by the said majority vote the trustees appointed by the said party may appeal to the chairman to veto the proposed action of the majority, and if the chairman, after full discussion, is of the opinion that the said proposed action would do substantial injustice to the said minority, he shall have the power to forbid it and to cancel the resolution agreed to by the said majority.

In other words, the American chairman has the veto power.

The agreement makes provision for the formation of so-called national companies for the conduct of radio communications between South America and other parts of the world. In these companies the trustees shall control at least 60% of the voting power. Each company is to be managed by a board of directors and shall be directly operated by a general manager assisted by four operators, one of whom shall be nominated by each party to the agreement. The latter shall, however, be subject to the orders of, and to dismissal by, the general manager. The president of the National Company shall be a citizen of the Republic in which it is incorporated, and the general manager also shall preferably be such a citizen. The original agreement provided for either the formation of new Argentine and Brazilian national companies, or the taking in and changing the names of the then existing corporations in those republics.

Substantial progress in this plan has been made. The local organizations in the Argentine and Brazil have been made over into national companies; the British station at Bogota, Colombia, and the German station at Cartagena, Colombia, have been purchased; the territory has been extended so as to include Central American countries except

European possessions, Cuba, Porto Rico, and those of the United States.

It should be noted that the rights extended to the trustees include only those pertaining to external communication. The South American Radio Corporation was kept in existence, and all the stock is now owned by the Radio Corporation. This company was retained to develop those rights which are outside the scope of the trusteeship; that is, the "development of continental and internal radio communications and the merchandising of amateur, experimental, and commercial apparatus."[1] Likewise, the South American subsidiaries of the four contracting parties have been kept in existence. By a subsequent agreement the Radio Sud America was formed by the trustees to handle the sale of radio apparatus in South America. Each of the four contracting parties agreed to limit its individual selling activities and to make use of this organization as the sole distributing agency for its products.[2]

ADVANTAGES OF TRUSTEESHIP ARRANGEMENT

The advantages of this trusteeship arrangement for South America are manifold:

1. Because of the great amount of static in the heated air over the tropics, and because of the projecting high land over and through which the waves must pass,[3] very high power is required for radio transmission from South America to the other continents of the world. This fact makes the cost of constructing and operating these stations very great.

---

[1] Quotation from *Report of Directors of Radio Corporation of America for Year Ended December 31, 1921.*

[2] For an account of the recent dissolution of the Radio Sud America, see Chapter XV. The trusteeship is still in effect for external radio communication from South America.

[3] Statement of Admiral Bullard of the United States navy. Cable Landing Hearing of Subcommittee of U. S. Senate Committee on Interstate Commerce on bill S 4301, January 11, 1921, p. 344.

2. This arrangement tends to eliminate or at least to reduce to a minimum the controversies which would surely have arisen under the former system of separate concessions.

3. The field is not sufficient to pay an adequate return to many independent companies operating a large number of expensive, high-power stations.

4. It makes for economy of wave lengths, the number of which is limited.[1]

5. It facilitates prompt construction of a station when the need for it is seen, since the resources available to the trustees are much larger than could be mustered by one single concern.

THE CHINESE SITUATION

The Chinese situation resembles in many ways that of South America before the organization of the trusteeship. Various foreign interests are obtaining concessions in China. The British Marconi Company and the Chinese Government own, together, the Chinese National Wireless Company, which has acquired concessions. The Federal Telegraph Company of California, in 1921, obtained certain rights. Japanese and Danish interests also hold concessions from the Chinese Government.[2]

The Radio Corporation of America early suggested a trusteeship arrangement in most respects similar to the South American, as this would "give China a direct international communication within six months or, at the outside, a year. It would insure an open-door policy in communica-

---

[1] But see statement of Senatore Marconi appearing in the August 16, 1924, number of the *Literary Digest*, in which he says that better long-distance transmission is possible with the short wave lengths—that is, feet and inches—than with the lengths running up into the thousands. If Marconi's statement is correct, it would mean the opening up of a considerably larger number of wave lengths than we consider available at the present time.

[2] Letter from Owen D. Young to James R. Sheffield, December 7, 1921. The full text of the letter is given in the *Report of the Federal Trade Commission on the Radio Industry*, pp. 60-62.

tion, cooperation of all the principal governments, and bring China the technical and financial resources of the principal wireless companies of the world."

Owen D. Young also suggested to Elihu Root that this question be taken up by the Disarmament Conference meeting in Washington at the call of President Harding. Mr. Root, however, declined to place this problem on the agenda, on the ground that it was too complicated a subject in the limited time allowed for the conference. For this reason and because of the fact that the Navy Department was lukewarm toward Mr. Young's proposition, the plans failed to materialize.

AGREEMENT WITH THE FEDERAL TELEGRAPH COMPANY

Besides the American Marconi Company, the Federal Telegraph Company of California was, prior to 1919, the only radio company operating on the Pacific Coast. In 1921 this corporation entered into a contract with the Republic of China for the erection of five high-power stations in China[1] and their operation for a period of ten years in partnership with the Chinese Government, China to pay by means of a bond issue. The Federal Telegraph Company asked the Radio Corporation of America to cooperate in the carrying out of this contract. Accordingly, the latter, under date of September 8, 1922, agreed with the California corporation to form a new company, the Federal Telegraph Company of Delaware, to take over the contract and obligations with the Chinese Government. The Radio Corporation of America acquired the controlling interest in the new company, and Owen D. Young became its chairman.

NATURE OF RADIO CORPORATION SERVICE

The Radio Corporation of America classifies its business as shown on the following page.

----

[1] One 1,000 kilowatts; three 100 kilowatts; and one 200 kilowatts.

1. Traffic department, which handles the international, as well as the marine, radiogram traffic.[1]

2. Sales department, which sells radio apparatus to foreign and domestic customers, which include governments, commercial companies, amateurs, experimenters, and the radio broadcast audience.

3. Marine department, which sells and rents radio apparatus to steamship owners and wireless companies.

4. Engineering department, which maintains or improves the standards of radio efficiency. The corporation conducts extensive research projects.

This corporation has made substantial progress. Formed especially to carry on point-to-point communication and for the sale of radio apparatus, its activity has been enlarged by the advent of popular broadcasting. As a competitor of the cable, it has drawn to itself an increasing proportion of international traffic and has been a pioneer in the lowering of rates.[2] The occasional breakdown of cable facilities has demonstrated the usefulness of the Radio Corporation's work. The interruption of the transpacific cable during the Japanese earthquake of 1923 threw an additional load on the American-Japanese radio circuit. The internal strife in Ireland resulted in the crippling of some of the transatlantic cables, and the Radio Corporation handled the extra traffic.[3] Occasionally the corporation's facilities have served as a valuable supplement to the land line telegraphs and telephones. An important part of the organization, in fact, consists of the traffic agreements which it has made with foreign nations and companies, as well as with the Western Union and the Postal Telegraph in the United States.[4]

---

[1] The work and policies of the traffic department will be discussed in greater detail in Chapter VIII.

[2] For discussion of relation between radio and the cable, see Chapter XIV.

[3] Nine of the eighteen transatlantic cables make relay landings in southwestern Ireland.

[4] For a description of these agreements, as well as of the method of handling international and marine radio messages, see Chapter VIII.

GROWING IMPORTANCE OF BROADCASTING

Table 6 shows the classified gross income of the Radio Corporation of America for the years 1921 to 1924.[1]

TABLE 6

CLASSIFIED GROSS INCOME OF RADIO CORPORATION OF AMERICA, 1921-1924

Kind of Business	1924		1923		1922		1921	
	Amount	Per Cent	Amount	Per Cent	Amount	Per Cent	Amount	Per Cent
Total....	$54,848,131	100.00	$26,394,790	100.00	$14,830,856	100.00	$4,160,845	100.00
Gross Sales....	50,747,202	92.5	22,465,091	85.1	11,286,489	76.1	1,468,920	35.3
Transoceanic Communication.	3,358,584	6.1	3,191,559	12.1	2,914,283	19.7	2,138,626	51.4
Marine Service..	742,345	1.4	738,140	2.8	630,084	4.2	553,299	13.3

While the aggregate receipts obtained from transoceanic communication and marine service have made a substantial and healthy progress, the greater increase in sales indicates the growing dependence of the Radio Corporation upon broadcasting. While in 1921 transoceanic communication tolls yielded a little more than 51% of the total receipts, this percentage has been constantly falling until, in 1924 only 6% of the gross revenues were obtained from this source. On the other hand, the proportion from the sales of radio apparatus, a large part of which was for broadcasting receiving sets, became larger and larger until, in 1924, it was 92% of the total.[2] This necessitated setting up an organization for the developing and merchandising of the newly popularized apparatus.

[1] The six months ended June 30, 1925, show a total income of $19,814,389, of which 15 million was earned during the first quarter. A deficit of $391,-000 resulted in the second quarter. The second and third quarters are adversely affected by the seasonal nature of radio, while the last quarter is as a rule the most prosperous.

[2] Many of the sales were, of course, made to foreign countries and companies to establish their ends of transoceanic communication circuits.

IV

THE RADIO INDUSTRY OF TODAY

Nature of radio service. Lack of authentic early figures. Radio communication after 1913. Broadcasting activity in the United States. Increased earnings of Marconi companies. Effect of telephonic broadcasting. Component parts of 1923 production. Production in 1924. Comparison of radio with other industries. Occupations in radio. Telegraph operating. Broadcasting station operating. Radio engineering. Manufacturing and selling. Increasing number of operators licensed.

THE radio renders a service of communication, the various types of which may be classified as follows:

$$
\text{Radio}
\begin{cases}
\text{Telegraphy}
\begin{cases}
\text{broadcasting} \\
\text{point-to-point}
\end{cases} \\
\text{Telephony}
\begin{cases}
\text{broadcasting} \\
\text{point-to-point}
\end{cases}
\end{cases}
$$

It will be noted that radio communication can be grouped in two ways: (1) when voice and sound waves of various kinds are transformed into electromagnetic waves, carried through the ether, and reconverted into sound waves, it is called *telephony*; (2) when a message is transformed by hand or machine into a system of dots and dashes, carried through the ether, and by means of the proper rectifying agency, reconverted into dots and dashes to be read by machine or by ear, it is called *telegraphy*.

Both telephony and telegraphy may be of two general types. Messages, reports, dots and dashes, the voice, may be addressed to no one in particular so that any one who has the necessary apparatus, skill, ambition, and interest may hear. The transmitting station does not call any definite station or person; neither does the receiver acknowledge the receipt of the message. This is broadcasting. Then we have the system of point-to-point communication wherein the sending operator calls a certain receiving station, which must answer with the "go ahead" signal before the message will be sent. Such messages are always addressed. Even here there may be eavesdroppers, but in most countries the contents of the radiograms may not be divulged to or by any unauthorized person under heavy penalty. There are also methods making for a limited secrecy, such as the use of the code, high wave lengths, unusual rapidity of sending, and the beam system.

There are thus four kinds of radio communication. When using the term "radio," people ordinarily think in terms of telephonic broadcasting. But telephonic broadcasting, significant as it may seem to the average man, is slightly, if at all, more important than point-to-point telegraphy. The Radio Corporation of America, which has a monopoly of the American end of private commercial transoceanic point-to-point telegraphy, handles about 30% of the messages crossing the Atlantic and 50% of those crossing the Pacific. Practically all stations, except those licensed only to broadcast, do a large amount of their business through point-to-point telegraphy. Telegraphic broadcasting has been common for more than a score of years, especially for the sending of time and weather signals, news items, and orders to ships at sea. Point-to-point telephony has been used, but is not considered practicable or desirable, except for communication to isolated points or to ships at sea, because, on account of the congestion of the ether, the land lines should handle all such conversation. Experience has taught that for point-to-point communication the system of dots and dashes is the best; whereas for broadcasting, telephony is the most adaptable.

To furnish the apparatus for the carrying on of these four distinct types of service, there has been a rapid growth in radio manufacturing. It may be logical, therefore, to discuss the growth and extent of the radio industry under the two general aspects of communication and production of equipment. When present-day statistics of manufactures and sales of radio are given, they include by necessity both the equipment used for point-to-point communication and broadcasting. It is impossible to know beforehand for which of these purposes a piece of antenna wire, a battery, or other radio apparatus is to be used.

LACK OF AUTHENTIC EARLY FIGURES

Though figures are available as to the number of radio stations prior to 1913, they are regarded as inaccurate, for the reason that most of the nations of the world did not then require a license or permit of the operators even of transmitting sets. In the year 1904 Great Britain passed her first act for the regulation of wireless telegraphy, which provided that "a person shall not establish any wireless telegraph station, or install or work any apparatus for wireless telegraphy, in any place or on board any British ship except under and in accordance with a license granted in that behalf by the Postmaster-General."[1] This law was, as far as the writer knows, the pioneer in this field. But Great Britain, the home of the Marconi Company, was naturally the first to legislate upon this subject. Other nations were not so prompt. Canada passed her original radio regulation law in 1913, and the United States in 1912.[2] It is true that the Radiotelegraph Conventions made an effort to classify and to give governments certain regulatory powers over stations, but not all nations had subscribed to these covenants.

The United States Bureau of Navigation reported that in the years 1906-1912, inclusive, the number of radio stations in the world was as follows:[3]

---

[1] 4 Edw. 7. ch. 24.

[2] A preliminary act had been passed in 1910.

[3] Compiled from annual *List of Radio Stations*, issued by Bureau of Navigation.

Year	Number	Year	Number
1906	627	1909	1,480
1907	784	1910	1,979
1908	1,016	1912	2,619

Lloyd's Register reported in 1911 that there were 1,013 vessels equipped with radio throughout the world.[1]

DATA ON RADIO COMMUNICATION AFTER 1913

From the year 1913 up to date we have relatively authentic statistics. Table 7 indicates the number of wireless stations in the world from 1912 to 1924.

TABLE 7
CLASSIFICATION OF WIRELESS STATIONS*
(All Stations American Except Sixth Group)

Class	1912	1913	1914	1915	1916	1917	1918	1919	1920	1921	1922	1923	1924
Amateurs...	†	1,224	2,796	3,805	4,870	‡	‡	‡	5,922	10,809	15,504	16,570	15,545
Special Land	†	22	53	118	183	‡	‡	‡	164	383	525	566	665
U. S. Commercial Land.....	†	75	91	117	129	38	38	38	94	139	185	236	289
U. S. Commercial Ship......	367	483	555	585	604	836	1,478	2,312	2,808	2,978	2,773	2,723	2,741
Government Stations..	†	306	385	421	442	§	§	1,849	1,574	1,385	1,478	1,299	1,249
Foreign Stations..	†	302	3,899	4,403	3,748	4,365	4,356	4,669	6,842	8,154	11,462	11,349	11,979
Broadcasting (U.S. only)											382	573	535
Total	367	2,412	7,779	9,449	9,976	5,239	5,872	8,868	17,404	23,848	32,309	33,316	33,003

*Compiled from figures furnished by W. F. Downey, supervisor of radio, Bureau of Navigation, Department of Commerce.
†No record kept.
‡War period, no amateur or special land stations.
§No listing during war period.

BROADCASTING ACTIVITY IN THE UNITED STATES

The first broadcasting licenses were issued by the United States Department of Commerce in September, 1921, and from that time the growth of broadcasting in the United States has been rapid but spasmodic. Table 8 shows the

[1] *Report of U. S. Commissioner of Navigation*, 1911, p. 44.

TABLE 8

BROADCASTING STATION ACTIVITY DURING EACH MONTH—FROM
SEPTEMBER, 1921*

Year	New Stations	Deletions	Increase	Decrease	Total
1921					
September........	3		3		3
October...........	1		1		4
November.........	1		1		5
December.........	23		23		28
1922					
January...........	8		8		36
February..........	24		24		60
March............	77		77		137
April.............	76		76		213
May..............	97		97		310
June..............	72		72		382
July..............	76		76		458
August...........	50		50		508
September........	39	23	16		524
October...........	46	22	24		548
November.........	46	29	17		565
December.........	31	20	11		576
1923					
January...........	28	34		6	570
February..........	24	13	11		581
March............	30	29	1		582
April.............	21	14	7		589
May..............	27	25	2		591
June..............	32	50		18	573
July..............	19	25		6	567
August...........	7	11		4	563
September........	15	16		1	562
October...........	22	14	8		570
November.........	12	33		21	549
December.........	12	34		22	527
1924					
January...........	27	20	7		534
February..........	21	7	14		548
March............	32	11	21		569
April.............	27	19	8		577
May..............	23	11	12		589
June..............	27	81		54	535
July..............	22	13	9		544
August...........	7	18		11	533

*Furnished by courtesy of W. E. Downey, supervisor of radio, Department of
Commerce, Bureau of Navigation.

number of new stations, discontinuances, increase, decrease, and total for every month from September, 1921, to August, 1924.

Several interesting points may be mentioned regarding this table:

1. The number of casualties in the radio broadcasting field has been great. The total of new stations established and licensed up to August, 1924, was 1,105. The total of discontinuances during the same period was 572. In other words, a little more than one-half of the stations have dropped out. Five hundred and thirty-three had survived up to August.

2. The greatest mortality occurred in June, 1924. There were several reasons for this. In the first place, the demands of the music writers for royalties became most insistent at about this time. Many stations, rather than pay the fee of $500 or more demanded by the Society of Music Composers, Authors, and Publishers, discontinued their operations. The demands of the American Telephone and Telegraph Company tended to have the same effect. In the second place, the competition among stations was becoming very severe and a considerable number of broadcasters were beginning to ask themselves the question: Does broadcasting pay? A large number dropped out on account of financial difficulty. In the third place, public interest in radio waves decreases appreciably during the summer months.

3. The reader will note the consistent growth from September, 1921, until the high point in the number of stations was reached in May, 1923—591. From that time the number has been fairly steady, though in May, 1924, it reached 589.

INCREASED EARNINGS OF MARCONI COMPANIES

The gross revenues of the British Marconi Company and of the Marconi International Marine were, for the years 1915-1923, as shown in Table 9.

TABLE 9

GROSS REVENUES OF BRITISH MARCONI COMPANY AND MARCONI
INTERNATIONAL MARINE, 1915-1923*

Year	British Marconi	Marconi International Marine
1915	£581,125	£ 208,927
1916	485,995	270,230
1917	539,856	470,855
1918	765,700	563,444
1919	946,997†	772,462
1920	563,314	933,723
1921	553,729	1,084,590
1922	556,289	1,104,135
1923	552,113	976,231

*Source, Moody's *Manual*, and *Reports* of the companies.
†Does not include the £590,000 damages for breach of 1912 contract by English Government.

The earnings of the Marconi Wireless Telegraph Company, Limited, have been comparatively steady because of the fact that it is largely a holding company. On the operating side this company is interested in wireless services from Great Britain to most of the other points in the world. The stations at the other end are controlled by subsidiary or associated companies, or by the government. On the other hand, the International Company is only to a slight extent a holding company. Its field is maritime operation and installation of wireless. As a result, its business has fluctuated up and down with the prosperity of the shipping industry. From 1915 to 1922 the receipts of this company have been multiplied by six. The year 1923 saw a decline due to the continued depression in the shipping business.

Both the British and the International companies have been practically independent of the business of broadcasting, and their growth has been due to the development of point-to-point communication. The broadcasting end of British radio has been taken over by the British Broadcasting Company, on the board of which the Marconi Company has representation.

EFFECT OF TELEPHONIC BROADCASTING

In telegraphic point-to-point communication broadcasting, for which radio was primarily intended by its first enthusiasts, it has maintained a steady, normal increase. The development of telephonic broadcasting, however, gave to this industry an impetus which made for an appearance of mushroom growth. Fully 3,000 manufacturers are producing sets or parts of sets.[1] *System* estimates that there are about 1,000 radio wholesalers and 20,000 radio retailers in the United States.[2] Every little village and hamlet has its dealer in radio, be it electrical shop, furniture store, or restaurant. The characteristic sign of the spark is evident over the doors and on the windows of numerous shops. Mail-order houses and chain stores are taking up the new business. The English language has swollen. A writer in the *Century Magazine* has estimated that 30 magazines have been poured out upon an enthusiastic and receptive public.[3]

The *Census of Manufactures of the United States* reports the following statistics for radio production in round numbers. (Returns only from concerns which produced $5,000 or more worth of product per year.)

1904..........	$114,000	1919.........	$ 8,074,000*
1909..........	448,000	1921.........	9,549,000
1914..........	792,000	1923.........	43,460,000†

*Figures for 1919 include motor generators, which were not included in the other years' reports.

†The figures do not include radio tubes for sale as such. These were, in 1923, valued at $4,572,251. "A part of these tubes were sold to manufacturers of complete receiving sets (and their value is, therefore, included in the total value of such sets) and the remainder were sold to individual purchasers for use in the construction of home-made sets."

[1] *The Radio Dealer Year-Book for 1924-25*, issued by the Radio Dealer Magazine, New York, contains almost 200 pages (exclusive of advertising) of names of radio manufacturers.

[2] *System*, A. W. Shaw Company, Chicago, January, 1925, p. 9. This article also gives the following figures: radio periodicals, 30; books about radio, 250; people connected with the industry, 250,000; radio audience, 8,000,000; receiving sets, 2,500,000.

[3] Bruce Bliven in June, 1924, issue, in article "How Radio is Remaking Our World."

Radio exports are taken up in Chapter XV.

COMPONENT PARTS OF 1923 PRODUCTION

The total of $43,460,676, for the year 1923, is composed of the items in Table 10. (The figures in Table 10 are taken from an announcement of the *Census of Manufactures*, issued October 9, 1924, and are stated to be subject to correction.)

The indirect expenditures for radio are also significant. Take, for example, the copper in radio sets. A survey of the radio industry, just completed by the Copper and Brass Research Association, discloses that on the basis of an estimated total of 2,500,000 sets in use today, radio apparatus

TABLE 10

PRODUCTION OF RADIO APPARATUS, 1923
(Reported by 290 Establishments)

Total value*	$43,460,676
Loudspeakers:	
Number	508,001
Value	$ 5,620,961
Head-sets:	
Number	1,889,614
Value	$ 5,352,441
Receiving sets:	
Tube type—	
Number	414,588
Value	$12,065,992
Crystal type—	
Number	116,497
Value	$ 550,201
Transmitting sets:	
Number	1,073
Value	$ 900,230
Transformers:	
Number	1,700,024
Value	$ 3,773,213

*Not including tubes for sale as such.

in the United States has consumed 5,000,000 pounds of copper—2 pounds being necessary to a set.[1]

PRODUCTION IN 1924

As to the production of radio for the year 1924, only estimates are available. The Babson Statistical Organization has calculated that $350,000,000 will be spent in the United States for radio equipment in 1924, of which $50,000,000 will go for tubes and $250,000,000 for sets and parts. The Radio Manufacturers Association says that the 1924 production of radio is approximately $400,000,000.

TABLE 10 (*Continued*)
PRODUCTION OF RADIO APPARATUS, 1923
(Reported by 290 Establishments)

Rheostats:	
Number	1,089,721
Value ....$	716,774
Lightning arresters:	
Number	355,161
Value ....$	196,534
Miscellaneous parts, value........$	14,284,330

RADIO TUBES, FOR SALE AS SUCH

Total:	
Number	2,601,575
Value ....$	4,572,251
Under 5 watts:	
Number	2,559,206
Value ....$	3,788,167
5 to 50 watts:	
Number	15,167
Value ....$	80,529
Over 50 watts:	
Number	27,202
Value ....$	703,555

[1]"The Copper Used in Radio," *American Industries*, July, 1924, p. 39.

Charles H. Porter, the executive secretary, predicts that the radio business for 1925 will exceed $700,000,000.[1]

Taking Babson's statistics, for example, as a basis, we would conclude that the total manufactures for the year 1924 amounted to about $175,000,000. This is on the assumption that the manufacturers' price is about one-half of that paid by the consumer. This is probably a rather liberal estimate.

TABLE II

THE VALUE OF THE PRODUCTS OF VARIOUS INDUSTRIES, 1904-1923*

(*In thousands of dollars*)

Year	All Industries	Radio	Phonographs	Sporting Goods	Automobiles
1904...	$14,793,000	$ 114	$ 10,237	$ 7,032	$ 26,645
1909...	20,672,000	448	11,726	11,052	193,823
1914...	24,246,000	792	22,116	13,235	503,230
1919...	62,418,000	8,074	158,548	23,840	2,387,903
1921...	43,653,000	9,549	98,212	31,811	1,671,386
1923...	60,481,000	46,460†	107,276	41,797	3,163,327

*From *Census of Manufactures.*

†The total value of radio apparatus manufactured in the United States was $43,460,-676. This figure does not include the radio tubes valued at $4,572,251. Some of these tubes were used in the complete sets; the most of them, however, were probably sold direct to the consumer. Assume that for every one tube used in the complete sets two were sold to the private consumer for replacement or construction purposes. This is perhaps a reasonable ratio. Therefore, in the interest of accuracy, the value of two-thirds of the total tubes, or about $3,000,000, has been added to $43,460,676, making about $46,460,000.

COMPARISON OF RADIO WITH OTHER INDUSTRIES

From these tables and the logarithmic graph, Figure 4, it will be noted that other industries have experienced as phenomenal a growth as radio. Compare, for example, the automobile and the radio curves. They are at all points practically parallel, indicating a similar proportional increase. From 1904 to 1909, however, the automobile manufactures increased more rapidly than the radio. For the period from 1914 to 1919 the radio curve is steeper, showing that radio developed more rapidly proportionally.

[1]Letter to the writer, October 3, 1924.

From 1921 to 1923 the increase of radio manufactures has far exceeded that of automobiles.

Moreover, when practically all other industries, as well as the total manufactures, were suffering relapses during the hard times from 1920 on, the radio and the sporting goods industries were enjoying a period of great prosperity.

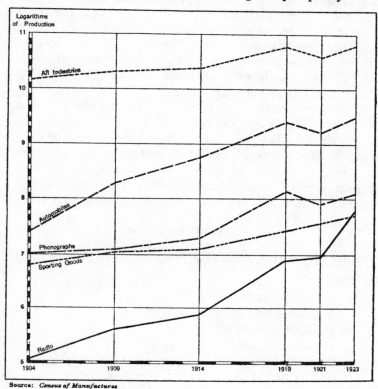

Source: *Census of Manufactures*

Figure 4: Value of products of various industries in the United States, 1904-1923.

The increase in radio, as well as in automobiles and phonographs, has been more rapid proportionally than the increase in total manufactures. This indicates that these industries have risen in the scale of importance. For example, radio has grown from an insignificant industry until today it ranks among the foremost in total product.

The fact that radio continued its development during the recent depression is not due to any superior soundness in the industry, but to the rise and popularization of radio telephonic broadcasting and to the interest caused by the early sense of popular curiosity. Radio, being a relatively new industry, naturally increased very rapidly. It will be seen that the automobile and the phonograph industries suffered their first severe setbacks during 1920 and 1921, and had successfully tided over the unfavorable conditions in 1903-1904, 1907-1909, and 1914.[1]

In comparing with other industries one notes the fact that for every dollar spent for radio, almost $69 is spent for motor vehicles, about $20 for boots and shoes, $15 for cane sugar, $13 for railroad cars, $1.12 for typewriters, 98 cents for sewing machines, 88 cents for chewing gum, 53 cents for lead pencils, 52 cents for matches, 43 cents for fountain pens, 36 cents for bicycles, 13 cents for writing inks.

OCCUPATIONS IN RADIO

Radio as an occupation may be classified in the following groups:

1. Telegraph operating
2. Broadcasting station operating
3. Radio engineering
4. Research radio engineering
5. Manufacturing and mechanical skilled work
6. Salesmanship and store management

TELEGRAPH OPERATING

To a person interested in the operating end of radio, service as wireless operator aboard a passenger or a freight vessel provides a good approach. Aboard ship a person

---

[1] For a consideration of the saturation point in radio, see Chapter XV.

learns the practical side and, what is more important, develops the reliance which comes only from first-hand experience and responsibility. Normally he must first procure a license from the Department of Commerce before beginning such service. The examinations for such licenses are given regularly at United States Customs-Houses and Federal Buildings in the important seaports, also in Detroit and Chicago. The test covers operation and knowledge of the care and construction of radio apparatus, as well as a few questions on the international regulations regarding radio. To receive a first-class license the applicant must pass the written examination with a grade of 75 and must copy at least 20 words of continental code per minute. A grade of 65 and 12 words per minute will make the applicant eligible for a second-grade commercial license. Night schools, trade schools, and a few resident high schools will give the training necessary to pass the examinations.

Upon receiving the license, the operator will be eligible for a position aboard ship or, in exceptional cases, in a land station. At the present time jobs are rather scarce on account of inactivity in our shipping due to the slump in foreign trade and demand for American goods. Ship positions pay from $75 to $125 a month and living expenses. The ship operator has ample opportunity to study and improve himself for the trade. From a position aboard ship, a person may ascend into the rank of operator in a land station, and thence, possibly, if he is apt, into the position of chief operator, the superintendent of a station, or a radio supervisor.

The prospective operator may ask: How can I know whether I am fitted for the trade? If one is of a nervous or fidgety temperament or has a tendency to work slowly, one should seek another occupation. A good radiotelegraph operator is born, not made. Large concerns, such as the United Fruit Company, are more and more requiring that the operator be able to handle a typewriter at his work both on land and at sea.

BROADCASTING STATION OPERATING

The writer has been informed by Mr. Downey, radio supervisor of the Department of Commerce, that until a short time ago most of the holders of second-class licenses failed to renew them at the end of their term, but either dropped out or took first-grade commercial licenses so as to be eligible for a better position aboard ship. With the advent of popular broadcasting, however, there was a change. A second-class operator is now allowed to operate a broadcasting station. Hence many of the second-class licenses are renewed. Thus there has been made available to the radio enthusiast a new occupation, which is becoming very popular. Though fully as difficult, this position does not require the peculiar nervous system essential to a good commercial ship, or land, operator. The October, 1924, radio conference recommended a new type of examination and a special license for those who plan on entering this field of activity.

RADIO ENGINEERING

A radio engineer may or may not be able to receive or send messages. He must, however, be an expert at the handling of the radio apparatus from the engineering point of view. A few colleges and universities are granting bachelors' degrees in radio engineering. When this type of degree is stabilized, it will correspond to the equivalent degrees in electrical and mechanical engineering. The large broadcasting and commercial stations and companies have their radio engineers, whose duty it is to handle and design the apparatus used and to make suggestions for the improvement of the service.

From radio engineer to radio research engineer is only a short step. One man may perform both functions. The radio engineer, in making plans for the construction of the apparatus in which he is interested, often anticipates what will happen in the future, sees far ahead, and seeks to develop new devices and methods for the improvement of the service. John Hays Hammond, Jr., though technically not even a radio engineer, has made very substantial improvements in the radio service, especially in the field of remote control. In this respect at least he may be spoken of as a radio research engineer, just as the expert accountant may be interested in practicing and at the same time in improving the methods of his profession. The big manufacturers of radio and electrical apparatus have large research staffs engaged in the development of the business.

MANUFACTURING AND SELLING

In radio manufacturing there is need for a large number of skilled men who understand mechanics and are able to apply themselves to the production of wireless apparatus. Herbert Hoover has estimated that more than 200,000 men are dependent on the radio industry for their livelihood. (*System* estimates 250,000.) The business is of such a nature that a large proportion of the work must be done by hand.

For the person who is interested in selling radio apparatus, a fair knowledge of radio theory and practice is usually necessary. The National Radio Institute of Washington, D. C., reports that a large number of its graduates are entering the selling and store management branch of the business.

INCREASING NUMBER OF OPERATORS LICENSED

Table 12 shows the number of commercial and amateur operators licensed by the Department of Commerce during each year from 1913 to 1924.

The increase in the number of commercial operators licensed from 1,645 in 1919 to 4,652 in 1920 is largely due to the fact that many discharged army and navy operators took the examination. Some of these men actually entered the merchant-marine service; others took the tests in order to have one more choice in the location of a job.

The increased number of amateurs after 1920 is one indication of the great interest taken at the present time in radio. Many of them will be future inventors and commercial and broadcasting operators.

TABLE 12

RADIO OPERATORS LICENSED BY UNITED STATES DEPARTMENT OF COMMERCE, 1913-24*

Year	Commercial Operators Licensed†	Amateur Operators Licensed†
1913................	1,932	1,841
1914................	339	1,172
1915................	1,653	3,067
1916................	1,278	4,199
1917................	1,682	3,302
1918................	1,616	....‡
1919................	1,645	....‡
1920................	4,652	5,988
1921................	2,722	6,207
1922................	3,136	8,920
1923................	2,860	9,908
1924................	3,370	9,545

*From figures by W. E. Downey, radio supervisor, Department of Commerce.
†Since operators are licensed for a term of two years, it is necessary to take the sum of two succeeding years in order to find the total number of licensed operators at any time. This method, of course, does not allow for withdrawals and cancelation of licenses.
‡No radio operators licensed.

Though in the past the demand for men trained in the various phases of radio has probably exceeded the supply, the result being relatively high wages, the operation of economic laws is rapidly bringing about a readjustment. In the absence of artificial restriction, the returns from one industry or occupation cannot long exceed those in another requiring equal skill and training. A person entering the work of radio would do well to keep this fact in mind, so as to avoid possible disappointment.

ECONOMICS OF THE RADIO INDUSTRY

PART II

BRINGING RADIO SERVICE TO THE PEOPLE

V

THE MARKETING OF RADIO

Nature of early demand for radio. Effects of shift in demand. Radio in disrepute. Progress toward standardization. Unfair price-cutting. Preventives of unfair price-cutting. Resale price maintenance. Radio manufacturer is center of marketing process. Manufacturers' representatives. Manufacturer—Wholesaler—Retailer. Direct-to-retailer system. Extensive advertising as a stabilizer. The place and functions of the radio wholesaler. Need of market analysis. Desirability of exclusive franchise. Relations between manufacturers and wholesalers or retailers. Direct selling not practicable. Proposed marketing plan.

WITH the rise of popular telephonic broadcasting, there have been two main developments in the marketing of radio: (1) the efforts of the existing companies to elaborate their selling machine so as to take full advantage of the new fad; (2) the entering of this field by a considerable number of new radio manufacturers and business men—some reputable, conscientious, farseeing, and eager to aid in the development of a sound marketing and merchandising policy; others, and their numbers were great, laboring under the impression that radio was an ephemeral fancy, and attempting to exploit it before the popularity waned. Time has demonstrated the error of the latter group, but not before their unsound business practices had wrought some injury to the industry.

Under these conditions, the development of a consistent marketing policy was the first problem to be met. Radio, like any young industry, had to go through "growing pains." People were at first interested in distance reception and in volume. Selectivity in receiving sets was not so necessary on account of the relatively small number of broadcasting stations. When radio was still a novelty, enthusiasts were satisfied if they heard screeches on the wireless—just so

they were numerous and of sufficient variety. The quality
and purity of the signals was not so essential. The early
manufacturers, of course, catered to the needs of the people,
placing emphasis upon quantity rather than quality, ignor-
ing selectivity and accuracy of tuning and the elimination
of static. At first the operating mechanism of the sets was
visible, just as some of the readers will remember was the
case with the early automobile and the phonograph. The
purchasers were willing to tinker with the apparatus which
they bought, and expected to do so. They did not demand
ease and convenience of operation.

EFFECTS OF SHIFT IN DEMAND

A large number of manufacturers and dealers, both jobbers and retailers, thinking that radio would last only a
few years, produced or bought an oversupply of receiving
sets and parts. As the number of broadcasting stations
increased and as the people began to regard this new creation as a parlor utility instead of "an attic experiment,"
the nature of the demand shifted. Consumers now looked
for apparatus which would enable them to tune out a larger
number of stations, thus eliminating interference and diminishing static; they entered the market for sightly apparatus
which would be an ornament in the home, and above all,
they wished for sets which could be as readily operated as
a phonograph with very little tinkering and experimentation.
As a result of this change in the public desire, however,
many manufacturers and dealers found themselves over-
stocked with obsolete apparatus.

The period of the popularization of radio corresponded
roughly with the depression following the crisis of 1920.
A large number of business men found themselves either in
or on the verge of bankruptcy. Some of these naturally
turned to radio as the last resort. They did this whether
they knew anything about radio or not. Consequently,
many inadequate radio sets, hardly worthy of the name,

were turned out on a gullible public. When the consumer became educated, these concerns were naturally forced out of business, and the radio market has not yet entirely recovered from the resulting demoralization.

Into the scene entered the predatory price-cutter. Extensive price changes should be the result of basic economic conditions, such as changes in the value of gold, or the quantity of money, changes in costs, or variation in demand. But in order to stimulate the sale of other lines, some retailers and wholesales would cut the price on a comparatively standard article so as to result in a probable loss. They hoped that the additional sales of other articles would make up for the deficit. So many manufacturers were permitting their products to fall into the hands of such cut-rate dealers that the effect on the trade was unhealthy. Practically every day the buying public would read in the newspapers of further price reductions.

With such a large number of manufacturers entering a relatively new field at the same time—some experienced, others inexperienced, some with good motives, others with purely selfish intent—there was sure to be, in addition to diverse business policies, lack of uniformity in products. There was a need of standardization in nomenclature, of standardization in certain parts which can be used indiscriminately with different kinds of sets and apparatus.

RADIO IN DISREPUTE

With the unloading on the market of a heterogeneous mass of products, some of which gave satisfaction, others not, some of which had given the purchaser too great aspirations on account of the dealer's puffing talk, the interest of the public began to wane. Prospective purchasers often argued after hearing a set demonstrated, "If that is the way radio works, I guess I will wait a while before buying." Furthermore, in more recent times, the radio market has, it seems, shifted from a seller's to a buyer's market. On account of these facts, manufacturers and dealers turned to advertising as a way of recovering the good-will of the public and of introducing uniformity and soundness into the marketing methods.

Finally arose the question of the proper agency for the distribution of radio apparatus among the public. Should radio continue to be sold by the storekeeper with a niche in the wall, the hardware dealer, the department store, the music dealer, the furniture dealer, the electrical dealer, or the exclusive radio shop? If it could not be handled exclusively by any one shop, should it be retailed in connection with music, electrical supplies, or other allied or non-allied line? This can be termed the problem of ultimate outlet.

These are a few of the marketing problems confronting the radio industry today. Some of them are to a certain extent engineering in nature, such as uniform nomenclature and standardization. Most of them, however, are of a purely economic character. Several are marketing problems; others belong in the field of retailing or merchandising. To aid in the stabilization of selling policies, associations of various kinds have been formed, such as the Radio Manufacturers Association, with headquarters at Chicago, the Radio Trade Association of New York City, and the Radio Apparatus Section of the Associated Manufacturers of Electrical Supplies. These organizations are valuable in collecting and spreading information as to trade practices and in the making of recommendations for the benefit of their members.

PROGRESS TOWARD STANDARDIZATION

As already indicated, the entrance of a large number of both experienced and inexperienced radio manufacturers into the production of broadcast receiving apparatus resulted in the placing on the market of a variety of types of products which should be readily interchangeable among sets of different makes. It is generally admitted that while sets cannot very well be standardized without discouraging originality, there is a real need for uniformity in the case of parts which are used in common with sets of all kinds. Thus, the Radio Division of the Associated Manufacturers of Electrical Supplies has undertaken the standardization of battery sizes, marking of receiving set terminals, sizes and types of terminals for head-phone and loudspeaker cords, package marking for variable condensers, and many other parts.[1] The need for standardization can be concretely illustrated. It was at first common for manufacturers of condensers to describe them on the carton as containing a certain number of plates. It is apparent, however, that the number of plates has very little significance; the purchaser is interested in the capacity of the condensers. Hence the "size" should be designated in terms of microfarads. Another illustration may be drawn from the field of batteries. The sizes and shapes must be uniform so that the manufacturers of portable receiving sets may design compartments which will hold any make of battery that the user may choose. It is also essential that the marking and the location of the terminals and the amount and pressure of the current supplied by the various makes of batteries be uniform.

The pressure for standardization has come from three sources: from the United States Government, which is a large purchaser of radio apparatus, and which by the standards it sets has a far-reaching effect on the efforts of private producers; from the manufacturers, dealers, and wholesalers who benefit from standardization in that it makes for lower costs per unit, wider market, and larger sales; and from the general public, to whom uniformity in parts means an additional convenience and economy in that they will be able to buy parts with a designated advertised name, and

---

[1]For a complete list of standards adopted by the Radio Division of the Associated Manufacturers of Electrical Supplies, see *Minutes of the Annual Meeting* of this section at the Ambassador Hotel in Atlantic City, June 17-18, 1924. The standards are very detailed, and space does not permit their enumeration in these pages.

will be assured that the parts can be used with any type of standard apparatus.[1]

UNFAIR PRICE-CUTTING

In any new industry or in the sale of low-priced standard commodities such as groceries, drugs, and shoes, the practice of price-cutting is likely to arise. The process is relatively simple: a store, in order to stimulate the sales on certain of its products, will advertise reduced rates on some standard and well-known commodity. The salesman, after selling this article, is often instructed to attempt to induce the customer to purchase other articles in the store. In other words, to make up for the loss on this purchase, the dealer hopes to sell products yielding a substantial profit.[2]

PREVENTIVES OF UNFAIR PRICE-CUTTING

For this system of price-cutting a number of remedies have been devised. One of the earliest was the manufac-

---

[1] The interest in standardization has been especially apparent since the autumn of 1923. Besides the Bureau of Standards and the Radio Apparatus Section of the Associated Manufacturers of Electrical Supplies and the Radio Manufacturers Association, work has been done by a committee organized by the American Engineering Standards Committee. This committee has 26 members, representing various producing, consuming, distributing, and general radio interests. The Interdepartmental Radio Advisory Committee gives attention to the standardization of radio equipment for government use through the work of its subcommittee on technical problems. A Committee on Radio Apparatus has been formed by the Federal Specifications Board. This committee adopts standard specifications for use in the purchase of radio equipment by all government departments. The Standardization Committee of the Institute of Radio Engineers is preparing a revision of terms and symbols used in radio. (See Radio Service Bulletin, October, 1924, p. 9.) The Bureau of Standards, the Signal Corps, and the Bureau of Engineering of the Navy Department are working in cooperation with practically all the government and private standardization committees.

[2] The dealer does not always lose on the advertised and cut-priced commodity, though he likes his customer to believe so. A store can handle some line on which there may be a loss as far as the total expenses are concerned, but, unless the selling price goes below the variable expense attributed to the sale of that commodity, the loss is nil; in fact there may be a profit, because the overhead is not necessarily increased by the selling of that article.

turer's fixing the resale prices either by a formal contract or by an "understanding" through circularization of uniform price-lists, and then punishing the price-cutters by refusing to sell them more goods. But by a series of Federal Court decisions this practice has been held illegal. A manufacturer or a wholesaler who has parted with the title cannot legally fix the resale price. The goods are then under the exclusive control of the buyer.[1]

It will be noted that the condemnation of price-fixing applies only when the title has passed. It is obvious, therefore, that if the manufacturer can retain the legal title to the goods until they reach the ultimate consumer, he will be able to maintain the uniform price. Thus, some of the larger radio concerns have established territorial and district sales agencies throughout the United States, so that the title never passes out of their hands until the consumer is reached. These agencies sell for the manufacturer on commission. It is difficult for the ordinary manufacturer to carry out this policy because of the expense of maintaining and difficulty of choosing these agencies. They must of necessity represent only the one line and must live from the fruits of their labor in this particular field. This method, though effective, is, therefore, of very limited use.

The second method is that of exclusive franchise for jobber and dealer. A Long Island corporation, finding that too many manufacturers were permitting their merchandise to fall into the hands of cut-rate houses, and that there was

[1] For a brief account of the most important Federal Court decisions, see Copeland "Problems in Marketing," pp. 733-734. The case of Dr. Miles Medical Co. v. Park and Sons, 220 U. S. 373 (1911), condemned the practice of price maintenance. Later the U. S. Supreme Court apparently reversed itself in that it failed to declare the successful maintenance of a resale price an offense under the federal laws (United States v. Colgate and Co., 250 U. S. 300 (1919)). In the case of United States v. A. Schrader's Sons, Inc., 252 U. S. 85 (1920), the same court held price-fixing illegal, justifying its apparent inconsistency with the Colgate case by means of the naive argument that in the Colgate case the manufacturer had merely indicated his wishes as to the resale price to be maintained by the dealers, and had stipulated that in case of departure from these prices no more goods would be sold to them; while in the Schrader case there was a formal

a danger of the buying public being demoralized, found that this condition was due "only to the fact that the manufacturers' sales departments had established too many competitive dealer situations in the same towns or city zones." Since competition resulted among the dealers in the same sets, there was a tendency for them to talk price and not quality—hence, an attempt to underbid each other. The remedy then seemed to this corporation to be an exclusive franchise for jobber and dealer. Manufacturers' agencies or representatives are, as a rule, where the manufacturer follows the policy of marketing through them, given exclusive territory. These manufacturers' agencies in turn, though not usually granting wholesalers exclusive franchises, appoint a limited number of jobbers so that there are only enough for the territory. The exclusive franchise may tend to reduce price-cutting. But in a large measure, it is difficult to see how it will eliminate this evil practice. Suppose a dealer acquires the exclusive rights for a certain receiving set or type of apparatus of national renown. What is to prevent him from advertising reduced rates on this apparatus in order to attract customers to the store and then induce them to buy other goods? Exclusive franchise does not mean that the retailer will deal in this line and no other; it merely means that nobody will compete with the wholesaler or the dealer in his district. It must be admitted, however, that the price-cutting evil is most common in groceries and drugs, where the exclusive franchise has been found to be impracticable.

---

contract between the defendant and the dealers. It is apparent that the effect of the two practices is the same. See *Harvard Law Review*, Vol. XXXIII, pp. 966 ff, quoted in Schaub and Isaacs, *The Law in Business Problems*, pp. 277 ff. For a statement of a few of the numerous state and federal cases on the legality of price-fixing, see Williston on *Contracts*, Sec. 1,649; 13 *Corpus Juris* 483; and the *American Digest*, subject "Legality." Price maintenance is legal in Canada and England.

The Federal Courts are rather confused on the question of legality of price maintenance, but the decision in the Miles Case has, as a rule, been regarded by business interests as controlling. The Federal Trade Commission has frequently ordered companies to cease and desist from the practice of resale price maintenance.

RESALE PRICE MAINTENANCE

Thus, it will appear that the system of marketing through sales agencies on a pure commission basis is too expensive and will result in the covering of a very limited field. Difficulty will be incurred also in the choosing of the proper agencies and in the collection of accounts. It also is evident that the granting by the manufacturer of exclusive territorial franchises will only partly remedy the evil and does not strike at the root. Some more fundamental and far-reaching measure may be needed—namely, legalization of the practice of resale price maintenance. By the Kelly and Merrit bills[1] any manufacturer or producer shall have the right in interstate commerce to prescribe the uniform prices charged and manners of settlement made by any wholesaler or retailer with whom he does business. The bill provides that the schedules of prices shall be filed with the Federal Trade Commission. If the dealer or wholesaler is going out of business or decides to discontinue the handling of this particular article, he is by this bill permitted to sell the goods at less than the specified price, if he has first offered them back to the vendor at the wholesale price, and if the manufacturer or producer has refused the offer.

Much may be said both for and against the principle of resale price maintenance. Its advocates argue that the Sherman Anti-Trust law, being aimed entirely at group price-fixing, was not intended by its framers to condemn individual price maintenance; that the prevalence of stable standard prices will cause the competition among dealers to become wholly one of quality; that, since all manufacturers' fixed prices will be open to the public, the competition will not be ignorant, but will be healthy and enlightened; that the public does not gain by price-cutting, since the dealer, not being in "business for his health," is sure to make up the supposed loss by concealed profits on other sales;

---

[1] H. R. 11 and 6, respectively. Similar bills have been presented before Congress at practically every session since 1914.

that on account of the publicity of prices, dealers will be prevented from overcharging their customers.

On the other hand, it may be urged that legal price-fixing will tend to obstruct the normal progress of the rapidly changing radio industry, because the dealer will be forced to dispose of obsolete apparatus at the old price instead of selling at a loss in order to make way for newer goods. Furthermore, by keeping in business inefficient dealers, who are very numerous in this new field, it may tend to prevent the working out of the law of the survival of the fittest.

As to the comparative merits of these arguments, it seems that radio is today becoming relatively stabilized, and is in much the same position as the automobile of 10 years ago. Since there has already occurred a sifting out of the unworthy dealers and manufacturers, these objections to the principle of resale price maintenance are not as strong as they once were. Moreover, even under the price-maintenance principle, a dealer would not be forced to dispose of obsolete goods at their former prices, since he would have the privilege of offering them back to the manufacturer or the wholesaler, who would be obliged to repurchase them at the original consideration or permit their sale at reduced prices. Further discussion at this point regarding the merits of resale price maintenance would lead us far astray. The reader is referred to any marketing book for detailed comment on this much controverted subject.[1]

RADIO MANUFACTURER IS CENTER OF MARKETING PROCESS

Since radio manufacturing is an "assembling" process, the manufacturer of the complete sets or parts ready for

---

[1] For testimony regarding this question, see the reports of the hearings on the several price-maintenance bills before the House Committee on Interstate and Foreign Commerce; for arguments in favor of the principle, see the publications of the American Fair Trade League, New York City. For the case against price-fixing, see Harry R. Tosdal, "Price Maintenance," in *American Economic Review*, March and June, 1918. This author also cites numerous articles on this question. For pros and cons see Nystrom, *Economics of Retailing*, chap. xv; Ivey, *Principles of Marketing*, chap. xv; and Converse, *Marketing Methods and Policies*, chap. xxv.

use by the public stands in the center of the chain. At the same time that he is disposing of his products, he is a buyer of the products of other factories. From a cabinet manufacturer he purchases the cabinets and panels. From the copper producer through the respective middlemen, he buys the necessary copper. And so after obtaining other parts, he assembles the complete sets.

MANUFACTURERS' REPRESENTATIVES

The radio manufacturers have adopted in general three different methods of distributing their products. Some make use of the so-called manufacturers' representatives, usually granting them exclusive territory. They, in turn, sell to the jobbers in their districts, one such representative reporting that he served 300. The manufacturer usually carries on an extensive advertising campaign to bring the goods to the attention of the wholesalers, as well as to supplement the efforts of the retailers. Even though the jobber may place his order directly with the manufacturer, the representative in the district receives a commission on the sale.

A factory representative differs from a wholesaler in that he works on a commission basis and does not as a rule carry stock. Occasionally he carries a small stock on hand for the convenience of the wholesaler. A factory representative does not guarantee the credit of the account from which he secured the order, but simply acts as an order taker like any ordinary salesman, from whom he differs, however, in that he is permitted to sell more than one line. Very often he represents ten or a dozen manufacturers, or occasionally even more.

The exporting producer commonly markets his radio apparatus through such representatives. These middlemen then sell to the wholesale importers, either direct or through commission agents. This system for foreign trade possesses obvious advantages, especially in the fact that it relieves the manufacturer of the task of negotiating with foreign wholesalers. In the domestic field manufacturers' representatives are not in great prominence, being used chiefly by radio accessories companies whose main business is with the manufacturers of complete sets. Thus a radio manufacturer whose products go abroad may deal with a manufacturers' representative both in procuring parts of his apparatus and in the disposal of his products.

MANUFACTURER-WHOLESALER-RETAILER

The second, and it seems to the writer the more common, method used by the radio manufacturer to dispose of his products is the wholesaler-retailer system. There seems to be some tendency for the manufacturer to grant the wholesaler an exclusive franchise, and for the wholesaler to give the retailer a non-exclusive franchise.[1] Some manufacturers or manufacturers' representatives report that, though they grant no exclusive rights to their wholesalers, they limit the number to such an extent that there are only enough appointed to serve adequately the territory in which they wish to dispose of their products.

Of 33 wholesalers consulted by the writer:

        10 represent from 1-9 manufacturers
         4 represent from 10-19
         3 represent from 20-29
         5 represent from 30-39
         4 represent from 40-49
         2 represent from 50-59
         2 represent from 60-69
         3 represent from 70 or more

[1] In a questionnaire sent to wholesalers scattered throughout the United States, the following questions were asked, the replies being as indicated.
Question: Are you granted an exclusive franchise by the manufacturer?
Answer: Yes—12; No—13; In some lines—10.
Question: Is the use of the exclusive franchise common in radio as to wholesalers?
Answer: Yes—12; No—20.
Question: Is the use of the exclusive franchise common as to retailers?
Answer: Yes (or in some lines)—6; No—26.
Question: Do you as a wholesaler grant an exclusive franchise to your retailer?
Answer: In some lines—6; In all lines—1; No—26.

Of the highest group, one wholesaler stated that he handled products of 200 manufacturers, another 150, and the third 147. Some authorities argue that the system whereby the wholesaler handles a large number of makes of goods tends to cause him virtually to become an "order taker"— to talk price and not quality.[1] The question whether it is practicable for the trade to encourage the development of wholesalers handling only one line of goods, in other words, practically becoming manufacturers' sales agencies, will be discussed later.

DIRECT-TO-RETAILER SYSTEM

The third general method of marketing radio is the direct-to-the-retailer system. This is common in sales to mail-order houses and chain stores. Occasionally manufacturers maintain their own systems for retailing. Another common direct method is the radio show. Just as in the Middle Ages producers assembled at certain places to display their wares and to obtain social contacts, so radio manufacturers and dealers now congregate at designated points to display and sell their apparatus. While the enterprises of olden days were called "fairs," the modern meetings are known as "shows" or "expositions." Three national radio expositions have been held in the United States, besides a large number of local or district shows. At these expositions goods are actually sold to the retailers and wholesalers who are present. At the 1924 National Radio Show held in Grand Central Palace, New York City, $10,-000,000 worth of business was transacted. The total attendance was 200,000, the daily record being 27,000. About 200 manufacturers had exhibits at this exposition.[2] Considerable business is also transacted at the smaller district shows. These radio expositions are a "joint convention of America's two greatest parties, the producer and the con-

[1] See, for example, article in *Printers' Ink Monthly*, February, 1924, p. 17.
[2] Figures from the officials of the exposition quoted in *Radio Dealer*, December, 1924.

sumer." They are a powerful force in spreading information regarding the progress of radio, and are a direct facility
for the making of sales.[1]

EXTENSIVE ADVERTISING AS A STABILIZER

Advertising, on a wide national scale, is today a practical
necessity in radio. "There is a tendency," says a Chicago
electrical and radio wholesaler, "for the consumer to want
a set that is advertised. This desire for advertised products
is more apparent in radio than in many other fields. The
consumer wants an advertised product because he feels that
he is so ignorant about the principles of radio that the fact
that the article is advertised gives him a feeling of assurance." The retailer of radio, as a result, prefers to handle
apparatus that is backed by national advertising because
he feels that the manufacturer or the wholesaler has, as it
were, broken and paved the way for him.

Advertising seems to be more extensively engaged in by
manufacturers and wholesalers than by retailers, who often
lean back and rely on the publicity which has been given
their products. During September, 1924, the six main Chicago newspapers published a total radio lineage of 76,000,
of which 43,000 was classed as "national advertising," that
is, placed by radio manufacturers and wholesalers.[2] The
Radio Corporation of America runs advertising in magazines
and newspapers with a total circulation of more than 23,-
000,000 readers.[3] Manufacturers and wholesalers often
publish "house organs" and distribute them to their trade.
Familiar examples are *The Philco Retainer*, *Town Crier*,
Colonial Merchandiser. These little publications contain

---

[1] Trade papers, such as the *Radio Dealer*, contain notes regarding all the
radio shows in the United States. *Commerce Reports*, of Department of
Commerce, occasionally contains accounts of foreign expositions.

[2] Figures by the Advertising Record Company, courtesy of the Chicago
Tribune.

[3] From *Radio Corporation of America Campaign Book* for Radiola dealers, fall and winter, 1924-1925.

statistics and pertinent facts on radio and helpful hints to the dealers.

The radio manufacturers and wholesalers supplement this national advertising service by furnishing the dealers with mats and displays and cuts and copy for the newspapers, besides pamphlets and form letters. The Colonial Radio Corporation sends a personal letter to every purchaser of its apparatus, assuring him that "Colonial will stand behind the receiver for a full year." This policy stimulates confidence on the part of its customers and assures them that the corporation is not only interested in making sales, but is also willing personally to recognize and thank every purchaser.

The early entrance into the radio field of numerous inexperienced and often short-sighted individuals tended to demoralize it. Sets which were advertised as enabling the listener to hear Europe sometimes failed to intercept the waves from the nearest broadcasting station. Inefficient demonstrations often prejudiced prospective customers against immediate purchase. Home-made sets failed to function properly. Thus it happened that in the late autumn of 1922, radio distributors, who only a short time before were unable to supply the demand, found themselves in danger of being unable to dispose of their stock. The Manhattan Electrical Supply Company, a wholesaler, "taking over a function which is commonly supposed to belong to the manufacturer," initiated a vigorous advertising campaign in New York City in an attempt to secure the cooperation of 200 dealers in convincing the public that the trouble with radio was one that confronts any rapidly growing industry. The company attempted to teach the people "how to buy radio safely" and the dealers how to demonstrate and sell it properly. This campaign was very successful, and tended to stabilize the industry.[1]

It is true that national advertising has been a great force in stabilizing the radio market. The public is being edu-

---

[1] *Printers' Ink*, December 21, 1922, p. 17.

cated to judge the value of radio merchandise. As goods become standardized, the flood of inferior apparatus subsides. The constructive policy of magazines—for example, of the *Radio Broadcast*— in "starring" the sets of its advertisers which it has tested and approved, is helpful. The time ought soon to come when the buyer of a radio receiving set can be as assured of its quality as is the purchaser of a piano or a phonograph or an automobile. To make the manufacturer's efforts of greater value, the dealer in radio should supplement his publicity efforts by means of appropriate local advertising. The dealer and the manufacturer must cooperate for the good of the industry.

The question is sometimes asked whether advertising pays. Advertising, of course, tends to stimulate demand and to increase the sales of the manufacturer and the dealer. Is the difference enough to make up for the cost? Radio business men testify that it is much easier to sell an advertised than a non-advertised product, that the customer comes into the shop able to call for the articles by their trade names, and, as a result, requires less demonstration of the good qualities of the set or part.

THE PLACE AND FUNCTIONS OF THE RADIO WHOLESALER

Production consists in the creation of form, time, and place utilities. It is an axiom that, "Things are not fully produced until they are in the form in which they are wanted, at the place at which they are wanted, at the time when they are wanted."[1] Some one must carry the goods from the manufacturer to the consumer, and some one must hold the goods until the consumer demands them. But as to the methods of performing these necessary steps in the productive process there is a great deal of disagreement. Some argue that the radio manufacturer should eliminate the wholesaler and sell direct to the retailer and possibly even to the large consumer. Others argue that the wholesaler

---

[1] Ely, *Outlines of Economics*, 4th Ed., p. 109.

performs a valuable and peculiar service and, hence, should be retained.

The American Radio and Research Corporation several years ago eliminated the wholesaler from its marketing system. As reasons for its attitude toward the average electrical jobber, this company states:[1]

1. The average jobber carries various makes of equipment and his efforts are concentrated on being able to supply whatever is ordered of him by dealers, and not upon pushing the sale of any one product. Further, the average jobber handles other electrical lines, and as the seasonal demand increases for them, he is disposed to drop all effort to *push* radio equipment.

2. Jobbers standing between us and the dealers have tended to cause us to lose the "dealer contact" which is essential in handling a specialty such as radio, where the public requires so much detailed information, which must be continuously fed to the dealers.

3. The jobber is not organized to render proper technical service to dealers.

These reasons caused the American Radio and Research Corporation to assume the jobber's function and to sell to the dealer through its own branches. It will be noted that this company did not deny the legitimacy of the wholesaler's function. The corporation divided the country into four territories: Eastern, Central, Southwestern, and Pacific. These territories were subdivided into districts, in charge of each of which there was a district manager, who might employ on his own account the necessary salesmen and assistants. All orders taken by the agents were forwarded to the district manager, who in turn passed them to the territorial manager. The district manager was to get credit for all orders received from his territory whether taken by him or not. Twice a month he reported to his territorial manager the number of orders and names of agents to whom the credit was due. The commissions, payable twice a month, were only half earned when the salesman obtained the order, the other half being credited to him when the

---

[1] *Standard Book of Reference* issued by the corporation in 1923.

company received final settlement from the purchaser. All the orders taken under this system were subject to acceptance at the home office.

The plan adopted by this corporation, one of the oldest establishments in the field of radio manufacturing, was watched with much interest by the trade. Such sales agencies are common in other lines, but probably no other important company had yet applied the principle to radio. The plan makes for a close connection between the corporation and its retailers, encourages greater activity on the part of the dealer, and enables the company to keep in closer touch with his methods of advertising and seeking business. It permits giving detailed instructions to sales representatives and making recommendations direct to the dealers.

Furthermore, this system enables the home office to maintain uniform terms and discounts,[1] as well as uniform prices, for the managers and agents are not permitted to vary from the listed prices. Then, too, since the managers and the agents are handling only one type of apparatus, they are more likely to push it with full force than the wholesaler or agent who represents a large number of houses. The latter is probably prone to talk price instead of quality, while a district manager and his salesmen must stress the quality of the articles.

This system was put into effect and given a trial by the corporation, but it was not successful for "two reasons, first, the inability to get proper personnel, and second, the difficulty experienced in collecting accounts." The corporation has, therefore, gone back to the method of selling to wholesalers, who, in turn, sell to retailers. The company has found this reversal necessary at the present time, but still believes the plan is theoretically sound.[2]

---

[1] At the present time, however, under the manufacturer-jobber-retailer system there is a tendency for manufacturers' and wholesalers' terms to become uniform at 2% 10 days, net 30 days. This is largely the result of the activities of the various trade and manufacturers' associations.

[2] Letter from H. M. Taylor, advertising manager, dated February 3, 1925.

For the average radio manufacturer the wholesaler-retailer route is the most adaptable. The functions and services of the radio wholesaler may be summarized as follows:

1. Because the wholesaler handles a large line of goods, the selling cost per unit is likely to be less than if he confines himself to one product. The traveling man calls on the retailer with a long price-list, and it is comparatively seldom that he fails to make some sort of a sale. This is a fundamental advantage over the plan of the American Radio and Research Corporation.

2. The wholesaler assumes part of the risks of distribution, taking them from the shoulders of the manufacturer. He is nearer to the retailers in his district than the manufacturer; hence, he is able to study his market. He has more opportunity to learn of the bad risks in his community. Under the direct sales representative system, though all orders are subject to approval by the home office, it is difficult for distant individuals to consider all phases of the credit problem.

3. The wholesaler is able to keep in touch with the small dealer as well as the large. With a system of manufacturers' selling agencies the large retailers may be overcanvassed. If the manufacturer wants to get into contact with all the retailers of radio in the United States, the expense would be tremendous.

4. The wholesaler stands ready to serve the retailer as often and in as small quantities as is needed. His capital and storage facilities and the fact that he handles a large assortment of goods make this possible. Thus long hauls and delayed shipments are minimized.

5. The wholesaler tends to even out the seasonal fluctuations in the trade. He takes regular amounts from the manufacturer, and classifies and holds them until they are in demand. In foreign trade the manufacturers' representatives and the import wholesalers enable the manufacturer to

dispose of radio products to the Southern Hemisphere in the spring and summer when sales in this country fall off.

6. The wholesaler furnishes advice to both the retailer and the manufacturer, serving, in fact, as a go-between.

NEED OF MARKET ANALYSIS

Many are the examples of manufacturers' and wholesalers' coming to grief because of inadequate study and analysis before entering a certain territory. A manufacturer, in extending the sale of his products, must consider the peculiarities of the market. A company, before developing a market in China, for instance, will have to consider climatic, political, and social conditions. As to the climate, the humidity is intense from February to November. The static is bad. Poorly insulated apparatus should never be sent to China. As to the political and social conditions, China (except Hong Kong) is as yet very antagonistic to the private use of radio receiving or transmitting sets. If the country is opened up, it must be remembered that broadcasting stations will probably not be as numerous as in the United States. Hence a high degree of sensitivity will be necessary. Then again, the purchasing power of the average Chinese will not permit him to buy an expensive set, and in the absence of cheaper apparatus or probably outside development of broadcasting stations, the market will include only the well-to-do. Charging stations are very scarce in China; hence, sets to be used with dry cells are probably to be preferred.[1]

The peculiar customs of the people should be studied. It is stated that American companies in Hong Kong have been satisfied with staying in the large cities and waiting for trade, instead of sending agents into the field to learn of the habits and likes and dislikes of the people. The Americans, therefore, are thought to be indolent.[2]

---

[1] See *Commerce Reports*, January 14, 1924.
[2] *Radio Dealer*, April, 1924.

It also seems difficult for business men to learn that English is only *one* of the tongues of the world. We too often expect foreigners to adjust themselves to our language. In numerous cases directions for setting up and operating a set have been printed in English, in spite of the fact that the apparatus was intended for foreign consumption. Then again, to the uninitiated, at least, radio needs a practical demonstration. In an investigation of the market in Bilbao, Spain, the consular officers found five radio dealers, but only one of them seemed to have much knowledge of the subject. No one had been able to assemble one set of American origin. In most foreign countries representatives must make demonstrations of their radio wares for the benefit of the dealer as well as of the prospective customer. Radio is different from a bar of soap: its use must be taught.

DESIRABILITY OF EXCLUSIVE FRANCHISES

Is radio adapted to the system of exclusive agencies? Convenience goods do not lend themselves to this principle; on the other hand, specialties do. An individual who wants a prophylactic tooth brush likes to be able to get it at the nearest drug store. The same is true of all types of groceries, certain kinds of clothing, tobacco, and accessories of various kinds. On the other hand, dealers in men's suits, women's dresses, musical instruments, automobiles, furniture, and farm machinery are, as a rule, given exclusive territorial franchises.[1] It may be stated that exclusive articles lend themselves to the exclusive agency, while articles which any one may demand at any time lend themselves to the non-exclusive agency. There is, as already stated, a tendency in the radio field to grant exclusive agencies, though this is more common in the wholesale than in the retail trade. Radio, being a type of goods for which there is need of an intensive sales effort, and which will require special service from the dealer, ought to lend itself to the use of

---

[1]See Converse, *Marketing Methods and Policies*, 1924, p. 542.

the exclusive franchise. This holds true only of the complete sets; in parts and accessories of various kinds the nonexclusive agency, especially in the retail trade, should be the rule. People do not generally buy radio on the spur of the moment as they buy a bar of soap; hence, it is entirely logical to have only one dealer selling a particular type of set in any one town or zone of a city. The dealer or the wholesaler who has an exclusive territory will be encouraged to enter into special sales drives and advertising, and will not be robbed of the fruit of his labor through competition with others who sell the same type of set.

RELATIONS BETWEEN MANUFACTURERS AND WHOLESALERS OR RETAILERS

Some consumers buy as much radio apparatus as the large retailers, or even more. Should the manufacturer or the wholesaler sell direct to these over the interceding middlemen's heads, and, if so, on what terms? One wholesaler confronted with this problem was the Pettingil Andrews Company, of Boston, one of the largest distributors for the Radio Corporation of America. This company has a large number of industrial customers, who buy from $20,000 to $100,000 worth of electrical apparatus per year. These large consumers, purchasing as much as many retailers, argued that they were entitled to as favorable terms as the radio dealer. Sales Manager J. E. Livor, of the Pettingil Andrews Company, thought this concession would be unethical. Consequently, he decided to grant a discount of only 15% to the customers who are not radio dealers. He urged purchase from the dealer, on the grounds that this was fair, that the dealer will install the apparatus at a small charge, that the dealer stands ready to give continuous service, and that the manufacturer or distributor will render no special services, but will simply deliver the radio f.o.b. the shipping point.[1]

[1]*Electrical World*, March 8, 1924, p. 503, article entitled "A Resale Policy on Radio," by J. E. Livor.

This company's policy is very reasonable. Any other course of action would, it seems, have been unfair to the retailer and would tend to destroy the most effective marketing channels of the radio industry—namely, the manufacturer-wholesaler-retailer system.

In order to obtain information as to the extent of sales by the radio manufacturer or the wholesaler over the succeeding distributors' heads, the writer asked the following questions of wholesalers scattered throughout the United States:

Question: Do you note any tendency for the manufacturer to sell and ship direct to the retailer?
Answer: Yes—20; No—12.

Question: Do you note any tendency for the manufacturer to sell and ship direct to the large consumer?
Answer: Yes—14; No—15.

Question: Do you note any tendency for the wholesaler to sell and ship directly to the consumer?
Answer: Yes—20; No—12.

Several of the wholesalers answering "yes" specified that only the disreputable manufacturers or business men are guilty of this practice. One reported that a certain wholesaler sold direct to the consumer under an assumed name. Several retailers complain that some of their prospective customers have, after the dealer has incurred much expense in demonstration, obtained a catalog from the wholesaler and made the purchase through him, getting the advantage of the regular discount.

DIRECT SELLING NOT PRACTICABLE

A system of direct selling to the consumer by the manufacturer or even the wholesaler is not practicable in case of radio products. As a rule, manufacturers resort to the direct method only when a highly intensive effort to arouse interest is necessary. It is entirely conceivable that a firm back in 1919 or 1920, when the popular interest had not been aroused, would have had good reason to resort to direct sell-

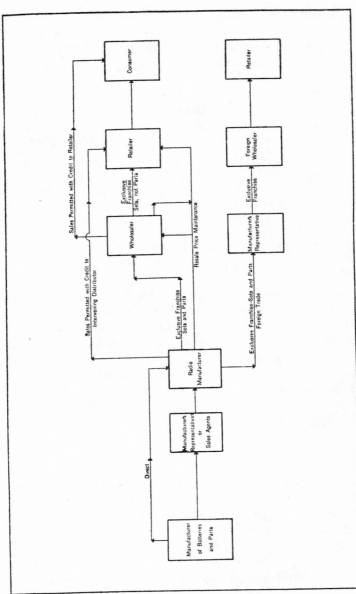

Figure 5: Proposed radio marketing system.

108

ing. At the time of the introduction of the sewing machine and the typewriter, it was common for these manufacturers to send their agents to call on the customer, demonstrate the machine, and take orders. Now, however, typewriters and sewing machines are, as a rule, sold through dealers, who sometimes, of course, send out agents to canvass their community. Radio is now not a novelty but a utility. Customers call at the radio store, where the apparatus is demonstrated to them. Then, after they have purchased, the dealer may be asked to install the set. But it is not necessary for the manufacturer to resort to intensive house-to-house selling.

PROPOSED MARKETING PLAN

Under the plan as described in Figure 5, the manufacturers of parts, batteries, and so forth, would dispose of their products through sales agents, or through manufacturers' representatives, to the radio manufacturers. On account of the small number of customers, the direct method would also be practicable, but either the direct or the indirect method should, if chosen, be consistently followed. The radio manufacturers, after manufacturing and assembling, should, in domestic trade, sell their products to wholesalers who are granted exclusive territorial franchises for sets and probably for parts. Each wholesaler could, of course, represent as many manufacturers as he deems advisable. The jobber is to grant an exclusive franchise to the retailer for sets but not for parts. Each retailer, though carrying as many lines as he sees fit, should limit himself to a small number so as to be able to concentrate sales efforts. In small cities there may be only one retailer handling a certain make of product; in large cities the territory ought to be zoned. If any goods are sold over the head of the intervening middleman, the profit should go to the dealer affected. If no distributors have been appointed for any area, the manufacturer or any succeeding middlemen may make sales direct.   The policy of resale price maintenance should be followed.

In foreign trade it would be advisable to introduce another step in the process, namely, the manufacturers' agent or representative, who would be given an exclusive right, and who could represent as many manufacturers as practicable. This agent is then to sell to the foreign wholesaler (possibly on an exclusive basis, so as to enable intensive sales effort) who will in turn sell to the retailer on an exclusive basis or non-exclusive basis, depending on commercial and political conditions.[1]

In a discussion of marketing problems the public welfare should be paramount.   The radio service must be made available to the people in the most economical and efficient way.   Therefore, it is also important to consider the condition of the manufacturers, wholesalers, and retailers.   The business morality in radio must be built up to a higher level. Unfair and predatory price-cutting, not being of any benefit either to the consumer or to the dealer, should be reduced to a minimum.   Dealers and jobbers should be protected in the performance of their legitimate function, so that they may take adequate steps to bring radio to the attention of the people with the reasonable assurance that they will not be deprived of the fruits of their efforts.

---

[1]To digress for a moment, we may mention at this point that according to figures received from 19 scattered wholesalers, the most common stock turnover seems to be between 4 and 6.   The lowest turnover reported was 4 and the highest 12.   As to the ratio of selling expenses to sales, the most common percentage reported was 17.   That is, the selling expenses were 17% of the sales.   The highest was 25% and the lowest 6½%.   The close similarity between the radio and electrical industries is indicated by the fact that the common ratio in the latter is 17-18%.   This bears out the statement made by some wholesalers who are handling both, that the costs of selling radio and electrical supplies are about the same.   For ratios in several industries including the electrical, see Converse, *Marketing Methods and Policies*, p. 241.

VI

PROBLEMS IN THE RETAILING OF RADIO

Which type of store can render best service? Location for service. Radio a specialty. Selection of stock. Arrangement of stock. Radio a service industry. Need of advertising the uses of radio. Importance of purchasing department. Need of expert and honest salesmanship. Chain store not practicable in radio. Ethics in radio trade. Accounting.

"SINCE radio swept its conquering way into the world of business, butchers, dressmakers, grocers, hardware dealers, electricians, shoe dealers, millinery shops, department stores, dentists, drug stores, ice-cream parlors, bootblacks, bankers, and newsboys have attempted to sell 'parts' and 'sets.' The 'craze,' like Coxey's famous army, has drawn its followers from every bypath, cowpath, and main traveled road, and, like Coxey's army, is leaving thousands stranded in a mire of sticky liabilities and depleted assets.

"Some of these retailers will survive. Radio, like youth, will be served. When the captains and kings of the radio bonanza depart, those radio dealers who possess merchandising vision and merchandising ability will still be doing business at the old stand; and they, with the new radio dealers coming on, whether they be in electrical stores or hardware stores or music stores or department stores, who possess the knowledge and ability to survive, will be the radio profit-makers of tomorrow."[1]

WHICH TYPE OF STORE CAN RENDER BEST SERVICE?

One of the most important problems confronting radio merchandisers today is that of outlet for their wares. Who shall do the work of retailing? This is important, not only

[1] *How to Retail Radio,* by editors of *Electrical Merchandising,* 1922, p. 3.

from the point of view of the business man, but also of the public which is interested in securing the best possible service. It is conceded that establishments unrelated to radio, such as hardware stores (except in the small towns, where they may be the only outlet), are not suitable for the retailing of radio. The controversy is mainly as to the relative merits of the electrical shop, the furniture and music store, and the exclusive radio shop. In favor of the furniture and music store as the main type of outlet may be summarized the following arguments:

1. The broadcast receiving set is primarily a musical instrument. It is used especially for listening to concerts. At the present time it is a drawing-room fixture; hence, the expert advice of the furniture or music dealer as to external appearance and models is necessary.

2. The musical instrument dealers have for many years been specializing in a full-grown, high-priced quality product. They have showed success in handling this, and they have been trained by their manufacturers for the greatest efficiency in demonstration; hence, they deserve to take on the selling of this new musical instrument.

3. Music and furniture dealers have a social standing in their home community; and this gives them a chance, which the electrical dealer does not have, of drawing trade through their acquaintances.

4. The furniture or music store is equipped in a more pleasing and attractive way than either the radio or the electrical shop, which establishments are, as a rule, noisy and crowded.

5. Radio is a seasonal industry. Trade falls off in the late spring and the summer, and builds up again in the fall and winter. Such being the case, it is not financially advisable for an exclusive radio shop to handle this business, as the receipts are too irregular. A business man must have a steady income; therefore, radio ought to be an adjunct to another well-established line, which logically would be that of furniture or music. Wholesalers and manufacturers are

not hampered by this difficulty, since a large number of them have customers in the Southern Hemisphere, where the seasons are the opposite of ours. The radio dealer has no such opportunity of evening out his sales.

In favor of the electrical shop we argue:

1. Although a broadcast receiving set is used to a large extent for listening in on concerts, it is, nevertheless, an electrical instrument which is likely to require attention. The proprietor of an electrical store knows more engineering than the furniture or music dealer. The owner of a piano which is out of tune does not summon the man from whom he bought it; he calls in an expert tuner. In case of trouble, on the other hand, the owner of a radio receiving set calls at once upon the dealer, perhaps the one from whom he bought it. The music dealer will be unable, through lack of training, to render these expert services. The electrical dealer, knowing the principles of electricity, is better able to demonstrate apparatus and to locate trouble.

2. The music dealer knows very little or nothing about the instrument which he is selling. If he adds radio to his stock, he will be entirely at a loss when some inquisitive customer inquires about the difference between two apparently similar but differently priced sets. He is not familiar with radio terms.

3. The electrical dealer may, or may not, be as socially respected as the music dealer, but, be that as it may, the electrical retailer has the advantage of knowing the atmospheric conditions of the community, the wiring in the residences, the nature of the ground available, and the opportunity for the erection of outdoor antennae.

4. The electrical dealer can install a radio section with very little extra expense. Since the electrical dealer has for a long time been the mecca of numerous radio amateurs, he has a market for construction parts which the music dealer lacks. On the other hand, the music dealer has never sold any piano or phonograph parts.

5. Radio may be a seasonal industry, but the electrical dealers' sales increase in the summer and decrease in the winter; radio decreases in the summer and increases in the winter. What better combination is possible?

6. Since many electrical wholesalers have added radio to their stock, the electrical dealer, being acquainted with the marketing procedure, has an advantage in the purchase of radio apparatus.[1]

But, though we reach the conclusion that the electrical shop is preferable to a furniture or music store for the handling of wireless supplies, it seems that, in the larger towns especially, radio could be handled by the exclusive radio shop or by a special section in a department store. The large cities are dotted with department stores which handle radio as one of their lines. The disadvantages of the exclusive radio shop are the large initial expenditure necessary, which is justified only in case the sales run up into large figures, and the seasonal aspects of the business. Certainly in cities below 15,000 in population the radio and electrical combination is desirable.

LOCATION FOR SERVICE

Copeland[2] classifies merchandise from the standpoint of the consumer into convenience goods, shopping goods, and specialty goods. Convenience goods are those customarily purchased at easily accessible stores, such as toilet articles, certain types of groceries, cigars, and other goods of small unit price. The store handling this class of goods must be conveniently located, because the unit of purchase is so small that people will object to going out of their way to obtain them.

Shopping goods are those in the purchase of which the

---

[1] For some arguments on one side or the other of this question, see *Radio Dealer*, August, 1924; and *Radio Broadcast*, November, 1923, and January, 1924.

[2] *Problems in Marketing*, p. 3. Fuller discussion in *Harvard Business Review*, Vol. I, pp. 282-289.

customer wishes to compare prices, quality, and style. The customer probably makes a special trip in order to procure this article, so she is prepared to visit several stores. Women's suits, dresses, and hats are examples. Stores handling goods of this class are usually grouped in the retail district of a city, so that the shoppers may readily pass from place to place.

Specialty goods are "those which have some particular attraction for the consumer, other than price, which induces him to set forth special effort to visit the store in which they are sold and to make the purchase without shopping. In purchasing specialty goods the consumer determines in advance the nature of the goods to be bought and the store in which the purchase is to be made, provided a satisfactory selection of merchandise can be effected in that store." The specialty goods resemble shopping goods in that purchases are made at irregular and infrequent intervals, "but in contrast to them, the exact nature of the desired merchandise or the store preference is well determined in the mind of the customer."

RADIO A SPECIALTY

Radio goods probably fall in the last named class, though there is evidence of the fact that at the beginning of the radio craze such apparatus possessed many of the characteristics of the second group. Individuals would go from store to store to listen in at the loudspeaker, to ask questions about the operations of the set, to compare prices, and to see which type of apparatus would present the best appearance in their living room, but with the growth of national advertising, with the standardization of products, and with the stabilization of styles, radio is rapidly assuming the characteristics of a specialty good.

One of the first questions confronting the prospective radio dealer is the location of his store. Space will not here permit a full discussion of this subject, but the fact that radio is, or at least is becoming, a specialty is significant.

"The store that handles this merchandise [Specialties] can easily make its location well known through advertising and other mediums. Since such a store depends upon the infrequent purchaser, the specialty store should be located so that it can attract trade from a wide area, but it is not essential, however, for it to be in the high-rent shopping area. Consequently, these stores frequently locate on the better side streets."[1] Radio can be governed by the same principles. An adherence to this rule will mean lower costs through decreased rents.

SELECTION OF STOCK

After acquiring the proper location and building, the problems of investment and stocking arise. Here a thorough analysis of the surrounding population ought to be made. Better still, this study should be undertaken before the location is chosen. A dealer would not be wise in establishing a store in districts where there is little enthusiasm for radio. The big influence making for interest is nearness to some efficient broadcasting station. Instances are very common where a dealer has created popularity by the construction and operation of a broadcasting station. But a prospective dealer is to be warned that the operation of such station is a real financial burden and that the addition of another to our already too large number would probably not be desirable.[2] If the dealer is located within 25 miles of a powerful broadcasting station, he can be reasonably certain of a demand for crystal sets, though these are, as a rule, unpopular in the United States.[3] However, a large number of indi-

---

[1]Trade Information Bulletin, No. 269, a supplement to the Commerce Reports, entitled *"Retail Store Location"* by Laurence A. Hansen. This bulletin gives a concise discussion of the factors to be considered in the choosing of a location. Other excellent discussions of this problem are found in Leigh, *Elements of Retailing,* New York; and Nystrom, *Economics of Retailing,* New York. For the peculiarities of urban land, see Ely and Morehouse, *Elements of Land Economics,* 1924, pp. 75 ff.

[2]See Chapter IX.

[3]The *Census of Manufactures* reported that in 1923, American producers manufactured 414,588 tube and 116,497 crystal sets. See Table 10.

viduals begin with the crystal, and later purchase tube sets. A Chicago wholesaler reports that he sells twice as many crystal sets as tube sets. Out of 20 wholesalers consulted, 13 reported the greatest turnover in complete sets, 7, in parts. If a dealer is not located within 25 miles of a station, his demand for crystals will be small. The occupations and the purchasing power of the people in the community must be considered. Retired farmers are likely to be enthusiastic purchasers of long-range sets. The nature as well as quantity of the stock must, then, be determined.

Stocking is a difficult problem, for the solution of which no fixed rule can be formulated. What proportion shall be kept in parts and what proportion in complete receiving sets? If the store is located in a community most of the inhabitants of which are workmen, there will be a large proportion of parts and of medium-priced receiving sets. On the other hand, if the shop is located in a fashionable and wealthy district, the relative amount of investment in expensive models will be greater, and the proportion of construction parts will be smaller. That is, the receiving sets will have to be of such a character as to add to the beauty and decoration in a room, but this does not mean that they will be of a greater sensitivity and selectivity. As to the absolute amount of investment required and needed, it has been stated by some that the retailers can reasonably expect to sell one radio set for every 20 inhabitants in the community served. Hence, divide by the number of retailers in the town and the result is the average trade of each store. We need not stop to criticise this statement, but it is necessary for the prospective retailer to make a market analysis and to set some standard or objective. Into the determination of this objective will enter the wealth of the community, the number of inhabitants, the nature and occupation of the population, the number of radio receiving sets already installed, the nearness to broadcasting stations, whether amusements are available to all the people, the number and location of the other stores in the city, the competition from the outside, such as mail-order houses, and whether the population is of the mail-order purchasing type. The investment should be made in stable and standard sets and parts. The store owner should aim to buy often and as little as possible at a time: in this way he will safeguard himself against overstocking and against the danger of obsolescence. Thus he will learn by experience the demand of the people. By a proper stock-control system, he will be able to regulate his inventory.

ARRANGEMENT OF STOCK

The next problem is the arrangement of the materials in the store. In the first place, as to the window decoration. Many radio retailers have fallen into the error of exhibiting so many articles and types of articles in their windows that the person on the street is confused by the chaos. A window display, like an advertisement, should contain only a few items. These should be arranged so as to appeal to the people's sense of beauty and utility. A conglomeration of nuts, insulators, and coils, with a set in one corner and a loudspeaker in another does not make the onlooker feel like taking the collection away with him. The window trimmer should appeal to the prospective customer's desire. Symmetry and proportion are essential. Hence the trimmings or exhibit should simulate a situation which the passer-by would like to create for himself. Some home scene, representing a person sitting by the fireplace with a complete radio set and a loudspeaker, with possibly a dog staring in wonder, gives a good impression. The window display should be varied so as to resemble certain seasons or events. During the last Democratic Convention one store, enlarging a picture of the gathering in Madison Square Garden so that the delegates were plainly visible to the street, placed it near a loudspeaker which sent forth the proceedings as broadcast from New York. The passer-by was in this case given a sense of reality.

Now as to the arrangement of materials within the store. In case of a department store the radio supplies may very well be on one of the upper floors, where the customer may make his comparisons and decisions away from the noise of the street and the crowds. In case of an exclusive radio store, there is some disagreement as to the proper location of the various types of apparatus. For the purpose of arrangement, goods have been classified as: (1) merchandise which the customer needs, (2) articles which he wants, (3) other articles which he may be induced to want.[1] Another writer has made the following classification: (1) impulse goods, (2) convenience goods, (3) necessities. According to the first grouping, goods which a customer may be induced to want should be placed nearest the front; next, those which he wants; and last, those which he needs. According to the other classification they might be arranged with the impulse goods near the front, convenience goods next, and necessities in less convenient parts. The systematic arrangement of merchandise is important so that the sale of one group will help the sale of others. The customer, in walking through the store, will see other articles which he may be induced to buy.

For radio it seems that neither of these principles will hold. Complete receiving sets are not, as a rule, bought on the spur of the moment; they are usually purchased only after the customer has been thinking about the matter for some time. Furthermore, the patron, in choosing a receiving set, and especially an expensive one, prefers to be away from the noise of the street and the crowd. He should be given the opportunity of quietly and leisurely examining the fixtures and testing the quality of the loud-speaker. He should be disturbed as little as possible by people brushing past him. On the other hand, these sets should not be placed too far toward the back of the store. The best arrangement would be, if the contour of the room

---

[1] Trade Information Bulletin No. 291, *Retail Store Planning*, prepared by A. L. Bush, a supplement to the *Commerce Reports*, November, 1924.

permits, to place these sets about the center, toward the side. Then, the necessities, such as tubes, should be placed near the front extending toward the back; so that the shopper, in looking for his desired counter, will notice the set section, but will not be forced to pass through it. General Manager R. M. Klein, of F. A. D. Andrea, Incorporated, New York, is of the opinion that the complete radio sets should be on display in the front part of the store and that the show cases and counters should range backward to the rear where the stable and simple merchandise, such as tubes, wire, insulators, and so forth, will be kept.[1] The only argument to hurt the logic of his scheme is the fact that receiving sets are specialties, the purchase of which people have before determined, and the fact that customers in buying radio sets, as in the case of phonographs and furniture, prefer to do their inspection away from the crowd and noise.

RADIO A SERVICE INDUSTRY

Radio more than any other industry can be termed a "service industry." A sale is not complete when the cash is rung up or when the order is taken, but the dealer must, as a rule, advise in installing, or actually install, the apparatus. He must stand ready to aid the customer in the elimination of difficulties, in the choice of apparatus and tubes, in the adjustments necessary to tune in on certain broadcasters, in the identification of previously unheard stations. The dealer must keep readily available copies of the daily programs of all stations within a wide radius. These may be called positive services.

There are also some important negative services to be rendered by the retailer. Not only should he tell his customer what he can do, and how to do it; he must also explain to him the limitations of radio. The purchaser of an automobile, on the other hand, knows the conditions of

[1] *Radio Dealer,* December, 1924, p. 59.

the roads and the topography of the country. The dealer should not sell a crystal set when the customer needs a tube set in order to hear even the nearest broadcasting station. When broadcasters are numerous in the community, he should emphasize in his talk the need of selectivity in an instrument; when stations are far away he should stress the advantage of sensitivity. The temperament of the prospective purchaser should teach the dealer whether he desires a means of reaching out as far as possible into space or a means of a steady evening's entertainment with a certain program. The former type will require a different class of apparatus than the latter. Sell the customer not what he thinks he wants, but teach him to want the thing which you know will bring him the most satisfactory results. This is a problem which is especially peculiar to the radio industry. A phonograph or an automobile will work as well in one state as another, but the distance of only a few miles may mean a big difference to the purchaser of radio.

NEED OF ADVERTISING THE USES OF RADIO

Another peculiar form of service is advertising. Any dealer owes it to his community to make himself known. This, you may argue, is certainly no duty to the public, though it may be a duty toward himself. The writer would suggest that it is also a duty toward the public. Many people today do not know the present status of radio; some are hardly aware of its existence; others think it is only a half-developed device which is of interest only to a few; still others regard a radio set as such a mysterious contraption that they do not have the courage and skill to operate it.[1] Advertising will tend to disperse these illusions. People who are ignorant of the advantages of radio should

[1]Some dealers today attempt to encourage the impression that radio is a mysterious thing. For some reason or other, they think such impression adds to their standing in the community. So when a customer comes in, one of this type of retailer will talk amperes, ohms, and connections, instead of service and utility.

be informed, so that they too may reap some of the benefits for themselves as well as their families. For instance, there are considerable farm areas where radio is practically unknown. A recent survey by the Bureau of Agricultural Economics reveals the fact that less than 400,000 farmers (exact estimate 364,800 in 1924) are supplied with radio. Fifty-one per cent of the population own and reap the benefits of nine-tenths of our national radio equipment.[1] This is not fair; it is the duty of the manufacturer, the wholesaler, and the retailer to spread information regarding wireless among the 49%. In this same connection it ought to be repeated that a considerable number of radio manufacturers and wholesalers carry on extensive national advertising. The retailers owe it to them to take up the burden and to notify the members of their communities where these nationally advertised sets may be obtained. National advertising will not, as a rule, directly result in the sale of equipment; it merely stimulates a desire. The dealer should cap the climax and lead, as it were, the radio enthusiast to his shop.[2]

Though radio is primarily a "service industry," the dealer should not render so much aid that his profits are absorbed. For example, after the set has been installed, there is no reason why he should not make appropriate charges for delivering small items to the residence of the radio fan, or for calling at the home and making certain tests and adjustments. The retailer should carry only standard receiving

---

[1]Fifty-one per cent of the American population live in towns of 2,500 population or above. Assuming, for example, that there are 4,000,000 radio broadcast receiving sets in the United States today, it will be noted that the farmers own less than one-tenth of them. In other words, the urban half of our people own 90% of our receiving sets. It must, of course, be borne in mind that the Bureau of Agricultural Economics counted only people on farms, while the Census draws the line at towns of 2,500.

[2]For special types of service to be rendered by the retailer, the reader is referred to the various trade papers such as *Electrical Merchandising* and the *Radio Dealer*, as well as the numerous house organs of manufacturers and wholesalers. The trade paper ought to occupy the same position to the business man as the professional paper to the doctor or the lawyer—as a means of spreading information regarding the news of the trade and the making of suggestions.

sets that are simple and not likely to get out of order.[1]
It may be advisable for the dealer to render services free
of charge when the customer brings the set or part down
to the store for advice, or when the service is one that can
be given without sending a man out at the expense of the
company.   In our present market there is such intense
competition among the retailers, especially in the larger
cities, that the rendering of free service is likely to be carried to an extreme for the purpose of procuring trade.   It
may become necessary for the dealers in a community to
agree on a scale of charges.

Another type of service which ought to be rendered to the
consuming public is the adoption of the principle "Money
back, if not satisfied."   This should work no hardship on
the dealer if he handles quality sets and parts produced by
reputable manufacturers who are willing and able to stand
back of their guaranty.[2]

IMPORTANCE OF PURCHASING DEPARTMENT

At the same time as it is the duty of the electrical or
radio dealer to attempt to sell apparatus which will operate
to the best advantage of the prospective customer, it is
apparent that in order to carry out this policy, the dealer
must exercise care and skill in purchasing his wares.   Writers today, as well as business men, stress too much the idea
of salesmanship and too little the principles of "purchase-
manship."   Concerning this point, a writer in *Radio Dealer*
says: "How many dealers realize the importance of proper
buying?   Remember that you are the purchasing agent for
a group of people who buy from you.   A purchasing agent
in a manufacturing plant is a highly important man.   You
are just as important to your customers.   They expect you
to cull the market for good merchandise correctly designed,

---

[1]For a good general discussion of the principles of servicing, see *How to
Retail Radio*, by editors of *Electrical Merchandising*, chaps. xi and xii.

[2]For instalment selling as a type of service, see Chapter VII.

correctly priced, and they expect you to tell them about it and to show it to them. They expect you not to waste their time with inferior merchandise. Out of the many good items which you have in stock, they will select the one that suits their needs."[1]

NEED OF EXPERT AND HONEST SALESMANSHIP

Radio salesmanship requires considerable skill of a special type. The man behind the counter must be a salesman and a demonstrator, as well as a clerk. One set sells for $100; another for $125. Since the external appearance may be practically the same, the salesman must be able to explain the difference in price. Though most customers wish to be told about the utility of a radio set, some will ask questions about the practical operation which the salesman must be able to answer. He should be abreast of the times, so as to be able to tell the customer of the constant new uses to which radio is put; this tends to whet the interest of the customer. Misrepresentation is known as one of the cardinal business faults. "Dealer's puff" is a common concept in the law of sales and contracts. The radio salesman should be taught to be honest. Too often has a customer been told that he could with ease hear Los Angeles from New York. When the purchaser was disillusioned, he was not only lost as a future customer, but he could do damage to the trade through his conversations and contacts with others. A radio store, like any shop, should aim to make not only sales, but friends and customers. A disillusioned radio fan is a poor future prospect. Perfect honesty with him at the beginning would have been better both for the public and the trade.

Retail store owners disagree as to the desirability of hiring a previously trained salesman, or whether he should be instructed in the proprietor's own way after his services have been accepted. But there is practical unanimity of

[1]Pierre Boucheron, of Radio Corporation of America, January, 1925, p. 54.

opinion that the radio salesman should have a knowledge of some of the fundamentals. Often stores will maintain "experts" to answer the especially difficult questions. Trade papers and house organs, by publishing articles and advice on the principles and operation of wireless, recognize the need of salesmanship.

CHAIN STORE NOT PRACTICABLE IN RADIO

As in almost every line of merchandising, the chain store is also developing in radio. One of the most successful radio chain systems in the United States is the Liberty Radio Chain Stores, Incorporated, chartered under the laws of Delaware. In March, 1922, David Kanofsky opened a radio shop on Liberty Street in New York City. Within a short time his business outgrew his limited quarters, and he was obliged to expand, establishing new stores, until by the end of 1923 he was operating a chain of five units. In order to obtain the advantage of the best possible prices, he organized a wholesale and manufacturing division to supply the chain of stores. In 1924 two other units were established, making seven in all, located three in New York City, one in Providence, two in Washington, and one in Long Island. The entire business was in the latter part of 1924 assumed by the Liberty Radio Chain Stores, Incorporated. Four stores were added in the early part of 1925, making eleven in all at the present time. A mail-order business has also been established.[1]

The extensive use of the chain store is not practicable in radio. This system lends itself especially to a business in which the price per unit is comparatively small, and where the selling requires only a small degree of skill; in fact, chain-store salesmen are clerks in the true sense of the word. Thus, such establishments are common in groceries, drugs, shoes, and novelties (five and ten cents). Radio does not lend itself advantageously to mass buying

[1] *Stanton's Wireless Bulletin*, January 23, 1925.

and selling methods, which are essentials of a chain-store system. Radio apparatus must be demonstrated to the customer; some system of instalment buying will be demanded; and more dealer service is required than the average type of chain store is willing or able to render.[1] Radio chain stores will continue to be a success only as long as the number of establishments is so small that they may continue to be under the direct supervision of the proprietor, thus preserving the personal touch. The fundamental difficulty with any large chain-store system is that of picking hired managers who are efficient and able, and who are willing to devote their best efforts to the service of the company. Some chain stores have been inaugurated by the manufacturer in order to prevent price-cutting in his products. This is a laudable motive, but it would be more desirable to legalize price maintenance.[2]

ETHICS IN RADIO TRADE

Due to the newness of large-scale radio retailing, there has been a comparative neglect of radio trade principles. Some of the obstacles to a sound development in the business side of this field have been:

1. The large number of inexperienced retailers who have entered temporarily, or have resorted to this because of failure in other lines. These men, in their anxiety to exploit what they considered a transient industry, have disregarded

---

[1] Neither is radio adapted to the mail-order business, because of the need of a personal touch and greater services than the mail-order house can render, even though it should be willing.

[2] "Radio lends itself advantageously to mass buying and selling, the practicability and profits of which have been thoroughly tested and demonstrated by such chain-store enterprises as Woolworth, Kresge, United Cigar Stores and other outstanding chain-store successes," says President Kanofsky of the Liberty Radio Chain Stores in a prospectus describing the company's activities. The reader will think of many points of dissimilarity between radio apparatus and a cigar or a box of Christmas candles. Though it may be true that radio lends itself to a certain extent to mass buying, it is not adapted to mass selling. Furthermore, the mass buying advantage may be offset by difficulties in management, changing of styles, and so forth.

all principles of sound merchandising. With the stabilization of radio and the operation of the law of the survival of the fittest, these individualistic and unscrupulous retailers are disappearing from the scene.

2. The large number of retail and wholesale failures in this field. This was at first inevitable, but failures result in social as well as individual loss, in that the goods of the bankrupt are thrown on a forced market and are sold at cut prices, thus tending to demoralize the trade.

3. The fact that many dealers sell standard radio apparatus at less than the list price.

4. The fact that some wholesalers give retailers' discounts to customers.

5. The fact that radio has been sold by dealers who know little or nothing regarding its technique. In their demonstrations of broadcast programs, they have been the cause of a great deal of public disgust and irritation and have led to the resolution to wait till the industry becomes stabilized.

6. The lack of uniformity in the accounting systems of the wholesalers and manufacturers as well as the retailers, thus preventing an accurate comparison of the individual members with the standards of the radio as well as other trades.

Progress is being made toward the solution of these problems. The first two will automatically diminish as radio becomes recognized as one of the main industries in the country. Cut prices will probably be eliminated through adequate legislation. Radio trade associations are adopting codes of ethics. These codes should stipulate the extent of service to be performed gratuitously and the point both in regard to time and nature of the service at which charges will be made; they should also contain a provision against unfair price-cutting, and should eliminate special discounts. There should be an agreement among wholesalers that if they give the retailers' discount to any consuming customer, the retailer in the territory should be given the credit.

ACCOUNTING

Notable progress has been made in the formulation and adoption of uniform accounting systems. Among the reasons for this improvement may be mentioned: (1) the activities of the Interstate Commerce Commission and the various state public utilities regulatory bodies, which have devised systems of bookkeeping for the companies under their jurisdiction; (2) the recent popularization of the study of accounting in our schools and colleges; (3) the work of research organizations, such as the Harvard Bureau of Business Research, which in its several bulletins has devised and recommended systems for various types of business men, including shoe and grocery wholesalers and retailers; (4) the pressure exerted on individuals by the federal and state income tax laws and regulations, which have imposed fixed procedures for the determination of income.

No uniform classification of accounts for radio dealers and manufacturers has yet been devised or generally accepted. Dealers might consider the advisability of adapting to their use the Harvard system[1] for shoe retailers, with appropriate changes. For the "shoe repairing" account, for example, could be substituted "service" account, in which the proper entries could be made covering receipts from, and expenses incurred in connection with, the rendering of service to owners of receiving sets. Appropriate allowance should be made for rent, both on owned[2] and leased property, and interest both on owned and borrowed capital.

A comprehensive survey of the various important balance-sheet and income statement ratios, such as selling expense to gross sales, turnover, and so forth, would be of great

---

[1]See "Bulletin Number 2," reprinted in Copeland's *Problems in Marketing,* pp. 750 ff.

[2]Particularly in the case of owned real property is this important. Mr. Herbert Dorau, of the Institute for Research in Land Economics & Public Utilities, is collecting data, as yet unpublished, tending to show that many retailers are not really making the profit shown in statements because they do not allow enough for rent on real estate owned by them and used in the business.

practical value. A study of these results would enable a radio business man to compare his individual results and policies with those of his own and other trades, and thus to take proper steps in the diagnosis and the removal of difficulties whenever they exist. A uniform accounting system would provide radio with a common standard of comparison.

VII

FINANCIAL PROCESSES

The investment bargain. No-par-value stock common. Few bonds. Liberal reserves. The sales bargain. Remedies for seasonal nature of radio. Prevalence of open accounts. Uniformity of terms. Advantages of trade acceptance. Use of partial-payment plans. The function of the credit company.

EVERY company, whether large or small, whether corporation, firm, or sole proprietorship, is concerned with two main financial processes. The first is that of securing capital, both borrowed and owned, for the construction and expansion of the plant. The second is that of buying and selling labor, raw materials, and stock in trade. The former involves an investment bargain, the second a sales bargain. Making use of machinery and plant obtained in the investment contract, the manufacturer transforms the raw materials and parts obtained by the sales contract into the finished product and then sends it on its way to the ultimate consumer. Though both of these transactions are of the nature of contracts, they will at this point be discussed under separate heads, since different principles and conditions feature each.

THE INVESTMENT BARGAIN

One of the first financial questions which will occur to the reader is the status of radio as an investment.[1] Though

[1] The latter part of the year 1924 witnessed an abnormal activity in radio production and an unusual rise in the prices of radio stocks. During the first half of 1925 the forced sale of much radio apparatus, coupled with the seasonal fall in demand, resulted in an enormous drop in the quotations of most radio securities. Counting as 100% the low prices for 1925 of 17 stocks dealt in on the New York exchanges, the writer found that the high for 1925 averaged 411%. The greatest variation was found among the securities of manufacturers of broadcast-receiving apparatus, while the most stable were those of the radio telegraph companies.

wireless is an old industry, still the popular interest in it is very recent. Such being the case, all securities in this field are still more or less in the speculative class. This has always been true of new and unstabilized industries. As time passes, and as the standards of the trade become stabilized, the rating of radio stocks and bonds will become higher. For the present, however, investors with limited means will do well to recognize the speculative nature of most of these securities. Moody's *Analyses of Investments* rates the Marconi Wireless Telegraph Company securities as follows:

> 7% cumulative preferred stock..*Aa*
> Ordinary stock (common)......*Baa*

It will be remembered that the Marconi Company has averaged about 18% on its common stock since 1911. Stocks carrying a *Baa* rating by Moody are issues of investment quality which do not measure up fully to the level where they can be classified as being entirely free from speculative influences. They are not quite in the pure investment class. Common-stock issues with good or improving records are, as a rule, in *Baa* class.

Moody rates the shares of the Radio Corporation of America as follows:

> 7% cumulative preferred.......*B*
> Common ....*Caa*

Stocks in *Caa* class have only speculative possibilities, according to Moody's. The Radio Corporation of America has paid dividends on its preferred stock since the spring of 1924, but has not yet begun paying dividends on its common stock.

In 1924 the company earned $2.91 per share on its no-par-value common stock (1,155,400 shares outstanding) compared with $0.28 in the preceding year (5,777,000 shares). The net current assets doubled during this period. Partly as a result of this, Moody raised the rating of the common stock from *Ca* to *Caa*.

Frank T. Stanton and Company, of New York and London, is the best known specialist in radio securities. This company furnishes analyses of the various radio stocks, such as DeForest Radio, Radio Corporation of America, Sleeper Radio, Ware, Hazeltine, Freed-Eisemann, Freshman, Incorported, British, International, and Canadian Radio. Space will not here permit an analysis of radio stocks, but the Stanton Company furnishes analyses of any stock on request.

NO-PAR-VALUE STOCK COMMON

An analysis of the capital obligations of the important radio companies reveals several features:

1. The practice of issuing no-par-value common stock is prevalent. Most of the radio corporations, being newly organized, could adopt this new kind of share without being bound by any prejudices or traditions on the part of its stockholders. The outstanding examples are DeForest, Radio Corporation of America, Freed-Eisemann, Hazeltine, Inter-Ocean, Liberty Radio, Rova Radio, Thompson Radio, and Ware Radio. In the case of the Radio Corporation, these no-par-value shares were listed in the balance-sheet as having the value found by subtracting the liabilities and reserves and preferred stock from the total assets. Recently, however, the corporation has built up a surplus account.

At the end of 1923 the Radio Corporation of America had outstanding 3,955,974 shares of 7% preferred stock, of a par value of $5, and 5,777,000 shares of no-par-value common stock. In May, 1924, the stockholders reduced the number of preferred shares by 90%, but increased the par value from $5 to $50. The old preferred stock is exchangeable for the new at ten shares of the old for one of the new. At the same time the number of no-par common was reduced by 80%; in other words, only one-fifth as many remain outstanding. The company will exchange the old common stock at the rate of five shares of the old for one of the new[1] These adjustments indicate an apparent increase in the stability of the stock.[2]

2. If the stock is of a par value, the denomination is usually small. The British Marconi common is of the par value of £1, the Magnavox, $1, the Canadian Marconi, $1, Spanish Marconi, £1, and International Marine, £1. This is a striking contrast with the orthodox $100 par value. With the stabilization of the industry, there will undoubtedly be a tendency to increase the face value, as was done with the Radio Corporation preferred stock.

FEW BONDS

Few of the capital obligations are in the form of bonds. The English Marconi Company has outstanding some one and a half millions of $6\frac{1}{2}\%$ convertible ten-year first debenture stock [bonds] each share with a par value of £1. These are convertible at the option of the stockholder into ordinary shares at a prescribed ratio, and are redeemable by the company after 1923 at par and previous to that time at a specified premium. But bonds are exceedingly rare in the radio field. The Canadian Marconi lists a mortgage, but no bonds, in its liabilities. The absence of bonds is due to the speculative nature of the business and to the large proportion of intangible and obsolescent assets.

LIBERAL RESERVES

The reserve policies are usually liberal. The question has sometimes been asked: Are the assets of wireless companies quickly wasting? A communication company, from the very nature of the case, needs large reserves. Many of the cable companies have built up reserves which are greater than the capital. One of the lowest ratios for the

---

[1]Public Utility Compendium of the *Commercial and Financial Chronicle,* November 1, 1924.

[2]The new common and preferred shares are listed on the New York Stock Exchange.

year 1921 for cables was that of the Eastern Cable Company, which carried a reserve of over three million pounds, and even this was more than one-third of its capital. The Radio Corporation of America, for the year 1921, applied all its net income to the amortization of its patents; in 1922 almost two and one-half millions out of a net income of three millions were so applied, for 1923 almost a million was used for this purpose. The unusually large amount in 1922 is due to the fact that some of the important patents were about to expire. For the year 1924 about 30% of the net income was applied to the building up of reserves, and for the writing off of certain investment losses and the balance of the organization expense. The patents and good-will of the company were, in 1924, valued at almost eighteen millions of dollars, offset by a reserve of 22%.

As indicated in Chapter II, the British Marconi Company recently has made drastic reductions in certain of its asset accounts, the value of which had depreciated. The most common causes of such fall in value were the political instability of the debtor nations and the depreciation of many foreign currencies in terms of English pounds. Thus, the company canceled the entire amount of the Russian debt and securities, pared down the overdue debts from other nations, and in general allowed for the depreciation of shares in foreign countries, so that they now stand as sterling values.

THE SALES BARGAIN

In introducing a discussion of the methods of financing purchases and sales of wireless apparatus, it seems advisable to point out the fact that radio is generally regarded as a *seasonal industry*.

REMEDIES FOR SEASONAL NATURE OF RADIO

On account of the general impression that static interference is more serious in summer than in winter, and that the range is not so great in warm weather as in cold, radio sales have always tended to fall off in the late spring and summer. Of 37 wholesalers from whom the writer received information, every one stated that the radio sales tend to slump in the summer. As a result of this tendency, the radio trade and papers have been waging a constant war on this prevalent view, arguing that summer static is a popular illusion, and advocating the extension of summer uses. What shall be the remedies for this situation? The most common views expressed by members of the radio trade are as follows in the order of the frequency of their suggestion:

1. *Education.* Through appropriate advertisements, news articles, and so on, the public should be taught that radio reception is very practicable in the summer. Knowledge of the summer uses of radio should be spread. In 1924 the radio apparatus section of the Associated Manufacturers of Electrical Supplies ran advertisements and interviews in radio magazines, trade and technical publications, and more than 150 leading metropolitan newspapers in the United States, the newspapers alone representing a circulation of fifteen million people. The total publications featuring the summer-time radio numbered about five hundred.[1]

2. *Better and more powerful broadcasting stations.* Admitting, for the sake of argument, that the reception and range are not so good in the summer as in the winter, it is apparent that one remedy is to make the broadcasting stations so powerful that they can blanket the country at all seasons of the year.

3. *The production of reasonably priced, simple, and good portable sets.* If portable sets are made more practicable, people will feel disposed to take such apparatus with them on their camping trips, and on excursions.

4. *Elimination of static through appropriate inventions.* Scientists are working steadily on this question. One of the

---

[1] Page 15, *Minutes of Annual Meeting*, June 17, 18, 1924, held in Atlantic City, New Jersey.

advantages of the short wave length is the lessened amount of atmospheric interference.

5. *The handling of other lines* by radio manufacturers and dealers. One manufacturer produces electric fans in the spring and summer and radio sets in the autumn and winter.

6. *More daytime broadcasting.*

7. *Chain broadcasting.*

Possibly the seasonal variations will never be entirely eliminated. About one-third of the persons answering the writer's question indicated that the various suggestions were mere palliatives, that the seasonal fluctuation is inherent, that radio is essentially an indoor diversion, that in the summer people are more interested in outdoor sports. There is, of course, a possibility of building up the summer sales by the production of simple and efficient portables, and the creation of interest in their use. Let the reader note the summer advertisements and he will invariably find a receiving set under the parasol at the beach or in the canoe or tourist automobile, or in some similar circumstance. This type of advertising tends to extend the uses of summer radio. More powerful broadcasting would, of course, be very valuable in the increasing of summer sales, but it seems that it would also stimulate winter business, and thus the fluctuation would still be present. The use of the short wave length will tend to make broadcasting equally effective as to range in day and night and in summer and winter. This is on account of the peculiar "bending qualities" of the short wave length. In 1924 Marconi discovered that the range by day increased very rapidly as the wave length was decreased. He also found that efficient communication could be established for all hours of the day and night between England and Australia with the employment of only 10 or 12 kilowatts and a 32-meter wave length.[1]

---

[1]Fleming, J. A., in *Nature*, January 24, 1925.

From the point of view of the individual, one of the best suggestions is the handling of other lines, the use of which increases in the summer and decreases in the winter. In this respect electrical apparatus seems to be an ideal adjunct. The exclusive radio manufacturer, rather than decrease his production in the summer and spring, would do well to arrange with his wholesalers to take goods all through the year on easy financial terms; the wholesaler to do the same for the retailer. The manufacturer would also do well to stimulate his foreign sales to the Southern Hemisphere during our late spring and summer months. The radio manufacturer has facilities for doing this through several manufacturers' agents, for example, the National Industries, Incorporated, which specializes in foreign trade and financing. The wholesaler can also in many instances turn his attention to foreign trade.

With the solution, or partial solution, of the seasonal variation problem, the financing activities of the manufacturers and dealers of all kinds will be greatly simplified, especially because of the more regular amounts of capital needed, the decreased turnover of labor, and the more efficient utilization of plant and machinery.

PREVALENCE OF OPEN ACCOUNTS

Three points especially will be noted about the short-time financing of radio: the prevalence of the open account system, the tendency toward uniformity of discount terms, and the increasing use of the instalment plan.

Of 35 wholesalers interviewed, 34 make use of the open account, the other selling exclusively for cash. Of the 34, only 5 reported the employment of both the trade acceptance and the open account. Of the 5, one indicated a 50-50 proportion between trade acceptances and open accounts. Another stated that about 85% of his sales were financed by the open account, 10% by the trade acceptance, and about 5% strictly cash. The other 3 did not report any difference in proportion between the methods. Three whole-salers said they use the promissory note in addition to the open account, especially for obligations over 60 days. Several indicated the employment of c.o.d. besides the open account. Although these figures represent only a small number of wholesalers, the conclusions drawn from them may be generally applicable, for the 35 firms are scattered throughout the United States. There was a time when many radio wholesalers refused to deal with the retailer at all except on a cash basis. This was unfair to the reliable dealer, but it was a protection against the "fly-by-night."

UNIFORMITY OF TERMS

The usual terms given both by the wholesaler to the retailer and by the manufacturer to the wholesaler are 2% 10 days, net 30 days.[1] Only 3 of the 32 reporting whole-salers indicated other terms to their retailers. Only 2 of 34 wholesalers reported a variation from the common 2% 10 days, net 30 days granted by the manufacturers.

The Radio Manufacturers' Association, with headquarters in Chicago, has a system for the interchange of credit information. Each member of the association reports accounts which are 30 days or more past due. These reports are made to the association on the tenth of each month, and a list of the delinquents is then sent to the members, who also have the privilege of requesting information from the association headquarters. This system, as will be noted, is not very extensive or complicated, but the association will extend it as the need arises. In this connection it must be remembered that an association has no power to enforce uniform credit policies without violating the Federal Anti-trust laws, but a uniform plan of discounts and credit procedure seems to be desirable. Such a system makes the competition among the members of the trade more nearly equal and tends to prevent unfair business practices.

[1] Discount of 2% allowed if cash is paid within 10 days. After 10 days, no discount. Bill due absolutely at end of 30 days.

ADVANTAGES OF TRADE ACCEPTANCE

The extensive use of the open account as opposed to the trade acceptance seems to have been carried over from the practices in the other trades and industries. Though the trade acceptance was employed in the United States during the period before 1840, its extensive use has been only very recent in this country. In favor of the trade acceptance as opposed to the open account may be argued the following advantages:

1. The trade acceptance is a credit instrument which, when properly made out so as to be negotiable, is conclusively presumed as to consideration. The holder in due course can enforce it according to its tenor. On the other hand, the open account will admit of numerous disputes as to the consideration.

2. The holder of a trade acceptance may sell it to a bank or to an individual more readily than he could dispose of an open account. The trade acceptance can be sold at its par value minus a reasonable interest charge, while the open account can very seldom be sold for more than 70% of its face value.

3. The debtor under an open account would be truly mortified if he found that his account had been sold to a stranger. Furthermore, he may arrive at the conclusion that the original creditor is in financial straits. The acceptor of a trade acceptance has no such feelings when he finds that his obligation has been sold.

4. The trade acceptance can be sold to a bank without its being included as a loan under the rule prohibiting any national bank to lend more than 10% of its capital and surplus to any one individual. This tends to increase the credit available to a borrower from a bank.

5. The use of the trade acceptance tends to discourage reckless and extravagant buying. It is comparatively easy for a purchaser to order goods by letter or telephone and forget the fact that he is incurring a legal liability. On the

other hand, if the purchaser has to sign his name to a trade acceptance before he can obtain possession of the goods, he is apt to realize more vividly that he is undertaking a financial obligation, which will have to be paid at a definite date. The open account has no definite due date, and, therefore, the debtor is likely to be more evasive when he is asked to pay his debts.

6. The trade acceptance is a two-name paper. This is probably not a strong argument, since, after all, the bank relies on the reputation of the indorser, instead of the one primarily liable. Certainly the trade acceptance is a safer investment for the bank than the open account. In this respect it may not be better than the promissory note. The objection commonly raised against the trade acceptance on the part of the buyer is that it is a reflection on his credit to be asked to accept a draft before getting possession of the goods. This ought not to be so regarded. The purchaser should welcome the trade acceptance as making his liability definite in amount and in time. It is a peculiar fact that business men like to be held to strict account for their obligations. A dilatory collection policy is not only a curse to the creditor, but is not generally appreciated by the debtor. The use of the trade acceptance makes for a strict collection policy. The purchaser knows, when buying on open account, that the transaction is recorded in the seller's books; he should have no objection to signing his name to a document and making the obligation definite both as to the amount and date of maturity.

USE OF PARTIAL-PAYMENT PLANS

The prices of radio receiving sets vary. Some are as expensive as automobiles, others as phonographs, sewing machines, and typewriters. There is practically a set for the means of every consumer. Very early it was seen that some system of instalment selling would eventually be necessary. This has been much used in automobile, typewriter, and musical instrument financing; it ought also to be judiciously used in radio, if the trade is to enjoy the full advantages of the market.

But radio styles were constantly changing and improving. The instalment-payment plans are applicable only to an industry when it has become well standardized. There was a time in the field of the automobile, the typewriter, and the musical instrument when it was not at all practicable. As long as changes and improvements are frequent, the prospective purchaser will very properly hesitate before buying, in the fear that before he has paid half of his instalments, the instrument purchased will be out of date, or will have fallen in value. A long period of service of the article is a prerequisite for the successful operation of partial-payment plans. Radio apparatus is now constructed so that comparatively good reproduction is possible. It is relatively easy to operate, with small chances of getting out of order. The elimination of the "A" and "B" batteries would tend toward further simplification. The sets are sensitive and selective. They are constructed so as to be an ornament in the house. This does not mean that changes and improvements will not be made in the future, but they will probably be as slight as the variation in the models of automobiles or typewriters. The tendency toward super-power and chain broadcasting in the United States will undoubtedly improve the quality of our radio programs, so that people will feel safe in making an investment in reliance on the continuation of the supply of entertainment.

Under the present conditions of relative stabilization, it is entirely natural that partial-payment plans should be introduced. It is probable that the future will see an increasing popularity of completed radio sets. Many retailers finance the deferred payments themselves, allowing the customer, after making an initial down payment, from 10 to 12 months in equal weekly or monthly instalments for the balance. This method is a great financial burden on the retailer, since it ties up part of his capital for a period of

10 to 12 months. In some instances the wholesalers assume the burden of carrying the deferred payment paper, but this has the same disadvantage. Furthermore, this method, whether practiced by the retailer or the wholesaler, tends to deflect the dealer from his proper field—the selling of radio apparatus—to that of banking. The majority of retailers cannot successfully be merchandisers and bankers at the same time, but the business men who carry their own instalment paper are virtually trying to accomplish this end, with the result that they cannot successfully accomplish either. Under these circumstances there has developed a tendency for the retailer or the wholesaler to shift the burden of financing instalment sales to some concern which has been organized just for this purpose, in fact, specializes in this form of banking.

THE FUNCTION OF THE CREDIT COMPANY

Under the plan of the Commercial Credit Company, a highly specialized organization of this type, when a dealer sells a radio set on the instalment plan, the customer pays a certain amount down and the credit company advances 90% of the balance, less a reserve sufficient to cover the service charge. The other 10% plus the reserve which has been held back is remitted to the retailer when the credit company has collected the final instalment from the customer, as the usual practice is for the finance company to make all of its collections direct from the individual consumer.

As stated, the collection of the monthly instalments, as well as the administration of the system, is done by the credit company. The retailer gets almost nine-tenths of his selling price immediately, which provides him with a working capital to buy more goods and increase his turnover. In numerous cases the retailer may be too small for the finance company to consider, and in such cases the business is handled through an arrangement by the credit company with the manufacturer or wholesaler of radio sets.

The retailer who handles sales on a monthly payment
basis is always compelled to establish both a cash selling
price and a time selling price, the difference between the two
serving as compensation to the credit company for its interest, risk, collection expense, and other costs of administration. For example, suppose the price of the set, including
the expense of installation, is $150, and suppose the cus-
tomer feels able and willing to pay $10 a month. Then,
according to definitely worked out tables, the retailer will
notify the purchaser that he can pay $41 cash and make 12
monthly payments of $10 each, or pay $58 in cash and make
10 payments of $10 each, or pay $76 cash and make 8 payments of $10 each, or pay $93 in cash and make 6 payments
of $10 each. If the purchaser cannot pay any of these fig-
ures down in cash, there are other possibilities. He can,
for instance, pay $31 in cash and make 12 payments of $11
each. Here is a concrete example of the operation of this
system:

Cash price of set including cost of installation... $150.00
Purchaser pays dealer $31, which he keeps......$ 31.00
Purchaser gives contract for $132, payable in 12
  instalments of $11 each. The dealer sends this
  contract to the credit company, which pays the
  dealer 90%, or $118.80, less $13 reserve for
  service charges, and so forth............... 105.80
When the instalments have all been paid, the 10%
  is returned to the retailer.................   13.20
    Total $150.00

It will be noted, however, that the purchaser has paid in
all $163, the balance of $13 being the gross profit of the
credit company. The big advantages of this plan are the
fact that it leaves the dealers their money for the carrying
out of their ordinary processes of trade, while it shifts the
burden to a company which has been organized for the
financing of such sales as one of its purposes. It also makes
for prompt payments, as the purchasers of sets are likely
to respect the calls of a strange company more than if a
local man demanded such payments. With the standardiza-

tion and stabilization of radio apparatus, the use of the deferred payment plans will be extended, but care should be exercised to prevent the abuse of the system and the over-selling of customers. At the present time not more than one-third of the wholesalers report this method of sales by their retailers, but the growth of the policy has been rapid.

VIII

THE HANDLING OF TRAFFIC[1]

The principles of wave motion. The operation of the vacuum tube. Tendency toward short wave length. Nature of traffic agreements. Position of Western Union. An anomalous traffic condition. Agreement with Postal Telegraph. Traffic and pooling contracts. Rocky Point.

BEFORE entering into a discussion of the method of handling traffic and of some of the problems connected therewith, it seems desirable at this point to consider a few of the physical principles upon which the art and science of radio are based.

THE PRINCIPLES OF WAVE MOTION

The reader is familiar with the fact that waves appear on the smooth surface of a pond when a stone is thrown into the water. These waves spread out in all directions and have the power to give motion to small substances that happen to be in their path. In other words, waves carry energy as they progress from their source. We may represent these waves by the diagram of Figure 6. They have a definite length in which one wave length is the distance from the highest part of one wave to the highest part of the next. This is represented in the figure as the distance from A to B, or from C to D, or from E to F. Again, if we watch the waves, we will notice that a definite number go past a given point each second. The number of waves passing a given point in a unit of time is called the "frequency" of the waves. The "velocity" (distance expressed in meters or feet that the waves go in one second) could be

[1]The sections on "The Principles of Wave Motion" and the "Vacuum Tube" in this chapter were prepared by Professor Richard H. Howe, of the Physics Department, Denison University.

found by watching the number of waves that go by in one second and by multiplying this number by the length of one wave. Thus:

Velocity=(number of waves per second) times (one wave length)

The velocity of radio waves is 186,000 miles, or 300,000,-000 meters, per second (a meter is a little longer than a yard). This velocity is the same for all radio waves, no matter how long or how short they may be.

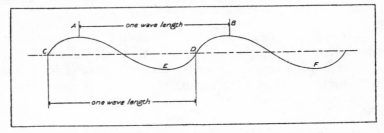

Figure 6: Diagram showing method of measurement of radio waves.

As all radio fans are aware, the lengths of the waves used in broadcasting vary from 200 meters to 545 meters. If the length of a radio wave is 600 meters, for example, then, by the above formula for velocity we can find the frequency or the number of waves passing us each second. There would be 300,000,000 divided by 600, which gives 500,000. The usual way of describing a wave has been by its length, but many people prefer to identify it by the frequency, so that we find stations listed both by their wave lengths and by their frequencies which are usually expressed in kilo-cycles per second (one kilocycle is 1,000 waves). This would make a station listed at 600 meters have a frequency of 500 kilocycles per second.

There are numerous methods of producing and receiving electromagnetic waves of this great frequency which will not be discussed in this chapter; however, of all the methods, the vacuum tube is so far superior that it will be treated briefly in detail of construction and operation, both as a means of creating the electromagnetic waves and of receiving them at a distant point and converting them into audible and intelligible signals of speech or code.

THE USE OF THE VACUUM TUBE

The ordinary vacuum tube used in radio consists of an evacuated glass bulb containing, (1) a filament which is heated by the current from a storage or dry cell, usually called the "A" battery in radio diagrams, (2) the positive electrode, which is a sheet of metal surrounding the filament but insulated from it, and (3) the grid formed by a wire wound in the form of a helix placed between the filament and the plate. Each of the elements is connected to the outside by wires coming through the glass and fastening to contacts on a convenient base. This arrangement of the elements in the tube is represented by the diagram of Figure 7. For the purpose of making clearer the description of the action of each element, the illustration shows the grid and plate as being only on one side of the filament, but in practice to secure the maximum efficiency (of electron emission) the plate and grid are placed on both sides of the filament.

In order to understand the function of the various elements of a tube, it will be necessary to recall some well-known laws of static electricity governing bodies that are electrically charged. There are two kinds of charges familiarly known as positive and negative. The positive charge can be produced by rubbing a glass rod with a piece of silk. Similarly, the negative charge may be had by the friction of a piece of flannel on a hard rubber rod. The rods are then said to be electrified.

These charges may be placed upon any insulated material by simply touching the electrified rod to the insulated body. A simple substance to charge is a piece of pith from the inside of an elderberry bush. This pith is suspended from a support by a silk thread as in Figure 8, Sec. *A*. If

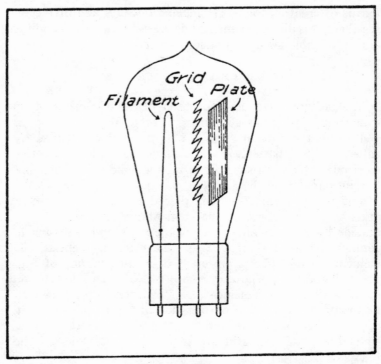

Figure 7: Sketch showing the elements in a radio vacuum tube.

the electrified glass rod is touched to the suspended pithball, it imparts to it a positive (+) charge. Likewise, the
electrified rubber rod gives a negative (−) charge. The
important laws may now be illustrated by this simple
apparatus. Let the pithball on the thread be charged negatively, then let the negatively charged rod be brought near
to the pithball, when the light piece of charged pith will be
seen to be pushed away from the rod. Similarly, if the
pithball is charged positively and approached by the positively charged glass rod, there will occur a similar repulsion.
But if the pithball is charged negatively and is approached
by a positively charged glass rod, there is evident an attraction between rod and pith. The three conditions are illus-

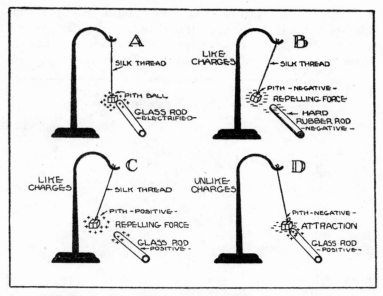

Figure 8: Sketches illustrating the basic laws of electrostatics.

trated in sections *B, C,* and *D,* respectively, of Figure 8. These experiments are summed up in the basic laws of electrostatics as *"Like charges repel and unlike charges attract."* A clear knowledge of these laws will greatly help to make plain the function of each element of the vacuum tube during the process of reception and transmission of radio communication.

When the metal filament of the vacuum tube is heated to a red or white heat, there are given off from the filament minute particles having a *negative* charge, provided the gases and air have all been removed from the tube. The presence of a gas will stop these small particles which are called "electrons." They are so small that they are invisible to even the most powerful microscope. A complete study of the electron has been made, however, and its weight and size have been measured with high precision.

When the positive pole of a battery is connected as in

Figure 9 to the plate of a vacuum tube, it puts the same kind of a positive charge on the plate that the glass rod did on the pithball. The negative electrons coming from the filament are attracted to the positive plate in large numbers.

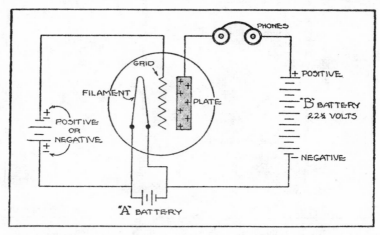

Figure 9: Sketch of vacuum tube hook-up showing positive charges on plate.

The presence of these numerous electrons between the plate and the filament renders this space conductive to the current in the "B" battery, which flows from the positive post of the battery through the tube to the filament and back to the negative post of the same battery. It is in this circuit that the headphones are placed as shown. Up to this point nothing has been said of the grid which plays a most important part. The electrons, in passing from the filament to the plate, have to pass through the grid. If now a charge is impressed upon the grid these electrons passing through the grid could be increased or decreased in number at will. Now since the current from the "B" battery is dependent upon these electrons to carry it across the space form the plate to the filament, this current could be varied in strength by simply changing the charge on the grid. This is exactly what the grid accomplishes in the various radio uses made of the vacuum tube.

Figure 10 shows a circuit in which the grid receives its plus and minus charges from the antenna which is energized by the passing electromagnetic wave. If the passing wave is broken up into dashes and dots, they are recorded as such on the grid which in turn controls the stronger "B" battery current in the plate circuit. In this case the headphones respond to the original dashes and dots created at the transmitter. On the other hand, the current in the antenna may contain variations caused by the voice which in turn varies the charge on the grid accordingly and causes the telephone current to change in response to speech, thus giving rise to the reception of radio telephony. The part of the circuit that determines which wave length shall energize the grid is the coil of wire, L, and the condenser, C, one or both of which are made variable to "tune in" to the desired wave length.

Thus the vacuum tube acts as a relay in which the moving parts controlled are the electrons, which are so small that

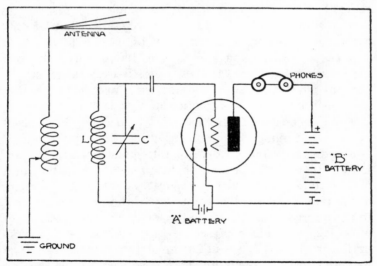

Figure 10: Sketch of circuit in which the grid receives its positive and nega-ive charges from the antenna, which is energized by passing electromagnetic waves.

they offer practically no opposition to the charges tending
to control them. This should make perfectly evident the
reason of the extreme sensitiveness of such a device for the
efficient detection of the energy obtained from the electromagnetic waves.

The recent advances in radio telephony and broadcasting
were made possible by the vacuum tube being able to function as a device for *creating* disturbances of a *radio frequency*, which ranges from 10,000 to 300,000 disturbances
every second. The vacuum tube is not only able to produce
this high a frequency, but is able to maintain these waves
constantly as long as the energy from the battery or generator at the sending station is properly supplied to the transmitting set.

The failure of the radio telephone to make its appearance earlier in the development of wireless communication
was due to the lack of such a device to supply this *constant* high frequency current, the absence of which would
make the voice distorted and unintelligible.

The electron tube is able to supply a current of this
nature by a particular arrangement of the circuit in which
it is used, in which the grid receives its charges to control
the plate current from the energy of a battery *in* the circuit
itself and not from an outside source (antenna) as in the
case when used for the reception of signals.

The direct current of a battery (Figure 11) is changed
by the controlling action of the grid into a pulsating or
alternating current of very high frequency which is connected to the antenna and emerges into space in the form
of electromagnetic and electrostatic waves as the carriers
of the radio signals. The frequency of the waves is changed
to the desired value by increasing or decreasing the amount
of wire in the coils represented in the figure by *P* and *G*
until a wave meter shows that the station is transmitting on
its authorized wave length. This wave length is assigned to
the station by the government.

The size is the chief characteristic that differentiates a

transmitting from a receiving tube. The sending equipment uses much larger voltages and currents than does the receiver; hence it is built proportionally larger and more rugged.

In the case of radio *telegraphy* the waves created by the transmitter are broken up into dashes and dots by

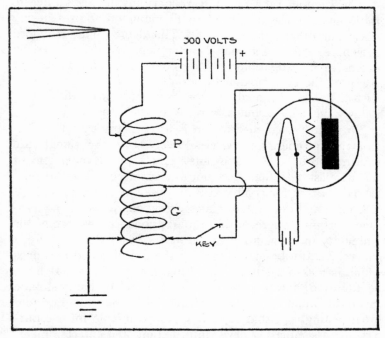

Figure 11: Sketch of circuit showing coil for controlling wave length.

the key; but when the voice is to be transmitted, the key is replaced by a microphone such as one speaks into on the ordinary line telephone. This microphone causes the grid charge to vary in accord with the vibrations of the speech; this also gives rise to similar vibrations of the high frequency electromagnetic waves which travel through space carrying these voice variations to the distant receiving station. The waves of radio telephony are not broken up, then, but simply varied in amplitude. In most broadcasting stations a separate tube is used to impart the voice variations upon the current in the generator tube. When used for this purpose, the tube is called a modulator, whereas in the case of a generator of the high frequency currents it is known as an oscillator.

The vacuum tube not only renders invaluable service to radio communication, but also to many other present-day devices in other fields of work. This device alone is indeed a rich reward to the many early pioneers who carried on extensive investigations and devoted years of time to the study of the electromagnetic wave and the electron theory, with little or no thought of the wonderful possibilities that today have come about as a result of their endeavors.

No matter what mechanism is used to transmit the electromagnetic energy in wireless *telegraphy*, the signals are transmitted by dashes and dots. The rapid development of the wireless telephone has not yet replaced the radio telegraphy system for commercial purposes to any great extent. The dash and dot system makes every character in the message certain, whereas the radio phone leaves room for ambiguity in enunciation to too marked an extent. Secrecy can very easily be maintained by the use of coded messages which is not so easily accomplished by telephony. It must be admitted, however, that the wireless telephone has made the most wonderful advances and improvements in radio broadcasting. In that capacity it is invaluable for the purpose of disseminating news, information, and entertainment. It is undoubtedly likely that wireless telegraphy will continue to hold its own in its present field, for it renders the same valuable service to the sea that the wire telegraph does to the land.

While the vacuum tube opened a new epoch-making era in the scientific world and seems now to have reached a maximum, there are a great many problems to be worked out, which, if successful, will perfect the present system to a very high degree. Considerable difficulty is encountered

from atmospheric disturbances, which present a most difficult situation, from the interference between stations using
the same wave length, and from the lack of secrecy where
required.

TENDENCY TOWARD SHORT WAVE LENGTHS

The majority of the broadcasting listeners are familiar
only with wave lengths from 200 to 600 meters; great
strides, however, have been made in the design of apparatus
for use on wave lengths far below 200 meters. Such equipment has been employed successfully in experiments with
wave lengths in the neighborhood of one meter. At such
low wave lengths static does not prevail to such a noticeable
extent, and the beam method of transmission, in which the
waves are transmitted in one direction only, gives good
results over remarkable distances. This method, if used
commercially, will tend to confine interference to one direction and help to maintain secrecy at the same time. Partial
elimination of interference between stations is now some-
what remedied by a more careful design of receiving apparatus, which is now made more selective. Interference due to
the old type of transmitting apparatus, having a broad
wave, is remedied by the substitution in its place of the
vacuum tube equipment.

NATURE OF TRAFFIC AGREEMENTS

Another phase of the mechanics of radio is the routing
and handling of traffic and the settlement of accounts.
Though these problems are present in all phases of point-
to-point communication, emphasis will here be placed on
transoceanic radio. Many messages originate at, or are
addressed to, places distant from the radio station. Land
wires must carry the messages to or from the terminals of
the transoceanic circuits. Furthermore, a circuit is no
stronger than its weakest link. A very powerful sending

station is of little avail if there is no receiving apparatus to hear the signals at a distance. Even if the receiving station is adequate, the communication circuit is not efficient unless there is also a sending set able to transmit back the answer.

These conditions necessitate traffic agreements, which, as entered into by the Radio Corporation of America, are of four distinct types:

1. This corporation has made contracts with certain foreign countries whereby they agree to construct and operate, or grant a concession to a private company to construct and operate, high-powered stations to work with it in an international circuit.

2. It has also entered into agreements with land wire companies or with foreign governments whereby they arrange to receive or deliver messages sent or to be sent via wireless.

3. Likewise, the Radio Corporation of America is the beneficiary of preferential traffic agreements whereby, other things being equal, certain companies agree to route relayed messages via the Radio Corporation, and vice versa.

4. Provisions have been made for the pooling of receipts.

Agreements of the first type have been made by the American Corporation establishing direct international communication circuits between the United States and Great Britain, Norway, Germany, France, Italy, Poland, Japan, Hawaii, and Sweden.[1] A direct commercial circuit has recently been established with points in South America. Operation with Argentina was begun in 1924. Plans have been approved for high-power stations in Brazil.[2]

---

[1] Besides the direct circuits with Hawii and Japan, there is one which includes both.

[2] The South American service is carried on with the stations owned and operated by the trustees of the American, English, French, and German companies. For details of this trusteeship, see Chapter III. A traffic agreement has been concluded for operation with Indo-China, a service which was to be inaugurated in 1925. See *Report of the Directors*, for 1924, p.4. The Philippine legislature has granted the Radio Corporation a concession for the erection of a transoceanic station at Manilla.

POSITION OF WESTERN UNION

Since it would be impracticable for a radio company to attempt through its own lines to collect messages from, or deliver them to, points distant from the terminus of the circuit, the need of agreements with the land line companies is apparent. The English Marconi Company has for a long time had a standing contract with the British Government providing for the cooperation of the telegraph lines in the forwarding or collection of messages. This is also true of a number of other countries. Likewise, the Radio Corporation has made similar agreements with our telegraph companies. The Western Union will receive and distribute messages at any of its offices to and from Hawaii, Japan, and the Far East. In other words, the reader can call the nearest Western Union office and dictate a message to Japan. The telegraph company will forward this radiogram to the San Francisco central control office of the Radio Corporation, which will place it on the air and send it to the Japanese Government station, whence it is delivered by wire again, if necessary, to the addressee. The procedure in the opposite direction is reversed.

Now, the Western Union is not financially interested in any transpacific cable companies. But it does operate transatlantic cables, with which the Radio Corporation of America competes. The Western Union was naturally very reluctant to make arrangements for picking up messages throughout the United States and forwarding them to the Radio Corporation for transmission eastward across the Atlantic, since it would be helping its competitor take some of the business for the handling of which it itself has facilities.

AN ANOMALOUS TRAFFIC CONDITION

The Western Union was willing, however, to deliver westbound radiograms. Thus, we were confronted with a peculiar situation. A Western Union messenger delivering a "via

RCA" message from England to your home or place of business, could not accept your reply. Your answer would have to be addressed to the Radio Corporation in New York. Upon its receipt, *if you had established a credit,* the Radio Corporation would send it by wireless to its destination. Obviously, rather than incur this trouble and delay, you would prefer to cable your reply, the handling of which would be completely taken out of your hands. Thus the Radio Corporation was constantly losing eastbound traffic. The following table reveals the traffic (number of words), both eastward and westward, of the Radio Corporation during specified months in 1920. The reader will note the wide variation between the amount of the eastward and westward traffic on the transatlantic circuits. On the other hand, the transpacific service in December was practically the same in both directions.

TABLE 13

TRANSOCEANIC TRAFFIC (NUMBER OF WORDS) HANDLED BY
RADIO CORPORATION OF AMERICA DURING SPECIFIED
PERIODS IN 1920*

Class of Service	Eastward	Westward	Total
British service:			
April	86,693	96,032	182,725
December	144,224	173,004	317,228
Transpacific service:			
March	87,890	61,401	149,291
December	105,358	105,295	210,653
Scandinavian service:			
June	81,255	139,596	220,851
December	114,958	142,840	257,798
German service:			
August	27,998	108,565	136,563
December	80,925	233,014	313,939
French service:			
December 15-31	8,193	22,104	30,297

*Statement by Mr. Winterbottom, traffic manager of the Radio Corporation, before the Senate Committee on Interstate Commerce, Jan. 11, 1921.

AGREEMENT WITH POSTAL TELEGRAPH

To remedy this defect, the Radio Corporation made an agreement with the Postal Telegraph Company providing for the delivery by the telegraph company of messages originating in Europe, Africa, or Western Asia to any point in the United States at which it has an office. Furthermore, under this pact the Postal Telegraph will receive at all its American offices all "transatlantic radio messages intended for and designated to be forwarded via Radio and will forthwith transmit and deliver same to the general transfer offices of the Radio Corporation at New York City, or at such other offices as may from time to time be designated by the Radio Corporation or mutually agreed to."

Thus both eastbound and westbound transatlantic as well as transpacific radio messages may today, if necessary, be handled at both ends by wire.

TRAFFIC AND POOLING CONTRACTS

Preferential traffic agreements and provisions for the pooling of receipts are found in all traffic agreements, though there are, of course, variations in their details. The contract of the Radio Corporation of America with the British Marconi Company illustrates the point. Every radiogram received by the British Company destined for points in, or routing through, the United States, is to be delivered to the Radio Corporation. Reciprocally, the American Company will deliver to the Marconi Company all messages originating in the United States and destined to or through Great Britain. All tolls from this British circuit are to be divided half and half between the companies. In regard to the pooling of the gross receipts, though the usual provision is half and half, other arrangements are found. For instance, in the American Marconi agreement with Japan (which was assigned to the Radio Corporation) the provision is made that if the messages are sent direct between Japan and the

United States, the Japanese Government and the Radio Corporation shall each be entitled to one-half of the gross tolls; but if the message is relayed via Hawaii, one-third shall accrue to the Japanese Government and two-thirds to the Radio Corporation—on the theory that since the relaying is done by an American station, it ought to get more than one-half of the receipts. The agreement with the French Compagnie Generale de Telegraphie sans Fil of October 26, 1921, stipulates that the transmitting station shall retain the tolls which it has collected.

ROCKY POINT

For a long time it has been the custom to construct radio stations in pairs about 50 miles apart and connected by telegraph wires—the one being a sending and the other a receiving station. In this way manual relaying of messages and duplication of telegraph staffs were necessary. Under its new central control system, inaugurated in 1921, all the Radio Corporation's transmitting stations (two in Tuckerton, New Jersey, one in New Brunswick, New Jersey, one in Marion, Massachusetts, and two[1] in Rocky Point, Long Island) are connected with and controlled by the central traffic office on Broad Street, New York. The sole receiving station, located at Riverhead, Long Island, has an antenna of two copper wires nine miles long strung on ordinary telephone poles. This antenna is constructed so as to permit uni-directional reception. The signals, which are simultaneously received from all transatlantic circuits are here intercepted and automatically relayed to the same traffic office, where they are interpreted. The tape method of both transmission and reception is used. The messages are punched on the tape by an apparatus operated by means of a typewriter keyboard. The letters are, therefore, uniform,

---

[1] The towers at Rocky Point are 410 feet high, and 1,250 feet apart. The cross-arms are 150 feet long. For detailed description of Rocky Point stations, see *Commercial and Financial Chronicle* for December 17, 1921, p. 2625, and *Electrical World* for November 12, 1921, p. 987.

and a speed up to 100 words per minute is possible. The received signals are recorded in ink on a paper tape, thus forming a permanent record to which reference may be made at any time.[1] The central control system is also in use on the Pacific Coast and has been adopted by several foreign nations.

Messages to or from ships at sea are handled by both the Western Union and the Postal Telegraph companies. Ships are required by international convention to communicate with the nearest land station. Such marine coastal stations are operated by almost a half-dozen American wireless companies.

[1]For detailed description of the method of handling messages, see "Electrical Plant of Transoceanic Radio Telegraphy," by Chief Engineer Alexanderson, in *General Electric Review*, July, 1923, also *Reports of Directors of Radio Corporation*, 1921 and 1922.

ECONOMICS OF THE RADIO INDUSTRY

PART III

PROBLEMS OF EFFICIENCY IN RADIO SERVICE

IX

BROADCASTING AND ITS PROBLEMS[1]

Development of radio broadcasting. Problems of radio communication. Present policy of control of service. Quantity of broadcasting service. Continuity of service. Operating costs. Income from radio broadcasting. Need for better quality radio service. Solution of problems. General Squier on "Who Shall Pay?"

THOUGH telegraphic broadcasting has been in use for more than a score of years for sending such things as time and weather signals, news items, and orders to ships at sea, only recently has the public interest been aroused. Radio amateurs have for a long time been active in the transmission and interception of telegraphic messages, but this hobby never appealed to the general public. It requires a certain amount of skill and patience to copy dots and dashes, and the effort is ordinarily prohibitive. Furthermore, comparatively few people are endowed with a capacity and desire for tinkering. Most of us wish apparatus and machines for service, and not as a means of experiment.

With the perfection of wireless telephony the situation changed. When people can hear the human voice and music coming through the air, they will sit up and take notice, whereas they will regard the system of dots and dashes as a mere jumble, intelligible only to a select few. How many of us would be willing and able to communicate over the wire if we had to operate a telegraph key and a pencil instead of the receiver and the mouthpiece?

The war effectively stopped wireless communication by private individuals. When the restraints were lifted, the people only needed some one to supply the incentive for a

---

[1] A portion of this and Chapter XIII appeared in the April, 1925, issue of the *Journal of Land & Public Utility Economics* in an article by the writer entitled "Public Policy toward Radio Broadcasting."

tremendous interest in radio. This spark was furnished by
the Westinghouse Electric and Manufacturing Company,
which, on presidential election night in 1920, transmitted
from its East Pittsburgh station the complete news of the
Republican victory. While relatively few (mostly amateurs)
heard these messages, the idea immediately became popular.
The electrical and radio shops in the vicinity of Pittsburgh
reported an unprecedented demand for their products. So
many listeners expressed their pleasure at the entertainment,
that the Westinghouse Company, deciding to enter this field
permanently, applied for and received permission from the
United States to broadcast regular programs.[1]

The radio became a fad, especially in the United States.
We are known as a nation enjoying the maximum of individual freedom with the minimum of official restriction.
Few formalities are necessary for the erection and operation
of transmitting stations and none at all for the establishment
of receiving sets. In most foreign countries, on the other
hand, the private use of radio is narrowly restricted by governmental regulations. Even private receiving sets have
been prohibited by some nations. So, while most of the
world has been forbidding or narrowly limiting the use of
radio, we have opened the field for all, imposing only the
necessary police regulations. The American Boy has been
allowed to tinker with transmitting as well as receiving
apparatus. While in 1913 there were 1,224 licensed amateur
sending stations in the United States, in 1924 there were
15,545.[2] The freedom which has permitted such expansion

---

[1] The impression must be avoided that the Westinghouse station was the
first to engage in telephonic broadcasting. DeForest and Fessenden had succeeded in broadcasting the human voice in 1908, some claiming that the
latter had projected his voice across the Atlantic in that year. At about this
time Caruso sang by radio to a few scattered listeners. By December, 1916,
the American Radio and Research Corporation was broadcasting concerts
two or three times a week.

[2] In 1913 only 483 American commercial vessels carried radio apparatus;
by 1924 this number had increased to 2,741. In 1912 there was only one
transoceanic station in the United States; today there are 12. Government
land and ship stations have increased in number from 77 and 229, respectively, in 1913, to 298 and 951 in 1924. The exclusively broadcasting stations
have increased from 3 in September, 1921, to 555 in January, 1925.

has had a very salutary effect on our technical progress. Many a valuable wireless device has had its origin in the woodshed or the attic. John Hays Hammond, Junior, who has made great progress in the problem of remote control, may be mentioned as one of our foremost inventors who began his wireless career as an amateur.

Another factor in the expansion of our wireless communication resources is the motivation of those who have entered the broadcasting business. Individuals have established stations because the fever was in the air. Radio manufacturers and dealers, department stores, hardware stores, newspapers, state experiment stations, universities and colleges, churches, secondary schools, various associations—these are some of the group which have entered this fascinating and mysterious field. Some have entered it to promote good-will, some to facilitate the sale of radio, still others for many various purposes. But a large number have begun the broadcasting game for no ulterior motive at all. They have gone into it merely to satisfy their desire for a hobby, or because they wanted to learn the tricks of the new game, or as a method of giving vent to their pent-up enthusiasm and restlessness—the desire to reach out into space and explore the unknown.

On this point the replies received in response to the writer's questionnaire to broadcasters throughout the United States are suggestive. The results are given in Table 14. If this is a fair sample, most broadcasting stations were established for some private end and only incidentally to serve the public generally.

PROBLEMS OF RADIO COMMUNICATION

Although our generally *laissez-faire* attitude toward the radio has been beneficial to the development of the science and to the popularity of this form of communication, it has at the same time resulted in many economic and legal problems of recognized public utilities. Generally speaking,

TABLE 14

PURPOSES OF BROADCASTERS

Purpose	Total	Number of Stations Reporting as the Only Purpose	Number of Stations Reporting as One of Two or More Purposes
To help maintain sale of receiving sets..........	31	2	29
To profit from advertising received and good-will developed.............	44	8	36
To profit by direct sale of advertising time.......	2	0	2
To serve public generally.	146	46	100
To serve some special group or clientele...........	26	6	20
Research purposes.......	13	4	9
Police information.......	8	2	6
University extension work	1	1	0

these outstanding problems pertain to the control, quantity, quality, and continuity of the service of radio telephonic broadcasting.

PRESENT POLICY OF CONTROL OF SERVICE

Radio communication in the United States is still operating under the Wireless Regulation Act of 1912. This act, beside incorporating the provisions of the 1912 Radiotelegraph Convention of London, stipulated that "A person, company, or corporation within the jurisdiction of the United States shall not use or operate any apparatus for radio communication—except under and in accordance with a license revocable for cause—granted by the Secretary of Commerce upon application therefor." This law was an attempt to regulate radio as it was at that time. Congress could not then foresee the future popularity of radio and the advent of broadcasting as we think of it today. The hearings in the committees indicate that Congress had in mind primarily radio for point-to-point communication and for broadcasting by means of the wireless telegraph. Radio telephony had not as yet been made practicable on a large scale.[1]

This act, however, gives the Secretary of Commerce no discretion as to the granting of licenses. His only discretion is in the assignment of a wave length. Under this power he has allocated wave lengths among the various uses.[2] The extent of the power of the Secretary was the issue in the case of *Hoover* v. *Intercity Radio Company*.[3] The Intercity Company had been engaged in the business of wireless telegraphy between New York and other cities in the United States under licenses issued by the Secretary from time to time. When the last license on one of its stations expired in January, 1924, Mr. Hoover refused to grant a renewal on the ground that there was no wave length available for the company which would not interfere with private and government stations. In other words, this was an attempt by the United States Government to prevent interference through a refusal to grant a license to a radio transmitting station.

The company argued that the Secretary had no such discretionary powers. It had in all respects complied with the requirements of the law; and so it petitioned in the Supreme Court of the District of Columbia for a writ of *mandamus* directing the Secretary to issue the license.

The Supreme Court of the District of Columbia granted the writ, and Mr. Hoover appealed to the Circuit Court of Appeals, which affirmed the decision on the ground that Congress, and not Mr. Hoover, had the power to regulate the radio business. Congress had not delegated any discretion to the Secretary of Commerce, but had merely com-

---

[1]Congress did realize that radio would appeal to the people as a hobby; so provision was made for the licensing of amateur transmitting stations. It will be noted that this act placed no restrictions on the construction and operation of receiving sets. A penalty was, however, provided for unlawful disclosure of information and messages obtained from the air.

[2]For a complete list of wave length allocations see *Recommendations for Regulation of Radio* adopted by the Third National Radio Conference, October 6-10, 1924.

[3]286 Fed. 1003.

manded him to grant the license when certain requirements had been met by the applicant. The issuance of the license was a ministerial act.

QUANTITY OF BROADCASTING SERVICE

People are, therefore, in a position after erecting a station to demand a license from the Department of Commerce. As a result, radio broadcasters are scattered throughout the United States in a haphazard and uneconomical way, with very little regard for the needs of the public and the amount of interference caused. Some idea of the quantity of telephonic broadcasting service now available to consumers can be gained from the distribution of the 555 licensed stations as shown in the accompanying map (Figure 12). It is to be noted that California boasts of 49 stations, Pennsylvania 39, Texas 29, New York 31, Ohio 29. The three Pacific Coast states have 77 stations, whereas the Atlantic states have 146.

This may seem to be a fair distribution, but radio resources cannot be measured merely by the number of stations; their power must also be considered. There are altogether 138 stations in the United States having a wattage of 500 or over. Ninety-two of this total are in New York, Pennsylvania, Illinois, Ohio, California, Michigan, Missouri, Texas, Nebraska, Minnesota, and Wisconsin. In other words, 67% of the stations of 500 watts or over are in 23% of the states. New York state has 17 of these high-power stations, while Montana, with three times the area, has none.

If apportionment of stations according to resources and population is a measure of good distribution, New York may be justified in its large number of high-power stations. But atmospheric conditions and area are additional factors that should be considered. The act of reception itself does not weaken radio signals, just as the human voice, carried by means of sound waves, can be heard by all within range

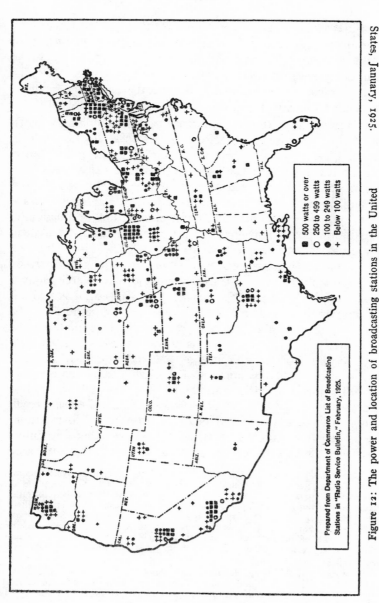

States, January, 1925.

500 watts or over
250 to 499 watts
100 to 249 watts
Below 100 watts

Prepared from Department of Commerce List of Broadcasting
Stations in "Radio Service Bulletin," February, 1925.

Figure 12: The power and location of broadcasting stations in the United

without loss of strength.[1] Thus, in many parts of the East, radio messages can, if necessary, be intercepted by means of cheap crystal sets which have a range up to 25 to 50 miles, whereas in certain isolated sections of the West, listeners must use expensive multiple-tube receivers in order to hear the nearest station.

Consequently, the present more or less haphazard distribution of broadcasting facilities tends to result not only in virtual sectional discrimination, but also in interference, which is the bane of the radio enthusiast's existence. Furthermore, interference has been aggravated by the "mushroom" growth of broadcasting and by a tendency toward concentration of control and the elimination of financially weak, low-power stations. At the present stage of technical progress the number of passes through the air is limited. All broadcasting stations operate on wave lengths between 200 and 545 meters. But, as Secretary of Commerce Hoover has said:[2] "Within this range [200-600] we have about seven possible bands for sending in any one community. The number of telephone or broadcasting stations that can be operated from any one place is, however, more limited than this because of interference of one locality with another. . . . No doubt the number of available wave lengths will steadily increase with improvements in the art and better adjustment between different purposes." As the reader will note in Figure 12, many localities attempt to foster more than seven broadcasting stations. Hence there is interference, as can be attested by a large number of radio

---

[1] There are, however, certain atmospheric obstructions, and physical obstacles affecting atmospheric conditions, which interfere with the reception of messages. The southern end of Central Park in New York is but six miles from the powerful WEAF, yet, because of the tall apartment buildings, there is a remarkable reduction in the energy received in this area. (See *Wireless Age*, May, 1924, p. 47.) It is interesting to note, also, that instances are recorded where obstructions to good radio service have affected the desirability, and values, of residential real estate. (See *Literary Digest*, February 14, 1925, p. 23.)

[2] Statement of Secretary Hoover before the Committee on the Merchant Marine and Fisheries of the House of Representatives in regard to H. R. 7357, a bill to regulate radio communication, March 11-14, 1924, p. 9.

"listeners in." The interference, however, is not only among the broadcasting stations. In 1924 there were 2,741 American commercial ship stations, 951 government ship stations, 298 government land stations, 15,545 amateurs, and 12 transoceanic stations. The first four of these classes operate on wave lengths which are more or less capable of interfering with broadcasters.

Unless technical advances remedy the situation, the tendency will be for certain broadcasting stations to establish property rights to wave lengths as a protection against interference. In effect, this is what happens when wave lengths are assigned by the licensing authorities.[1] The combination of claims to property rights and interference is likely to result in conflicts, or, in order to minimize interference, in abstention from service—thereby disappointing receivers.

As a result of the 1924 Radio Conference, the wave lengths available to broadcasting stations were extended by lowering the amateur to 150 and below and raising the marine to a range between 600 and 835, and by the preparation of a new system of zoning, whereby the stations on the Pacific Coast (Zone 6) will use exactly the same wave lengths as those in Zone 1. The net result is that there has been an increase of 30 possible channels, bringing the total up to 100. The conference assigned to Class 1 broadcasters (the old Class B, power 500 watts or above) the wave lengths ranging from 280 to 545, making 63 channels available for broadcasters in this class. Therefore, since there are more than 100 Class 1 broadcasters, few, if any, of them will be given exclusive wave lengths. The conference recommended that in a given locality not more than two Class 1 stations be licensed on a given wave length. Thus, the stations are obliged to observe silent nights and to divide the time in other ways. Our present system results, therefore, in a great amount of social waste.

Another aspect of the service problem, from the standpoint of both quantity and quality, is the duplication of

---

[1] These wave lengths may at any time be changed by licensing authorities.

programs. Under our present broadcasting system there is a large amount of waste. We say that capital and energy are wasted when two or three telephone companies serve the same community. Likewise, if several broadcasting stations duplicate the same service, there is loss to the community of receivers. One radio fan heard the song *I Love You*, "eleven times in one night." This is probably a record, but the rendition of the same piece of music and the announcement of identical news items during the same evening are not uncommon.

CONTINUITY OF SERVICE

In the case of recognized public utilities, continuity of service is a standard requisite. In the case of radio communication, there are no restrictions preventing broadcasters from ceasing to operate, and the discontinuance of service is assuming large proportions. The United States began to license broadcasting stations in September, 1921, only a little more than three years ago. By August, 1924, the Department of Commerce had licensed 1,105 broadcasters, but only 533 had survived; 572 had fallen by the wayside, indicating a total mortality of more than 50%. In other words, for every two stations granted a permit, one has ceased operation. Discontinuances during this period averaged 24 per month; new stations more than 30 per month.

The question of discontinuing business is mainly a concern of the broadcaster alone, but it has significance also from the consumers' standpoint in so far as the consumer comes to prefer, and depend upon, the service of a particular station.

This high mortality rate is apparently due chiefly to three factors: the large capital investment, high operating expenses, and the absence or intangibility of the income. Table 15, prepared from answers to the questionnaire previously mentioned, indicates the relative importance of capital outlays among 106 stations.

TABLE 15

EXPENSE OF INSTALLING BROADCASTING STATIONS

Expense of Installing, in Dollars	ABSOLUTE NUMBER		PERCENTAGE	
	Simple	Cumulative	Simple	Cumulative
0— 1,000 Inc...	12	12	11.3	11.3
1,001— 2,000 ...	20	32	18.9	30.2
2,001— 3,000 ...	19	51	17.9	48.1
3,001— 5,000 ...	14	65	13.2	61.3
5,001— 10,000 ...	11	76	10.4	71.7
10,001— 25,000 ...	15	91	14.2	85.9
25,001— 50,000 ...	7	98	6.6	92.5
50,001— 75,000 ...	3	101	2.8	95.3
75,001—100,000 ...	2	103	1.9	97.2
100,001—above........	3	106	2.8	100.0

It will be noted that 51 stations, or almost one-half, indicated a cost of $3,000 or less. These are almost entirely the stations of colleges and churches. Eight stations, or almost 8%, reported an initial expense of more than $50,000. These are, as a rule, constructed by large manufacturers or dealers in radio apparatus. Fifteen reported an original outlay of more than $25,000, while one dual station revealed an expense of $400,000.

Variations in the cost of installation are due primarily to the fact that some stations are built without the purchase of Western Electric sets; in colleges the parts are constructed in the physics department; construction costs of buildings are not included in the case of stations housed in sheds or attics; and there is also the difference in the power and elaborateness of the machinery installed.

OPERATING COSTS

The cost of operation, as given in Table 16, shows one of the chief reasons for the great number of stations discontinuing business.

Among the reasons for the variations in the annual operating costs of the different stations may be mentioned:

TABLE 16

ANNUAL OPERATING EXPENSES OF BROADCASTING STATIONS

Operating Expenses, in Dollars	ABSOLUTE NUMBER		PERCENTAGE	
	Simple	Cumulative	Simple	Cumulative
1,000—or under.....	39	39	42.4	42.4
1,001— 2,000......	11	50	12.0	54.4
2,001— 3,000......	9	59	9.8	64.2
3,001— 5,000......	8	67	8.7	72.9
5,000— 10,000......	9	76	9.8	82.7
10,001— 25,000......	7	83	7.7	90.4
25,001— 50,000......	3	86	3.2	93.6
50,001— 75,000......	2	88	2.1	95.7
75,001—100,000......	1	89	1.1	96.8
100,001—above........	3	92	3.2	100.0

1. Many stations, such as schools, churches, and hobby stations, operate only part time at irregular intervals, and the work is done by non-paid persons.

2. Only a few of the broadcasters are making any payment for the services of the artists and performers. Home talent is used, but the demand for compensation is increasing. A few pay regularly, others only occasionally.

3. Some must pay copyright royalty fees, usually $500 a year, while colleges pay only a nominal fee of $1. Others are paying no fee at all.

A striking characteristic is the fact that the operating costs of the broadcasting stations are large in comparison with the initial expense of installation. In many instances the former are larger than the latter, while the average expense seems to be about $75 a year for keeping the station going in comparison with $100 in original outlay. That is a ratio of three to four. It seems, therefore, that the great financial burden is the cost of upkeep.

INCOME FROM RADIO BROADCASTING

The relation of operating costs to original outlay is insufficient explanation by itself of the high mortality rate.

Broadcasters of the type being considered have little or no direct income. Several stations are supported by interested business men or clubs. Church stations continually receive donations from the members of the congregation. Students and alumni help support their college broadcaster. Such contributions can, however, be considered as payments by the owners, be they congregations, student bodies, or business clubs. Though a small number of broadcasters indicated that occasionally they received a check from a far-off "listener in," only 3 out of 110 reporting stations stated that they received more or less regular contributions from their radio audiences. This business aspect of broadcasting is not often remembered by radio "fans." Up to a recent date, the American Telephone and Telegraph Company station was the only one which charged for advertising. For example, its station will permit any concern to broadcast a program and announce its name and position in connection with the rendition. For such advertising WEAF charges $10 a minute or $400 an hour. But even the American Telephone and Telegraph Company has stated that its broadcasting is unprofitable, "receiving a revenue of less than half the operating expenses" in 1923.[1]

The ordinary broadcaster has, then, no source of direct income. He relies on the indirect benefits, such as the building up of good-will. But these indirect receipts are very uncertain. In his questionnaire the writer asked the broadcasters whether the average number of applause cards received after each program was considered satisfactory. Of the broadcasters replying, 36% answered in the negative. A considerable number of those added the comment that the response from their audiences is "not what it used to be." Only about one-fifth of the stations reported difficulty in obtaining talent, but of this small number three said the

---

[1] See Hearings before House Committee on Merchant Marine and Fisheries, on H. R. 7357, a bill to regulate radio communication, March 11-14, 1924, p. 88. Testimony by Mr. Harkness, a vice-president of the Bell System. Mr. Harkness stated that the cost of operating WEAF for 1923 was about $250,000, and that the revenue to the company, including that from its licenses to other companies, was "less than half that amount."

complaint was "lack of appreciation." The point is this: If a large percentage of the audience are not interested and appreciative of the programs rendered for them free of charge, there seems to be a good reason to believe that the indirect gain through the advertising and publicity may not be very great. With large sums of money going out, and uncertain and unmeasurable indirect benefits coming in, many stations are asking themselves the question: "Does it really pay?" Broadcasting may have been profitable for the first in the field, but the situation seems to be changing, now that the novelty has worn off, the stations are many, and the radio fan has a wide choice of programs. That broadcasting does not always adequately compensate the owner is presumably indicated by the heavy mortality rate in this field.[1]

"Last winter," writes the proprietor of a middle-western 500-watt station, "our talent cost us $700 per month, besides $200 for an operator and many other expenses too numerous to mention. We have put about $50,000 of our money into radio during the past 12 months and we have never received back one dollar in cash returns. We no doubt have lots of good-will and are nationally advertised, but we cannot cash in on our advertising. Furthermore, we cannot see our way clear to withdraw; we have too big an investment to throw it away; yet, every day we stay with it, we put in more money without hope of cash return."[2]

One newspaper reported that radio broadcasting did not tend to increase its circulation. A number of stations admitted that "they had no way of knowing whether their purpose in broadcasting was being successfully fulfilled or not." Another broadcaster, an Illinois concern, writes: "We may have to discontinue on account of the large license fee which the American Telephone and Telegraph Company

---

[1] WEAF, after its Bori-McCormack concert in January, 1925, received huge quantities of letters from fans. In one month this station received as high as 54,000 responses from its audiences. Practically every radio enthusiast knows of WEAF. And still this station does not pay.

[2] Letter to writer, dated July 24, 1924.

wants us to pay. We hate to quit, but guess we can't afford to pay the fee as we don't figure that our broadcasting brings us much net return, if any."

NEED FOR BETTER QUALITY RADIO SERVICE

These are only samples, but a study of the 130 answers to the questionnaire sent out by the writer indicates a growing feeling of unrest and speculation among broadcasters as to how it will end. To make matters worse, there are increasing demands for the broadcaster's money. Besides the requests of some artists for pay, and of the copyright owners for royalties on the broadcast music, the fact must be faced that radio audiences are becoming more and more critical. They are beginning to regard radio no longer as a plaything or as a mystery, but as a utility for the rendering of genuine service, to be placed alongside of the piano and the talking machine. Americans are popularly noted for taking things for granted. Three years ago the average citizen was satisfied, if he heard a *voice* on the radio. Today he must not only hear the voice or the music; it must come in clearly and steadily and must be of good quality such as he could expect in his theater.[1] The broadcasters must prepare to face this situation. The time is rapidly passing when the radio fan will be satisfied to hear selections rendered night after night by local talent. The fact that one-third of the broadcasters answering the writer's questionnaire complained of a diffidence and a lack of interest on the part of their audiences, a "not-as-it-used-to-be" cry, may be of some significance.

We must also face the fact that the period is slipping by when the concert singer will be willing to sing gratuitously before the microphone. The listener will not remain satis-

---

[1] A large number of listeners do not, even now, care so much for quality as distance and number of stations "logged." When the novelty of distance wears off, quality will be more in demand. Surveys conducted by large stations, for instance, WEAF, indicate that audiences are tiring of "jazz" and are demanding better music and better entertainment.

fied with local performers; and skilled and renowned talent must be paid. If the broadcaster pays, his already great expenses will be increased; if he refuses to pay, his audience will dwindle, decreasing further the questionable advertising value of broadcasting.

Many of the stations report that they have more talent available in the locality than they can possibly use. Others report that their programs are easily filled from the large waiting list. Universities and colleges state that their talent is furnished by the students and members of the faculty of their respective institutions. Churches report that there is adequate talent in the congregation to take care of their program needs.

Are these reports such as to stimulate optimism? The writer thinks not. The situation for the individual broadcaster may be comparatively satisfactory. He may get all the talent *he* needs, but is it always the talent *his audiences* want? The writer has had occasion to study the programs offered by a large number of stations. Very seldom, indeed, did he run across a person of national renown. The reader will, of course, recall many instances of large broadcasters furnishing nationally and internationally famous talent. But broadcast programs are, as a rule, mediocre. Since broadcasters generally use local talent, should they manifest disappointment, if people throughout the entire nation do not respond?

After all, why do broadcasters rely so largely on local talent? In the first place, these stars are willing to serve free of charge, since their appearance, besides giving them a real thrill, also serves as an effective and economical advertising medium. They need this publicity and are willing to pay for it in kind. The stars of national renown do not need advertising. In the second place, when a person establishes a station, he hopes to create a demand for his goods, for example, receiving sets. Since he feels that he is supported by his community, he thinks it to be his duty to offer talent in which his audience is personally interested.

SOLUTION OF THE PROBLEMS

We are, thus, confronted with important questions. What shall be the solution? Chapters X and XI will discuss the copyright and patent problems. Chapters XII and XIII will deal with the problems of quantity, quality, and continuity of service which in the final analysis are all questions of control and compensation to the broadcaster. Let us conclude this chapter with a description of some of the proposed and actually used methods of raising money for the broadcaster without public compulsion.

Some broadcasters are requesting contributions from their audiences. So far not many have reported a success, although occasionally checks both large and small are received. The irregularity and the uncertainty of the remittances are the main defects of such efforts at raising funds.

The Sweeney Automotive and Electrical School, of Kansas City, Missouri (WHB), has adopted a very unique scheme, called the "Invisible Theater." The general plan is the sale of tickets of various classes—box seats, $10 per year; main floor, $3; loges, $5; circle seats, $2; second balcony, $1. The purchase of one of these entitles the holder to hear any programs which may be broadcast, besides receiving a monthly program and a year's subscription for the *Microphone,* the official paper of the Invisible Theater. In view of the voluntary nature of such contributions, the plan has so far been fairly successful.

A plan that is used extensively in foreign nations is the levying of a direct tax on the owners of receiving sets and the distribution of a large part of the receipts to the broadcasting stations according to some logical and equitable system. This method will be considered in Chapter XIII.

GENERAL SQUIER ON "WHO SHALL PAY?"

General Squier, in a recent article,[1] first criticizes the policy of the taxation of receiving sets as "repugnant to the

[1] *Popular Radio,* August, 1924, pp. 140 ff.

American mind," because it would mean the taxation of the people of low income as well as of large income. This would be unjust, he says. Mr. Squier suggests that hotels and apartment houses install first-class receiving sets. The material received would then be distributed over the electric lighting system to the various rooms and apartments. He then suggests that the guests and dwellers would be willing to pay a small monthly fee for the privilege of listening in. The individual rooms and apartments would be equipped with crystal sets and a pair of telephone receivers. If any individual guest did not wish to pay the fee, there would be no compulsion. A large portion of the money received could be distributed to the broadcasters, either by mutual agreement or under the direction of some central government agency.

General Squier is an authority in the field of technical wireless, especially wired wireless, and because of his eminence, his proposal deserves attentive consideration. This scheme seems to the writer to be weak in the following respects:

1. It is not compulsory. He provides that the guests may pay or not as they see fit. "There will be no compulsion." This would be no improvement over our present system. At the present time, listeners are perfectly at liberty to contribute to the broadcasting stations if they wish. But their contributions have, thus far, been small in the aggregate.

2. The plan is founded on the wrong political principle. Although ability to pay is properly the predominant principle which should be followed in any money-raising effort, the principle of benefits received should be invoked to *justify* such attempt. It is not a sound principle to tax the rich and not the poor, though the wealthy should bear the greater portion of the burden. Why should the farmer, who may be poor (or who may be rich) be exempt from the payment of his share for the maintenance of broadcasting stations? Why should the city dweller in residence houses

(who may be poor but is not always so) not pay his share? Why ask only dwellers in hotels and apartments (and not all these are wealthy) to pay for the privilege of being a part of the vast unknown and unseen radio audience?

3. The plan does not go to the root of the difficulty of the "who shall pay" problem. General Squier says nothing about the questions of pay to performers and royalty to owners of copyright.

X

COPYRIGHT AS A PROPERTY PROBLEM IN THE RADIO FIELD[1]

Constitutional and statutory provisions. What is a public performance? Statement of problem. Decisions involving restaurants and theaters. Is present-day broadcasting a public performance for profit? Bamberger case affirmative answer. Conflict in federal courts. Purpose of broadcasters generally indirect profit. Is broadcasting performance public? Meaning of term "public performance" constantly changing. Comparison with "due process of law." Comparison with terms "commerce" and "post-office." Final authority with Congress. Provision and purport of Dill bill. Case for bill. Arguments against. Need for settlement of question on basis of public service.

THE founders of our government saw that in order to have a strong development of American culture and science, it would be necessary to protect the property rights of authors and inventors. So they inserted in the Constitution the following section: "(Congress shall have power) To promote the progress of science and useful arts, by securing for limited times to authors and inventors the exclusive right to their respective writings and discoveries."

Several points must be noted concerning this provision. In the first place, copyright is not a natural right like life, liberty, and property. Though Congress has acted under this enabling clause with acts and amendments protecting the work of an author, still it may withdraw this protection at any time without doing violence to the Constitution. The section says in effect, "Congress may. . . ."

In the second place, though this section is undoubtedly for the benefit of the individual, the public interest is paramount. Congress may grant a monopoly for a limited time only. The exclusive right is granted for the purpose of pro-

---

[1] A part of the material in this chapter appeared in an article by the writer in the *Radio News,* for May, 1925, under the title "Radio and the Copyright Problem."

moting progress, in which, of course, society is interested. Conceivably, if it should be discovered that the social welfare can best be promoted by some other means than the granting of such rights, Congress would recall the grant. The revocation by Congress could not, however, be retroactive. The prior existing grants would continue in effect.

Under the United States Copyright Act approved March, 1909, the author, dramatist, composer, or other person entitled to such protection, is given, among other privileges, the exclusive right to print, reprint, publish, copy, vend, and translate the copyrighted work, as well as the exclusive right to perform publicly for profit.

WHAT IS A PUBLIC PERFORMANCE?

The real issue concerns the meaning of the expression "to perform publicly for profit." What is a public performance? What is a performance for profit?

"A performance is public," says Arthur W. Weil,[1] "when there is present a sufficient number of the public who would, presumptively, also go to a performance licensed by the author, as a commercial transaction, so that it may be said that, theoretically at least, the author has sustained a monetary loss." (That is, if he receives no compensation.)

STATEMENT OF PROBLEM

A large number of questions immediately suggest themselves: If I buy a sheet of music, what rights have I? I may certainly play it on the piano by myself; I may play it in the presence of members of my family; I may invite in a few neighbors and relatives to hear and enjoy the new selection. I may announce a housewarming and invite the entire community to my house and then play the record for the entertainment of my company.

Now, suppose I buy a hotel, restaurant, or theater. The

---

[1] *American Copyright Law*, Chicago, 1917, p. 89.

selection is rendered in the dining room or in the auditorium. I charge for the meals or for admission to the theater. The music forms a part (an essential part) of the dinner. May I play this piece without incurring further liability to the owner of the copyright? Exactly where does private performance end and public performance begin? When does a performance become one for profit?

Suppose now I played this selection into the microphone of the transmitting apparatus of a broadcasting station, which sends the music out upon the waves to an unseen audience of thousands scattered over a wide territory. Is this a public performance? Is it a performance for profit?

If the reader will visualize these situations, he will understand the crux of the copyright problem.

DECISIONS INVOLVING RESTAURANTS AND THEATERS

The federal courts have for some time been grappling with such questions. The Shanley Company conducted a public restaurant in New York City. Songs were sung and music was played for the entertainment of the patrons. The diners, of course, paid for their meals, but there was no direct charge for the musical entertainment. The song *Sweethearts* was sung in this place. The owner of the copyright asked for an injunction restraining the proprietor of this restaurant from having this song rendered. He claimed that his property rights were being invaded. In the inferior federal courts the plaintiff failed to get relief on the ground that, since no admission was charged, there was no public performance of *Sweethearts* for profit. Hence, the United States copyright law would fail to protect.

The plaintiff appealed the case, however, and it ultimately reached the Supreme Court for final decision. The highest tribunal granted the relief. The court, speaking through Justice Holmes, said in part: "If the rights under the copyright are infringed only by a performance where money is taken at the door, they are very imperfectly protected. Performances not different in kind from those of the defendant [the restaurant owner] could be given that might compete with and even destroy the success of the monopoly that the law intends the plaintiff to have. It is enough to say that there is no need to construe the statute so narrowly. The defendant's performances are not eleemosynary. They are a part of a total for which the public pays, and the fact that the price of the whole is attributed to a particular item which those present are expected to order, is not important. It is true that the music is not the sole object, but neither is the food, which probably could be got cheaper elsewhere. The object is a repast in surroundings that to people having limited powers of conversation or disliking the rival noise give a luxurious pleasure not to be had from eating a silent meal. If music did not pay, it would be given up. If it pays, it pays out of the public's pocket. Whether it pays or not the purpose of employing it is profit and that is enough. Decrees reversed."[1]

A certain theater owner employed a pianist to play appropriate music at his performances. The pianist was given discretion as to what selections he should perform. He played *Tulip Time* from Ziegfeld's Follies of 1919. No charge was made for the music, but a charge, of course, was made for admission to the theater. The owner of the copyright sought an injunction restraining the theater owner from playing this selection. The Federal District Court granted the injunction, holding that the playing of copyrighted music by a pianist in a picture theater was an infringement of the copyright.[2]

IS PRESENT-DAY ENTERTAINMENT BROADCASTING A PUBLIC PERFORMANCE FOR PROFIT?

With the advent of radio broadcasting, it became necessary for these stations to furnish music for the musicians

---

[1]*Herbert v. Shanley Company*, 242 U. S. 591.

[2]*Harms* v. *Cohen*, 279 Fed. 276. For similar case see *M. Whitmark and Sons* v. *Pastime Amusement Co.*, 298 Fed. 470 decided May 13, 1924.

to send out upon the air. It would conceivably be possible to make up a good popular program from the free list (on which the copyright has expired), but audiences demand up-to-date music as well as the popular songs of the past. So it is practically necessary for artists performing at broadcasting stations to resort to newly copyrighted music. But herein lies the difficulty. If I buy printed sheet music, the possession of the tangible property does not vest in me ownership or control of the thought and creation of the author for any other than my own and others' private enjoyment. May I legally sing that selection which I have learned from the sheet, into the wireless apparatus for the enjoyment of an unknown and unseen audience?

BAMBERGER CASE—AFFIRMATIVE ANSWER

The opinions of the federal courts are conflicting. In a 1923 case,[1] it was held that broadcasting from a department store was a performance for profit. L. Bamberger and Company conduct a department store in Newark, New Jersey. They have instituted a radio department, selling radio equipment of all sorts. This company also conducts a broadcasting station (WOR) from which vocal and instrumental concerts and other entertainment and information are broadcast. The station performed *Mother Machree*. The plaintiff, the owner of the copyright, claimed that its copyright was infringed, and sued for relief. The district court granted the injunction. Judge Lynch held that this was a public performance for profit for the following reasons: (1) The defendant charged the cost of the broadcasting station against the general expenses of the business; (2) While the Bamberger Company does not broadcast the sale price of its wares, it does broadcast a slogan, "L. Bamberger and Company—one of America's great stores, Newark, New Jersey," at the beginning and end of each

---

[1] *M. Whitmark and Son* v. *L. Bamberger and Co.*, 291 Fed. 776, decided August 11, 1923.

program; (3) If the purpose had been eleemosynary and not for profit, it is likely that it would have adopted some anonymous name or initial.

CONFLICT IN FEDERAL COURTS

Other federal courts have held that the act of broadcasting is not a public performance. In the fall of 1923 the American Automobile Accessories Company of Cincinnati, a manufacturer of radio receiving sets and parts, caused the rendition of *Dream Melody,* by means of singing and an orchestra, to be broadcast from its station in that city. The purpose of this broadcasting was to advertise its wares and to stimulate the public interest in things wireless. The owner of the copyright, arguing that this was a public performance for profit under the Act of 1909, petitioned for an injunction restraining the Automobile Accessories Company from further rendering this composition by radio.

The Federal District Court, speaking through Judge Hickenlooper, dismissed the case on the ground that this was no public performance for profit. The argument of the court may be briefly summarized:

1. A strict construction of the statute is necessary. The law must be read according to the natural import of the words used. Radio broadcasting was not within the mind of Congress when using the term "perform publicly for profit."

2. In order to be a public performance in the sense in which Congress intended the words, there must be an assemblage of persons. "We simply feel that the rendition of a copyright piece of music in the studio of a broadcasting station, where the public are not admitted and cannot come, but where the sound waves are converted into radio frequency waves and thus transmitted over thousands of miles of space, to be at last reconverted into sound waves in the home of the owners of receiving sets, is no more a public

performance in the studio, within the intent of Congress, than the perforated music roll from which emanates the reproduction of copyrighted music, by one without musical education, is a copy of such music.[1] A private performance for profit is not within the meaning of the act, nor is a public performance without profit. All contemplate an audience which may hear the rendition itself through the transmission of sound waves, and not merely a reproduction of the sound by means of mechanical device and electromagnetic waves in ether. . . . The auditor 'listening in' at Indianapolis, Cleveland, or Chicago would be surprised to learn that he had, that evening, attended a public performance in Cincinnati."[2]

The third important decision to be noted is that of *Remick* v. *General Electric Company.* The General Electric broadcasting station (WGY), at Schenectady, New York, had broadcast the song *Somebody's Wrong,* the copyright of which belongs to the Jerome H. Remick Company. The plaintiff petitioned the United States District Court of the Southern District of New York to enjoin the General Electric Company from further rendering this song by radio.

The court, speaking through Judge Knox, stated that if no public performance had been authorized, the broadcaster would be liable. But if a public performance had already been authorized, the mere broadcasting of the music, that is, making it available to a greater number of persons, would not render the broadcaster guilty of infringement. "So far as the practical results are concerned, the broadcaster of

---

[1] The United States Supreme Court has held that the making of a perforated music roll is not a copy within the meaning of the copyright act. "A 'copy' of a musical composition within the meaning of the copyright law is a written or printed record of it in intelligible notation and this does not include perforated rolls which, duly applied and properly operated in connection with musical instruments to which they are adapted, produce the same musical tones that are represented by the signs and figures on the copy in staff notation of the composition filed by the composer for copyright." The court said the perforated rolls are virtually *a part of the machine* which produces the music. *White Smith Music Co.* v. *Apollo Co.,* 209 U. S. 1 (1908).

[2] *Remick* v. *American Automobile Accessories Co.,* 298 Fed. 628 (1924)

the authorized performance of a copyrighted musical selection does little more than the mechanic who rigs an amplifier or loudspeaker in a large auditorium to the end that persons in remote sections of the hall may hear what transpires on the stage. Such broadcasting merely gives the performer a larger audience and is not to be regarded as a separate and distinct performance of the copyrighted composition on the part of the broadcaster. . . . The performance is one and the same whether the 'listener in' be at the elbow of the leader of the orchestra playing the selection, or at a distance of 1,000 miles."[1]

On the other hand, "If a broadcaster procures an unauthorized performance of a copyrighted musical selection to be given, and for his own profit makes the same available to the public served by radio receiving sets attuned to his station, he is, in my judgment, to be regarded as an infringer."

PURPOSE OF BROADCASTERS GENERALLY INDIRECT PROFIT

Thus, it is apparent that the Federal District Courts are in conflict. It is generally admitted that most of the broadcasting performances are for profit, not for a direct gain, it is true, but for indirect profit,[2] such as the building up of good-will and maintaining the sale of receiving sets and parts. The owner of a broadcasting station hopes, no matter what his business, to keep his name constantly before the public. The fundamental problem is this: Is a broadcasting performance a *public performance* as intended by the framers of our copyright act?

IS BROADCASTING PERFORMANCE PUBLIC?

The final adjudication of this question lies with the Supreme Court of the United States. The Copyright Law

---

[1] 4 Fed. (2nd) 160. The court denied the application for an injunction on the ground that the plaintiff had not properly pleaded his case.

[2] See Chapter IX.

of 1909 is very general. It merely says perform "publicly for profit" without mentioning any specific type of performance. Congress saw that a public performance of the future might not be the same as a performance in 1909; so it couched the statute in general terms. "It is a general rule," says Sutherland in his book *Statutory Construction*, section 589, "that courts must find the intent of the legislature in the statute itself. Unless some ground can be found in the statute for restraining or enlarging the meaning of its general words, they must receive a general construction: the courts cannot arbitrarily subtract from or add thereto."

Judge Hickenlooper gave a strict construction to a general statute and restrained the meaning of general terms. It is true that a penal statute must be interpreted very strictly, but the copyright law is not penal in its nature. It is true, that when a statute fixes obligations or grants privileges in specific terms, the courts will interpret it rigidly.[1] Beyond certain powers inherent in corporate existence and reasonable implied grants, a corporation has no authority to enter into activities not expressly mentioned in its charter or in the state laws as belonging to that organization. If a corporation has been granted certain privileges (for instance, exemption from taxation) it may not transfer that favor to a subsidiary. But the copyright law makes no such grants. The rule of strict construction ought to apply to all cases of grants in derogation of common rights. But the copyright is not of such nature.

Chester Lloyd Jones[2] cites an illustration of a Louisiana statute which provided that "every person who shall wilfully set fire to or burn, any bridge, shed, railroad, plankroad, railroad car, carriage, or other vehicle, or any goods, wares, or merchandise, or any stack, bale or heap of hay, fodder, grain, corn, or other produce, or any crop. . . ." should be guilty of arson. The defendant was accused of the crime of burning the wooden box seats of a merry-go-round outfit.

---

[1] See *Charles River Bridge Co.* v. *Warren Bridge*, 11 Pet. 420.

[2] *Statute Lawmaking in the United States*, 1912, p. 134.

The state's attorney argued that this was a burning of "goods" under the law. The judge ruled that such a burning was not a crime in Louisiana because "while the above statute enumerates a number of different kinds of property . . . it does not mention seats of the kind in question."

Sutherland[1] cites, among many other examples, a case in which power was granted to a corporation to take private waters "for the extinguishment of fires, and for domestic, sanitary, and other purposes." The last words were held to mean other like purposes, and did not include manufacturing purposes.[2]

This is known as the *eiusdem generis* rule; that is, if a law uses general as well as specific terms, the courts will hold that the general words used are not to be construed according to their ordinary meaning, but are to be restricted to persons or things of the same kind as those mentioned. So a strict interpretation of the law says that what it means is either the particular terms only, or allied concepts.

Courts will not, however, interpret this rule so as to destroy the intended meaning of the act. Suppose the enumeration exhausts the entire genus. Under this condition logically the general words cannot apply to things of the same kind. So the legislature must have meant the general term to refer to another group or groups of ideas.

MEANING OF TERM "PUBLIC PERFORMANCE" CONSTANTLY CHANGING

As already indicated, the Copyright Act of 1909 grants, among other rights, the exclusive power "to perform the copyrighted work publicly for profit if it be a musical composition." This is a general statement. There is no specific point mentioned in it. Congress saw that it was best, in laying down a general rule of action, not to mention specific

---

[1]Sutherland on *Statutory Construction*, 2 ed. Sections 422-441. This is a very detailed and authoritative treatment of the meaning, interpretation, and limitations of the *eiusdem generis* rule.

[2]*In re Barre Water Co.*, 62 Vermont 27.

points. The term "public performance" is constantly changing meaning. Not many years ago the only people who could hear the inaugural address of the president of the United States were those who were actually within range of his voice. Then the authorities installed loudspeakers, which so amplified the sound waves that his words could be plainly heard a mile away. Then the advent of radio telephony made his voice audible to millions. Are not all three of these groups audiences? The act contemplates a "public performance": not a public performance where there is a close assemblage of persons, not a performance in which the actual sound waves emanating from the performer directly reach the ears of the audience. Congress wisely saw that a public performance of 1909 might not be of the same nature as a public performance of 1925.

COMPARISON WITH TERM "DUE PROCESS OF LAW"

Consider an analogy. The Constitution of the United States provides that neither the federal nor the state governments may deprive a person of life, liberty, or property without due process of law. This is a very elastic prohibition. One hundred years ago the close relation between hours of labor and working conditions, on the one hand, and the health, safety, and morals of the general public, on the other hand, was not recognized. Much social legislation has been declared unconstitutional on the ground that the public health, safety, and morals did not justify such an interference with private rights of contract and property. At the present time a large number of our states (as well as the central government in some instances) have written on their statute books valid laws limiting the hours of women and, in certain hazardous occupations, of men, laws providing for compulsory accident insurance at the expense of the employers, and laws forcing the employers to establish certain standards of working conditions. Why the change in the attitude of the courts? Because, with the ever-increasing complexity and interdependence of our social life, the terms "due process" and "police power" are acquiring a larger and broader meaning. Individual acts, which yesterday had no direct social significance, today are seen vitally to affect the public well-being.

COMPARISON WITH TERMS "COMMERCE" OR "POST-OFFICE"

A decision of the United States Supreme Court in 1877 is also instructive. In that year Mr. Justice Waite said, regarding the "commerce" and "post-office" clauses of the United States Constitution: "The powers thus granted are not confined to the instrumentalities of commerce, or the postal service known or in use when the Constitution was adopted, but they keep pace with the progress of the country, and adapt themselves to the new developments of time and circumstance. They extend from the horse with its rider to the stage coach, from the sailing vessel to the steamboat, from the coach and steamboat to the railroad, and from the railroad to the telegraph, as these new agencies are successively brought into use to meet the demands of increasing population and wealth. They were intended for the government of the business to which they relate, at all times, and under all circumstances."[1]

---

[1]*Pensacola Telegraph* v. *Western Union Telegraph,* 96 U. S. 1 at p. 9.
As this manuscript was sent to the publisher, the United States Circuit Court of Appeals (sixth district) announced its reversal of Judge Hickenlooper's decision. Case No. 4190. In the course of his opinion, Circuit Judge Mack said:

While the fact that the radio was not developed at the time the Copyright Act was enacted may raise some question as to whether it properly comes within the purview of the statute, it is not by that fact alone excluded from the statute. In other words, the statute may be applied to new situations not anticipated by Congress, if, fairly construed, such situations come within its intent and meaning. Thus it has been held, both in this country and England, that a photograph was a copy or infringement of a copyrighted engraving under statutes passed before the photographic process had been developed. . . . . While statutes should not be stretched to apply to new situations not fairly within their scope, they should not be so narrowly construed as to permit their evasion because of changing habits due to new inventions and discoveries. . . .
A performance, in our judgment, is no less public because the listeners are unable to communicate with one another or are not assembled within an enclosure or gathered together in some open stadium or park or other public place. Nor can a performance, in our judgment, be deemed private because each listener may enjoy it alone in the privacy of his home. Radio broadcasting is intended to and in fact does reach a very much larger number of the public at the moment of the rendition than any other medium of performance. The artist is consciously addressing a great though unseen and widely scattered audience and is therefore participating in a public performance.

FINAL AUTHORITY WITH CONGRESS

The settlement of the copyright problem is an important matter of public policy. The problem is legislative rather than judicial. It is the duty of Congress to determine the rights of the owner of copyright. The courts interpret the law as it is, but Congress may change the statute so as to include broadcasting, if the courts say it is not included, or so as to exempt broadcasting, if the Supreme Court should decide that it is covered by the present law.

PROVISION AND PURPORT OF THE DILL BILL

In order to settle this question, Senator C. C. Dill, of Washington, introduced into the last Congress bill number S 2600, which was intended to amend the copyright law by exempting the radio and the telephone from the operation of its provisions. The important change in the law comes near the end of Sec. 1:

And provided further, That the copyright control shall not extend to public performances, whether for profit or without profit, of musical compositions where such performance is made from printed or written sheets or by reproducing devices issued under the authority of the owner of the copyright, or by the use of the radio or telephone, or both.

Let us examine the effects of this bill. If it should be enacted, I would have the right to purchase sheet music or a phonograph record, and have it played without extra charge in the public dining room, in the auditorium of a theater, or in a broadcasting station. The theory of the amendment is this: When I buy a sheet of music or a device for mechanical reproduction, I include in my purchase price an amount sufficient to pay the royalty accruing to the author or composer. He has already, then, received one fee, which is all the law ought to grant. It was never the intention of Congress that the composer should have the double right of selling his product to the public, and then of following it up and requiring further payment every time it is played in public. This is the theory and purpose of the bill.

CASE FOR THE BILL

The arguments for this bill may be summarized briefly as follows:

1. It will free radio broadcasting. On account of the great expense, the lack of direct income, and the instability of this new public utility,[1] the proprietors of these station: cannot afford to pay royalties.

2. It is unjust to permit the owner of a copyright to collect two fees for the same service, especially when the second charge is applied to a growing business such as broadcasting. The owner of the copyright has already got his just desert from the royalty included in the price of the record or sheet of music.

3. Broadcasting a new piece of music tends to advertise it and to stimulate its sales. Since the owner of the copyright does not lose, but probably gains, by the act of broadcasting, he should receive no extra compensation.

4. If the owners of copyrights are allowed to make this extra charge, the effect will be cumulative. For example, how about the bootblack who places a radio receiving set in his shoe shining parlor for the enjoyment of his customers? Here, again, would be another public performance for profit. Surely, the advocates of the Dill bill say, the 1909 law cannot be intended to have such far-reaching effects.

ARGUMENTS AGAINST

These are potent arguments. But against the passage of this bill may be advanced the following arguments:

1. Broadcasting should be placed on a sound economic basis so that royalties can be paid. The United States

---

[1] As to the question whether radio telephonic broadcasting is a public utility, see Chapter XII.

Government should limit the number and location of broadcasting stations, so that this new and important public utility may be placed on a scientific basis. Conceivably, it would be advisable for the government to favor a system of superpower stations to which the government would grant a subsidy. The funds for this subsidy could be collected in the form of a tax on gross sales of all radio manufacturers. Since this tax falls on all manufacturers, the conditions would be favorable for its being shifted to the purchasers of the sets and parts, in other words, the radio listening-in public. This would be just, as the people who own receiving sets and listen to the programs should pay the costs of broadcasting. If some system like this were adopted, the broadcasting stations could afford to pay royalties to the owners of the copyrights.

2. This is not a case of two fees for the same service, but of two fees for two different services. If I buy a sheet of music and have it played in a private entertainment for my friends or relatives, or in a public non-profit performance, I have paid one royalty charge. In return for that I acquire the privilege of reading physical notes from physical paper and transforming them into things spiritual and mental. If I had not bought this sheet, this transformation could not have taken place. This is service number one.

Now, if I render that selection before the microphone of a broadcasting station, the expenses of which I charge to my general business costs, I am enabling many people to hear it who, unless they had purchased the sheet, would not otherwise have had the opportunity. This is service number two, for which an extra payment is legitimate.

3. Whether broadcasting helps or hinders the sale of sheet music is really beside the question. As Judge Lynch said in the Bamberger case:

Our own opinion of the possibilities of advertising by radio leads us to the belief that the broadcasting of a newly copyrighted musical composition would greatly enhance the sales of the printed sheet. But the copyright owners and music publishers themselves are perhaps the best judges of the methods of bringing them to the attention of music lovers. It may be that one type of song is treated differently than a song of another type. But, be that as it may—the method, we think, is the privilege of the owner, he has the exclusive right to publish and vend, as well as to perform.

4. The owner's rights of copyright should be strengthened rather than weakened. Art, music, and culture can under our present state of society be encouraged by making special inducements to the authors. The private property rights in copyright should be maintained on a sound basis.

NEED FOR SETTLEMENT OF QUESTION ON BASIS OF PUBLIC SERVICE

The question of the balance between the rights of the copyright owner and the broadcaster must be settled on the basis of public service. If entertainment broadcasting is of sufficient importance to be classed as a public utility and to necessitate and justify its continuance on an economical basis, and if broadcasting tends to retard the sales of sheet music and devices for mechanical reproduction, it may be necessary to furnish the broadcasting stations a sufficient direct income so as to enable them to pay royalties. On the other hand, if broadcasting tends to stimulate the sales of music, then Congress may be justified in enacting the Dill bill into law. The problem as to whether broadcasting hinders or retards the sale of music is difficult of solution. Instances may be mentioned where broadcasting has practically ruined the sales of a certain selection. On the other hand, music publishers have reported sales of music or increased popularity of certain selections which apparently can be accounted for in no other way than that the placing of it on the air has made it popular. There is evidence tending to show that the Bori-McCormack radio concert in January stimulated the sale of Victor records.

Music publishers who complain that broadcasting of their selections has retarded sales often base their argument upon the fact that the constant repetition of a selection *ad nauseam* tends to prejudice the listener against purchase of a permanent record. If this is true, it may be advisable to decrease the quantity of our broadcasting service and to prevent the duplication of services. It is even conceivable that if Bori and McCormack had sung several nights in succession from each of a number of stations, the point of diminishing gratification would have been reached.

XI

PATENTS AS A PROPERTY PROBLEM IN THE RADIO FIELD

Nature of patent laws. Peculiarities of patent problem. Absence of basic patent in radio. Ease of constructing home-made radio sets. Diverse ownership of important radio patents. Interference proceedings. Interpretation and enforcement of the cross-licensing agreements. Cases arising out of cross-licensing agreements. Suits by patentees against broadcasting stations. Conclusion.

PATENT laws are founded upon the same essential principles as copyright laws; namely, the protection of the interests of the inventor and of the welfare of society. In case of clash between the social and the private interests, the good of the people will be held supreme. Congress could, if it saw fit, withdraw the patent protection from future inventions.

Under our present patent laws four things may be patented; namely, arts, manufactures, machines, or compositions of matter, or any improvement thereof. The thing patented must be *new* and *useful*. It must not have been known or used by others in the United States before the invention or discovery by the patentee. The same invention cannot be patented by two different persons. In case of conflicting claims, the authorities will attempt to determine the right of priority.[1]

---

[1] "Any person who has invented or discovered any new and useful *art, machine, manufacture, or composition of matter,* or any new and useful improvements thereof, not known or used by others in this country, before his invention or discovery thereof, and not patented or described in any printed publication in this or any foreign country, before his invention or discovery thereof, or more than two years prior to his application, and not in public use or on sale in this country for more than two years prior to his application, unless the same is proved to have been abandoned, may, upon payment of the fees required by law, and other due proceedings had, obtain a patent therefor." Barnes *Federal Code,* 1919, p. 2125.

In the copyright field, on the other hand, it is possible for two similar works to be granted a copyright monopoly. If two authors should publish simultaneously very similar treatises, the government will grant such rights to both, provided, of course, that each has done independent work.[1]

The patentee has the exclusive right to make, use, and vend the invention or discovery throughout the United States and its territories. This triple right may be sold and assigned in whole or in part by the patent owner. He may make, and assign the right to sell and use; he may make and sell, and transfer the right to use; he may assign all three rights, he may retain all; or he may refuse to make use of the invention, provided there is no restraint of trade involved. He may not, however, assign only one of these specified powers when its exercise alone by another would be an empty privilege. For example, the patentee could not retain the right to use and sell, and grant to another the right to make, because the presumptive purpose of the making is the sale or use. He could, however, assign the right to make and use, without transferring the right to sell.

PECULIARITIES OF PATENT PROBLEM

In the radio field the patent problem is unique. Three peculiarities ought at the outset to be mentioned:

1. The absence of a fundamental or basic patent;
2. The fact that individuals can construct home-made receiving sets and even transmitting apparatus with the purchase of only a few patented articles;
3. The large number of essential patents independently owned.

ABSENCE OF BASIC PATENT IN RADIO

As indicated in Chapter I, scientists have been working for many years on the problem of wireless. Though Mar-

---

[1] For a thorough and authoritative discussion of the legal phases of patents, see Walker, *Patents*, 5th edition, New York, 1917.

coni deserves the credit for making wireless commercially practicable, others before him had conceived the idea, but had looked upon it as only a bit of interesting theory. For example, the German, Heinrich Hertz, professor of physics at Bonn University, had discovered that electric waves travel through the air by means of the ether. That is the reason they are today called Hertzian waves. Professor Hertz actually made devices for both the radiation and the detection of such vibrations, but, as he never succeeded in producing waves which were detectable at more than a few feet, he did not realize that he had discovered the elements of a system of wireless telegraphy.[1]

As far as the writer is able to ascertain, Heinrich Hertz did not take out a patent. He may not have thought it worth while. Possibly, he did not consider it useful. Another, and it seems, a better reason, was that Hertz could not take out a patent. He conceived the idea, but not the operation of wireless. If I go out and discover a new continent, it would be an outrage on my part to ask for a patent, but I could write a book describing the new territory, and have it copyrighted. So with ether and electric waves. They have existed from time immemorial. My discovery of their existence does not give me the privilege of patent. Hertz could have written on the subject of ether and electric waves, and have had his work copyrighted. On this point Walker makes the following statement (page 3):

These things [arts, machines, manufactures, composition of matter] are not found, but created. They are results of original thought. They are inventions. Laws of nature, on the other hand, can never be invented by man, though they may be discovered by him. They exist as facts at all times whether known or unknown to human knowledge. When discovered, they may be utilized by means of an art, a machine, a manufacture, or a composition of matter. It is the invention of one or more of these, for the purpose of utilizing a law of nature, and not the discovery of that law, that may be rewarded with a patent.[2]

[1] See the opinion of the Court in 213 Fed. 815 at pp. 820-821.
[2] See also *O'Reilly* v. *Morse*, 15 Howard 62 (1853).

The revelation of the idea of wireless thus induced many to work upon its control and utilization. So it seems entirely natural that there should be conflict and interference, infringement charges and counter charges, in the radio field.

EASE OF CONSTRUCTING HOME-MADE RADIO SETS

The fact that individuals can construct home-made receiving sets and even transmitting apparatus with the purchase of a few or no patented articles has facilitated the infringement of radio patents and has also tended to decrease the monopoly value of such rights. The wonders of electricity are to a large extent matters of turns of wire and connections. If I should take some ordinary copper-insulated wire, wind it in a certain way, and connect it with batteries and devices, I might make a revolutionary radio invention. This device is patented. My specifications are open to the public. In the *Official Gazette* one is able to obtain a description of any patent registered in the United States Patent Office. Magazines and newspapers describe the innovation. When a corporation today hits upon a new method of manufacture, it very often refuses to patent it, in order to escape the deadly publicity. The very word "patent" implies throwing a thing open to the public.[1]

In the winter of 1922, while a resident of Madison, Wisconsin, the writer had occasion to construct a small receiving set in order to hear the State University broadcasting station. In setting up that apparatus all he bought was a pair of headphones and some copper wire. Somebody, undoubtedly, had a patent. He was legally robbed of the fruits of his efforts. The only patentee who benefited was the inventor of the headphones. In the construction of long-distance receiving sets the amateur has to purchase a greater number of parts. He cannot, as a rule, construct the audion himself; nor can he make the "A" and "B"

---

[1] Adam Smith, in his *Wealth of Nations*, mentioned the possession of secret processes as one of the sources of monopoly power.

batteries needed. But even so, the builder of a delicate receiving set can devise many of the parts himself.

Contrast this situation with that of the inventor of the typewriter which I am using in writing this, or the electric fan which is keeping me cool and comfortable, or the electric lights in the room, or the automobile in which my neighbor rides down-town. I would need to be a good mechanician to enable me to buy bolts and nuts and ivory and wire and a hundred other miscellaneous parts, and from them construct a good-as-new Remington typewriter. Most people would prefer to buy the machine complete.

DIVERSE OWNERSHIP OF IMPORTANT RADIO PATENTS

The large number of essential patents independently owned is in reality a corollary of the first two peculiarities. The absence of a fundamental patent left the field open. As a result, not only scientists and professional inventors, but also some of the folks who have constructed their own sets, have made important discoveries in the wireless field. Broadcasting companies are dependent upon the patents of the telephone companies. A station wishes to broadcast the speech or musical performance given at the local opera house one mile away. How transfer the sound waves from the microphone on the platform or stage to the transmitting apparatus? Construct your own line, you say, or use the regular telephone or telegraph line. Suppose the land line companies should refuse, or demand a fee for the service? Then, if the station does not desire to pay the charge, it might stretch its own wire. But in order to make this wire work effectively, certain devices which the telephone company owns and controls would be necessary.

Then again, the broadcasters are often dependent on the manufacturers of radio apparatus. The maker stipulates that the sets sold shall not be used for profit. Under the present United States patent law the owner has such a right. The broadcaster could not construct independently certain parts of the apparatus. One station reports by letter that it hired its own engineers and built its own set without the aid of the Western Electric Company. "We paid $2,000 patent license fees to the American Telephone and Telegraph Company which gives us all the rights and privileges we would have had, had we paid them $23,500 for one of their sets." The American Telephone and Telegraph Company controlled certain patented machinery that this "independent" broadcaster had to use and which he could not construct. Hence, the need of the license fee.[1] The president of the American Telephone and Telegraph Company estimates that approximately 400 broadcasting stations are using the Bell System's inventions without a license. He says that most of these are probably ignorant of the fact that they are infringing.[2]

As indicated above, the owners of sensitive receiving sets involving the use of the audion are also dependent upon the manufacturers of radio. The several manufacturers, too, are dependent upon one another. A company can make a perfect receiving or sending set, but unless it is equipped with the vacuum tube, it will not be satisfactory, especially for long-distance work.[3]

These three conditions have to a large extent encouraged patent litigation. Federal court records are replete with radio patent suits.[4]

---

[1] Even though the individual were able to construct these parts, a license fee would probably be necessary, on account of the fact that the broadcaster generally operates for profit.

[2] "The Radio Broadcasting Situation," a statement to the stockholders of the American Telephone and Telegraph Company, issued on March 25, 1924, by President H. B. Thayer. Reprinted in the Bell Telephone Quarterly, April, 1924, pp. 113 ff.

The remarks made in regard to this interdependency apply with equal force to commercial point-to-point wireless companies, which also must use land lines and resort to many kinds of apparatus.

[3] For other illustrations of this interdependency, the reader is referred back to Chapter III.

[4] Concerning the Fessenden United States patent No. 918306, there have been four cases in our national courts; the Fessenden U. S. No. 918307 four cases; the Marconi U. S. patent No. 763772 seven cases; Lodge U. S. patent No. 609154 eight cases; Fleming U. S. patent No. 803684 seven cases; Marconi U. S. patent 586193 five cases. Computed from the Patents Section of

Patent litigation may be classified under the following heads: (1) Cases in which the main question has been the ownership of the invention, that is, cases in which there have been interference proceedings; (2) cases arising out of the interpretation and the enforcement of the cross-licensing agreements referred to in Chapter III; (3) recent litigation involving the interpretation of the rights and liabilities of broadcasters who are making use of the patents owned by members of the Big Four,[1] especially the American Telephone and Telegraph Company. A separate class may possibly be made consisting of the cases involving the infringements of patents, but since the question of infringement is present in practically all patent litigation, no separate group will be assigned.

INTERFERENCE PROCEEDINGS

One of the earliest patent cases in the radio field was an infringement suit brought by the American Marconi Company against the DeForest Radio Telephone and Telegraph Company. The plaintiff alleged that the defendant was infringing a patent dated November 7, 1905, issued on application of John Ambrose Fleming on April 19, 1905, who had assigned his rights to the Marconi Company. Fleming had taken the Edison hot and cold electrode incandescent electric lamp and had utilized it as a detector of radio signals. This was a new and unusual use of an old, abandoned device.

Lee DeForest had for several years been experimenting on the heated gas flame as a means for the reception of electromagnetic waves. His theory was thus very different from Fleming's. In a lecture before the Royal Society of

Shepard's *Federal Citations*. It must be borne in mind, however, that some of these are appeals. Thus, if a District Court decides a certain patent case, an appeal can be taken to the Circuit Court of Appeals, making two actions concerning one patent.

[1] Radio Corporation of America, General Electric Company, Westinghouse Electric and Manufacturing Company, American Telephone and Telegraph Company including the Western Electric Company.

England in February, 1905, Fleming had described the operation of his invention. The court in its statement of facts indicated that DeForest read this address, and then shifted tactics. "He promptly used the knowledge so acquired" and began to experiment with the incandescent lamp.[1]

The Federal Courts upheld Marconi's contention on the grounds that Fleming had the right of priority and that DeForest had not consistently followed one concept or theory.

Another interesting early suit involved the same plaintiff and the same defendant joined with the Standard Oil Company of New York. The DeForest Company had installed wireless apparatus on certain vessels of the Standard Oil Company. In the installation of these sets the company had made use of devices patented by Marconi and by Lodge, but instead of putting the parts together in the normal, specified way, it had rearranged some of the apparatus so as to produce different circuits than those originally intended. The defense had argued that even though the apparatus was patented, they could take the several parts and so arrange and coordinate them as to avoid infringing. The court disposed of this defense by saying that "when this signaling apparatus was put together and used in the normal way, the easiest way, and the most effective way, it would infringe both the patents in suit."[2]

The early purpose of the vacuum tube was to receive wireless signals. However, soon several scientists saw that this device, if sufficiently powerful, could be used for the transmission as well as the reception of electrical oscilla-

---

[1]*Marconi Wireless Telegraph Company of America* v. *DeForest Radio Telephone and Telegraph Company,* 236 Fed. 942, affirmed by the Circuit Court of Appeals in 243 Fed. 560.

[2]The decision of the District Court (225 Fed. 65) was affirmed by the Circuit Court of Appeals in 225 Fed. 373 (1915).

On the attitude of the Marconi companies toward the "intercommunication" section of the 1903 and the 1906 Radiotelegraph Conventions, see Chapter II. Marconi, it will be remembered, argued that the enforcement of the "intercommunication" section would compel him to share his patents with others.

tions. Four men, E. H. Armstrong, Lee DeForest, Alexander Meissner, and Irving Langmuir, all entered contesting claims for the rights of priority to this new use of the audion. The main legal controversy was between the first two mentioned. The principal issues in this litigation were: (1) Who was the first to conceive clearly the vacuum tube as a producer of electrical oscillations? (2) Did the originator of the idea subsequently abandon it? The case was passed upon by all the tribunals in the United States Patent Office and by the United States District and Circuit courts, and all through the litigation Armstrong won consistently. Finally DeForest appealed to the United States Court of Appeals of the District of Columbia, the court of last resort in patent litigation, which decided in his favor. The court, through Associate Justice Van Orsdell, held that while Armstrong's earliest claim to the conception of the vacuum tube as an oscillator was in October, 1912, DeForest had conceived of the idea in August, 1912, as revealed by the fact that DeForest's notebook showed a diagram and notes inserted in that month,[1] which had disclosed the invention in a "clear workable manner." "In October DeForest had reproduced for a friend the drawing made in August, which so perfectly demonstrated the invention that the friend years later, when testifying in court, was able to reproduce the drawing from his recollection."[2] The court also held that DeForest had not abandoned the idea. Thus both questions were settled in favor of DeForest. This case is unique in the importance of the device in dispute, in the number of courts and tribunals which passed on it (this case, as far as the writer knows, was acted upon by every possible tribunal and court), and the lesson taught inventors as to the importance of keeping certified diagrams and data regarding their inventions.

[1]The assistant commissioner of patents had held that, though DeForest had thought of the oscillator in August, 1912, he had subsequently abandoned the idea, thus forfeiting his rights.

[2]*DeForest* v. *Meissner et al.*, 298 Fed. 1006. Court of Appeals of District of Columbia, decided May 5, 1924.

INTERPRETATION AND ENFORCEMENT OF THE CROSS-LICENSING AGREEMENTS

The court reports abound with cases involving infringement and questions of priority.[1] With the beginning of the World War, some of the large radio manufacturing and communication companies set aside considerations of patent ownership. As a result, the ensuing years saw a rapid and substantial progress in the development of certain types of radio equipment, particularly the audion.[2] With the signing of the Armistice, however, the need for this disregard of patent rights ceased. But "a valuable art had been developed, which no one in the business of communication could use without infringing upon the rights of others."[3] Progress then seemed to be at a standstill until the United States Navy Department asked several of the big manufacturers to attempt a solution of this problem.

"In response to this request, negotiations were initiated and carried through to an arrangement of cross-licenses to which other owners of patents in this field were afterward admitted. For practical operation under this arrangement it was necessary that the parties to the agreement be given the specific uses of the apparatus in question that were logical to their business."[4]

CASES ARISING OUT OF CROSS-LICENSING AGREEMENTS

The next series of cases is an outgrowth of this cross-licensing agreement. Figure 3 shows the details of these

---

[1]See, for example, *National Electric Signalling Company* v. *Telefunken Wireless Telegraph Company*, 221 Fed. 629 (1915); *United Wireless Company* v. *National Electric Signalling Company*, 198 Fed. 386 (1912); *Kintner* v. *Atlantic Communication Company*, 230 Fed. 829 (1916); *Marconi Wireless Telegraph Company* v. *Kilbourne and Clark Mfg. Company*, 239 Fed. 328 (1916); *Kintner* v. *Atlantic Communication Company*, 241 Fed. 956 (1917), and same 249 Fed. 73.

[2]See Chapter I.

[3]Statement of President H. B. Thayer, of the Bell System, to stockholders on March 25, 1924. In *Bell Telephone Quarterly*, April, 1924. pp. 113-117.

[4]President Thayer's statement.

contracts. The questions and issues are to a large extent of a procedural nature, though substantive rights are also involved.

The Radio Corporation of America brought suit against the Independent Wireless Telegraph Company for the infringement of the DeForest audion. As the reader will remember, whatever rights DeForest had were assigned to the DeForest Radio Telephone and Telegraph Company. The latter had in turn granted an exclusive license to the Western Electric Company, which had transferred the right to make, use, and sell to its parent, the American Telephone and Telegraph Company. The DeForest Company, however, had reserved non-exclusive, non-transferable, and personal licenses to make and sell the patented apparatus for certain specified purposes. Later (November 20, 1919) the General Electric Company made a contract with the Radio Corporation of America by which the former granted the latter an exclusive license to use and to sell for radio purposes all inventions then owned by it or afterward acquired. The agreement had a term of 45 years, and applied to wireless communication only. At this time the General Electric Company had no interest in the patents, but on July 1, 1920, the American Telephone and Telegraph Company and the General Electric Company agreed to exchange rights in the various patents owned and controlled by them. Certain of these rights were exclusive; others, non-exclusive. Thus, the Radio Corporation has licenses to use and sell the patented apparatus of the De Forest Company.[1]

The question in this case was twofold: (1) Did the Radio Corporation of America possess an exclusive license? To this the court answered, "Yes." (2) If the Radio Corporation of America has an exclusive license, can it sue an infringer in its own name? Again the court answered, "Yes." "An exclusive licensee may maintain an action in equity in his name and that of the owner of the patent right

Facts taken from the opinion of court.

and may prosecute his claim without the cooperation, indeed against the objection, of the owner."[1]

The case of the *Radio Corporation of America* v. *Emerson and LaFrance Import and Sales Company, American Telephone and Telegraph Company, et al*, involved practically the same facts as the preceding. The Radio Corporation of America alleged that two patents were infringed by the defendants. The patents were originally taken out by DeForest and were sold on May 24, 1917, to the American Telephone and Telegraph Company, which has continued in possession of the legal title. On August 23, 1922, the American Telephone and Telegraph Company licensed the Radio Corporation of America, the plaintiff, under these patents. The defendant alleged improper procedure in that there was a defect of parties, because the American Telephone and Telegraph Company was not joined in the action as co-plaintiff with the Radio Corporation of America. The American Telephone and Telegraph Company was the real owner of the patent, and action should be brought in its name, argued the defendant. Instead, the American Telephone and Telegraph Company had been named as defendant.

The American Telephone and Telegraph Company admitted that it had declined to become a plaintiff, though it had a substantial interest in the suit. Thus the main issue appeared to be the right of the Radio Corporation of America to maintain the action.

The court held that the action by the plaintiff was justifiable on the following grounds:

If "A" licenses a patent to "B" but retains the title, "A" is still the patentee. Suppose that after granting a license to "B," "A" for some reason becomes hostile or indifferent to the interests of "B." Somebody infringes the patent. The only legal recourse is a suit in equity. Suppose that "A" refuses to bring the action. Then, justice demands that

---

[1] *Radio Corporation of America* v. *Independent Wireless Telegraph Co.*, 297 Fed. 521, March 3, 1924. This is the decision of the Circuit Court, 2nd. District.

"B," who is the Radio Corporation of America in this suit, is entitled to maintain the complaint.[1]

The Westinghouse Electric and Manufacturing Company and the Radio Corporation of America had sold apparatus to the Independent Wireless Telegraph Company on the condition that it should not be used for the reception of continuous waves. A change in the connections enabled this apparatus to be used for the reception of such signals. The Independent Company, however, forbade its operators to tamper with the connections. Some of the operators disobeyed the orders, and connected up the apparatus in the forbidden way. The plaintiffs now brought suit, charging the Independent Company with violation of the terms of the agreement. The court held that:

1. The acts of the operators in the performance of their general duty are acts of the principal. Hence the tampering with the connections was really in law the work of the Independent Company, in spite of its orders to the contrary.

2. The sale of one element of a patented combination, which has other uses, carries no implied licenses to the buyer to furnish the other elements himself and to complete and use the combination. If the element could be used for only one purpose, the buyer would have the right to furnish the other elements himself. "It is only when the article sold must be used in the patented combination, if it be used at all, that a license is implied." Therefore, in this case the Independent Company had no authority to use the purchased devices in a forbidden way when there was another specified method available.

The court granted an injunction against both the company and the operators.[2]

---

[1] 296 Fed. 51, Circuit Court of Appeals, 2nd Dist., Jan. 7, 1924. The U. S. Supreme Court refused to review (certiorari) this case in 44 Sup. Ct. 456.

The thirty-seventh rule in equity reads: "Persons having a united interest must be joined on the same side as plaintiffs or defendants; but when any one refuses to join, he may for such reason be made a defendant."

[2] Westinghouse Electric and Manufacturing Company et al v. Independent Wireless Telegraph Company, 300 Fed. 748, June 3, 1924.

A large number of other cases could be mentioned in which the members of the Big Four, especially the Radio Corporation of America, have been (or are) the plaintiff. It will be remembered that the DeForest Company assigned its rights under the audion patent to the American Telephone and Telegraph Company, retaining for itself a personal non-exclusive, non-transferable right to make and sell. This right was not of much value as long as the Fleming patent of 1905 was still in force, but, when that expired in 1922, the DeForest Company immediately began the making and selling of the vacuum tube. At once the problem arose of defining the rights of the Radio Corporation of America and of the DeForest Company.[1]

SUITS BY PATENTEES AGAINST BROADCASTING STATIONS

The next group of cases are suits by the American Telephone and Telegraph Company against certain broadcasting stations for infringement of its patent rights. These raise the following issues:

1. The members of the Big Four impose certain patent restrictions in their sale of radio apparatus. One of these is that the broadcasting station shall not use the set for profit. Suppose a station purchases a set and then uses it for commercial purposes; that is, it sells advertising time to business men and politicians, is this an infringement of the patent?

2. Or suppose, this broadcasting station receives only an

---

[1] The Radio Corporation asked the DeForest Company to obtain an agreement from purchasers or lessees that the apparatus would not be used in commercial radio communication for pay or used by other than the original purchaser or lessee or used for any other purpose than radio communication. The DeForest Company refused to insert this provision in its sales contract, and in 1923 the Radio Corporation was granted an injunction restraining DeForest from manufacturing and selling audion bulbs. This injunction was subsequently dismissed by Vice Chancellor Lewis at Trenton, N. J. The effect of this recent decision is "to permit the DeForest Company to manufacture and sell parts of receiving sets without having its selling policies in any way dictated by the Radio Corporation of America." See *Commercial and Financial Chronicle,* November 1, 1924, p. 2074.

indirect gain, for example, building up good-will, is this an infringement of the patent?

3. Suppose a person builds most of his own broadcasting apparatus himself, and purchases independently certain devices, the exclusive patent rights on which are owned by the maker of the complete sending set, and then uses it for either of the purposes mentioned in 1 and 2 above, is this an infringement of the patent?

4. Suppose any broadcasting company using a set for either a direct or an indirect gain makes use of the telephone lines in transferring the sound waves from the theater platform to the transmitting apparatus, is this an infringement of the land line companies' patent rights?

These are confusing and difficult questions, which are now being fought out in the federal courts.

Loew's, Incorporated, is operating station WHN in New York City. The broadcasting set was not manufactured by the Western Electric Company, but Loew's had, in its installation, made use of a number of devices patented by the American Telephone and Telegraph Company. The American Telephone and Telegraph Company brought suit[1] for infringement of its patents. The case was settled out of court by WHN applying for and obtaining a license under the patents of the company.[2]

The American Telephone and Telegraph Company also recently brought suit against the North American Company and its subsidiary, Wired Radio, Incorporated. These companies were alleged to be sending entertainment without

---

[1]U. S. District Court for Southern District of New York on patents Nos. 1,201,270; 1,218,195; 1,377,405; 1,129,943; 1,231,764; 1,442,146; 1,442,147; and Reissue 14,380.

[2]Letter from George E. Folk, General Patent Attorney of Bell Telephone dated August 1, 1924.

According to the stipulations of the settlement, the American Telephone and Telegraph Company released WHN from all liability for past infringement of its patents. WHN paid $2,000 for a personal, non-transferable license to do general telephonic broadcasting, including for toll or hire, for the entire term of the patents. If at any time the power of WHN should be increased, the American Telephone and Telegraph Company will grant a new license on similar terms and for a proportionally larger fee.

authorization over the lines of the Bell System. This case has not yet been decided.[1]

Under a strict interpretation of the patent laws, it seems that all four of the above questions, with the exception of the second, must be answered in the affirmative. The vendor of a machine or device has a legal right to stipulate that it shall not be used for profit. In the case of the second, it is possible that since the usual primary or secondary purpose of a broadcasting station is the development of good-will or some other indirect benefit, the very act of sale could be regarded as a permit to use the apparatus for these purposes. Any other rule would virtually deprive the purchaser of the use of his machine. If the owners of patents or the assignees of certain rights thereunder prefer to lay down the rule that their articles shall not be used for purposes of gain, the courts must interpret the law as it is. It is the prerogative of Congress to fix the rights of patentees. If it should be desirable to deprive patentees of the right to stipulate in the sales contract that the apparatus sold shall not be employed for profit by the purchaser, such action lies with Congress and not with the courts. If Congress takes such action, may not the hardship wrought on patentees of other articles more than offset the benefits received therefrom in the radio field? It is not difficult to conceive of a situation where the power to specify that a device shall not be used for profit is an essential of a patent privilege. Another alternative, which would probably be undesirable on account of the precedent established, would be the nationalization of radio patents through government purchase and subsequent lease to any private individuals. Some of the German patents obtained by the government during the

---

[1]Suit was brought in the United States District Court for the Eastern District of New York. The patents sued on are numbers 1,129,943; 1,231,764; 1,442,146; 1,442,147; Reissue 14,380; 1,403,475; 1,448,550; 1,388,450, and 1,385,777. Letter from Mr. Folk, *supra*.

war are leased indiscriminately to applicants. Still another possibility, and perhaps a desirable one, would be the placing of broadcasters on an economic basis so that they can afford to pay for the privilege of using patented apparatus. If telephonic broadcasting is of value to the people and continues to be so, reasonable steps should be taken to enable the broadcasters to render efficient service. As to the marine communication field the government here ought to encourage cross-licensing agreements. Unlike transoceanic and international point-to-point communication, a state of competition in the marine radio service could logically be encouraged and demanded.

XII

PUBLIC POLICY AND CONTROL OF RADIO SERVICE

Need for consideration of service. Radio communication a natural monopoly? Radio communication a public utility? Point-to-point communication and public policy. Investigation by the Federal Trade Commission. Commission charges unfair competition. Is monopoly justifiable from point of view of public service? Need for monopoly in transoceanic communication. Monopoly to be strictly regulated. International problems. Competition desirable in making and selling of radio. Property in air.

THE problem of regulation and control arises in connection with both broadcasting and point-to-point communication, as well as with the manufacturing and selling ends of radio. In all questions of public policy the consideration of service should be paramount.

RADIO COMMUNICATION A NATURAL MONOPOLY?

The comments in this and the following chapter are based upon the premise that radio communication is a natural monopoly and a public utility. By a natural monopoly is meant a situation or business in which the number of individual concerns is limited by physical or economic conditions. For example, experience has proved that railways are a natural monopoly because of the great proportion of fixed to operating expenses,[1] because of physical obstructions and the small number of passes over mountain ranges, and because of the cutthroat competition in the case of rate wars always resulting ultimately in unity of action.[2] Though it may be too early to make a definite statement, it seems that radio communication in both its broadcasting and point-

---

[1]About $20 fixed to $80 operating. The cost of constructing a railroad system is so great that the number of enterprises is effectively limited.

[2]See Ely, *"Outlines of Economics,"* 4th edition, pp. 187-190.

218

to-point phases has certain elements, at least, of a natural monopoly. Transmitters of wireless must use a common medium, the air, or more accurately, the ether.[1] Under our present stage of technical progress the number of passes through this medium is limited. When too many pedestrians attempt to walk abreast on a sidewalk, they will bump into one another. So, if too many different wave lengths are sent out through the ether simultaneously, the passageways will become so crowded that interference will result. The generally used wave lengths run up to about 20,000 meters. The government has allocated these waves in groups to the various types of wireless stations.

RADIO COMMUNICATION A PUBLIC UTILITY?

Businesses rendering indispensable services to the people are sometimes stated to be clothed with a public interest and are hence termed public utilities. There is no rule of thumb by which we can determine whether an industry comes within this class or not. The manufacturing of iron bridges is not a public utility, but the operation of a toll bridge may be so termed. The operation of a grocery store is not a public utility; the furnishing of street-car service, gas, water, telephone or telegraph facilities, electricity, or most forms of passenger transportation, is so regarded. One test seems to be the indispensability of the article furnished or the service rendered, and the dependency of the public or certain groups of people on particular operating units.

Applying this test to radio point-to-point communication, such as ship to shore or transoceanic, it appears that we must conclude that this phase of radio is as much a public utility as the cables or the telegraph and telephone, since it is engaged in the carrying of messages for hire. The Interstate Commerce Commission Act, in so far as it applies to wireless, was apparently intended to cover this aspect.

---

[1] There is some doubt as to the existence of the ether. If scientists should definitely prove that there is no such thing, they will be forced to seek a new explanation of the carrying of electromagnetic waves.

Poors' and Moodys' *Manual, Consolidated,* and Moodys' *Analyses of Investments* list the wireless companies as public utilities. The problem in regard to telephonic broadcasting is more difficult. Can the material disseminated by means of the radio be regarded as a necessity?[1] Is the service rendered by this form of communication invested with sufficient public interest to justify classifying it as a public utility? Presumably, if the consuming public is apathetic, if it shows no appreciation of, or desire for, more and better service, a claim to the public interest in radio service would fall of its own weight. In other words, if the radio is only a fad, and the fad is waning, it would be absurd to seek to regulate it in the public interest.

It is difficult to obtain adequate information on this point. We know that over $400,000,000 has been invested in receiving apparatus and that this demand continues more or less unabated. We also are safe in estimating that the American radio audience numbers at least ten millions.[2] But there is no adequate way of learning whether this initial enthusiasm, which prompts the purchase of receiving sets, is sustained. It is well known that radio audiences are becoming more critical of the service offered, just as performing artists and holders of music copyrights are demanding compensation which boosts the operating expenses of those broadcasters who try to give better service.

The test, however, is rather with those receivers who have regarded radio service as indispensable to business or existence and neither duplicated nor possible of duplication by other agencies with the same efficiency. If this group is a small minority, or if it finds that it can dispense with the radio without loss of efficiency, one can hardly claim with reason that telephonic broadcasting is affected with sufficient public interest to justify treating it as a public utility.

---

[1] The term "necessity" is relative, of course, to time, place, and condition, so that things which were once luxuries are now necessities. Many commodities have made the transition.

[2] The number of radio receiving sets in the United States (probably four million) compares rather favorably with the ten million and sixteen million gas and electric meters.

Farmers probably constitute the largest single group of radio service consumers who would be likely to come within this class. The United States Department of Agriculture, not to mention agricultural colleges and experiment stations, has arranged, since 1921, for broadcasting marketing news and weather reports. The nine stations, which in January, 1922, were licensed to broadcast market reports, increased in number to 86 in January, 1924.[1] It has been estimated that the number of farmers having receiving sets has increased steadily to about 370,000 in 1924.[2] Generally speaking, radio broadcasting is performing a very important service for the farmer, which probably cannot be rendered as efficiently by any other agency, though the telegraph and the telephone have not been abandoned for the dissemination of market and weather reports.[3]

The question whether telephonic broadcasting is actually or potentially a public utility cannot be answered with finality until the service has become more stabilized, particularly in the quality of programs and service rendered. It is possible, however, to point out certain current tendencies, including the above, indicating public utility status. It is probable that the future may see such dependency upon radio that it can be classed as a necessity. The importance of the solution of this question lies in the fact that if radio broadcasting is a public utility, it can be regulated in greater detail than if it could not be so classified.

POINT-TO-POINT COMMUNICATION AND PUBLIC POLICY

As previously indicated, the Radio Corporation of America is the center of a series of cross-licensing agreements with other members of the Big Four, besides smaller concerns. These contracts, together with alleged restrictions

---

[1]Almost 120 stations broadcast weather reports. *Official Record,* United States Department of Agriculture, December 17, 1924, p. 1.

[2]Bureau of Agricultural Economics *"Survey of Use of Radio by Farmers,"* September, 1924, p. 3.

[3]See Chapter XIV for radio and the farmer.

in the use and sale of both receiving and sending radio apparatus, have recently been made the subject of an investigation by the Federal Trade Commission.

INVESTIGATION BY THE FEDERAL TRADE COMMISSION

The fact is that for several years Congress has considered legislation for the more effective regulation of radio communication. In its search for extensive and reliable information, the House, on March 3, 1923, passed a resolution requesting the Federal Trade Commission to investigate conditions in the radio industry and to report its findings. Besides this, in 1922 the Commission received an application for a complaint against several concerns in the radio industry, including the General Electric Company and the Radio Corporation of America. On December 1 the Commission made its report to Congress and on January 28, 1924, issued a complaint against eight companies for combining and conspiring "for the purpose and with the effect of restraining competition and creating a monopoly in the manufacture, purchase, and sale, in interstate commerce, of radio devices and apparatus, and other electrical devices and apparatus, and in domestic and transoceanic radio communication and broadcasting."

COMMISSION CHARGES UNFAIR COMPETITION

The principal reasons for the Federal Trade Commission's conclusions were the following:

1. The respondent companies had collectively acquired and pooled patents, both competing and non-competing, for all types of devices in the radio field.

2. To the Radio Corporation of America had been granted the exclusive right to sell such devices, restricting its purchases to certain of the defendants and apportioning such purchases among them. This has reference to the agreement whereby the Radio Corporation of America is

to buy 60% of its apparatus from the General Electric Company, and 40% from the Westinghouse Company.

3. The competition of certain companies in fields occupied by other of the defendants had been restricted.

4. There was an attempt to restrict the use of apparatus sold. For example, goods were sold on the condition that they would not be used for profit.

5. The companies had acquired apparatus essential for long-distance communication and refused to sell this apparatus to competitors.

6. They had entered into traffic contracts and preferential agreements whereby others were excluded from the field.

7. They had agreed to cooperate in the development of new patents and to exchange patent rights acquired in the future.

All these practices were held by the Federal Trade Commission to be unfair methods of competition under the Act of 1914. Each of the companies has filed its answer, but the Commission has not taken final action.

IS MONOPOLY JUSTIFIABLE FROM POINT OF VIEW OF
PUBLIC SERVICE?

The principal questions which arise in this litigation are these:

1. Are the Radio Corporation of America and its affiliated companies acting contrary to the Trade Commission and the anti-trust acts?

2. Did they make contracts which are not permitted by the United States patent laws?

3. Assuming, for the sake of argument, that they have a monopoly of the making and selling of radio apparatus, is such monopoly justifiable?

4. Assuming, again, that the Radio Corporation of America has a monopoly of external radio communication, is such a monopoly justifiable?

5. The cross-licensing agreements were really suggested by the United States Government through the Navy Department. They are now attacked by another administrative branch of our government. Does not this working at loggerheads indicate the need for a reorganization of our government so as to make for centralized authority and control?

The fundamental problem is not: Did these companies violate our laws? The question is: Should the United States Government foster and permit monopoly, whether private or public, in the external communication field or in the radio manufacturing and selling end of radio? This problem, involving the determination of policies of tremendous importance, should merit the attention and study of every American citizen. The writer wishes to suggest the following principles:

1. The United States Government should permit and foster a strict private monopoly in the American end of the external radio communication field.

2. Such private monopoly should be subject to strict governmental regulation and control as to rates, service, installations of new stations, and so forth. The cable companies should be subject to the same degree of stringency of control.

3. Since in external radio and cable communication, one end of the line is always in foreign territory, new international agreements are necessary to facilitate such control by the government.

4. There may be competition in domestic communication and between ship and shore.

5. There should be active competition in the making and selling of radio sets and supplies.

NEED FOR MONOPOLY IN TRANSOCEANIC COMMUNICATION

Monopoly is necessary in the American end of external radio communication, because foreign nations have granted

or are favoring such exclusive control. The American station engaged in foreign business must, by the very nature
of the situation, cooperate with the station at the other end.
This fact necessitates agreements between the two ends for
the routing of traffic and the pooling of the gross receipts.
Most of such agreements today provide for the half-and-
half system and for the preferential routing plan. Now
suppose that there is one station in a foreign country doing
business with the United States. and this is usually the
condition. Either the government has undertaken external
communication itself, as in the case of Japan, or it has
granted a concession to a private company, as in the case of
France. Suppose also that doing business with this foreign
station are four independent competing stations in the
United States. The foreign concern will handle 100% of
the direct radio messages, but each American station will
handle on the average only 25% of the total. Since radio
is, up to a certain point at least, a business of increasing
returns, each of these companies is presumably capable of
handling more than 25% of the total.

What will happen? The four stations will each, in the
absence of unity of action among them, strive for a greater
percentage of the traffic. Just as in any business, they will
do so by lowering the price of their products. This lowering of price may take either of two forms.

The first form of price-cutting could be a decrease in the
actual charge per word. This would draw more business.
The second and the more probable form can be illustrated
as follows: Assume the foreign station to have an agreement with each of the four United States stations, whereby
the distribution was in all cases 50-50 of the gross tolls;
that is, for each dollar collected the foreign company or
government takes 50%, and the American station handling
this end of the message takes the other half. Plainly the
foreigner would, if he could get it, prefer more than 50%.
So each (or several) of the American stations is threatened
that if it (or they) will not be satisfied with, say, only 40%

of the receipts, the foreigner will direct his traffic to one of the other American stations, which has or may easily acquire facilities to handle this extra business. The threatened station will be afraid of losing its business, and so will come to terms. Now, if it takes this percentage, and the others insist on the 50%, the traffic will go to the station agreeing to accept the smaller proportion.

The result will be that the American percentage will uniformly become 40%, until the foreigner makes up his mind that he wants a larger amount. Thus the foreign monopoly, by playing off the small competing stations against one another, will always occupy the favored position.[1]

Accordingly, one company should have an absolute monopoly of external radio communication, at least with a particular country or area. If several American companies wish to conduct transoceanic communication, each should be given an exclusive territory.

As additional arguments for this policy may be mentioned the facts that radio communication probably will prove to be a natural monopoly and that the certainty of the position of the wireless company will place it on an equal basis of competition with the cables so that it can proceed with its plans, knowing its tenure to be relatively safe.

MONOPOLY TO BE STRICTLY REGULATED

Since an absolute monopoly appears to be desirable, it would follow that the company holding this public trust should be subject to strict governmental regulation. Uncontrolled monopoly is contrary to our modern conceptions of government and industry. The rates in point-to-point com-

---

[1]There would be a limit to this process. With the decrease of the ratio accruing to the American stations, the profits will become smaller, until finally either of two things will happen (1) the weeding out of the weaker stations, or (2) unanimity of action for the common defense, which is monopoly. There is another possibility, however. If the American stations become too "obstinate" the foreign company or government may induce some other concern to take over the business, or it may organize an American subsidiary to operate a station in our territory. Under our present laws this subsidiary could demand a license.

munication should be fixed at a point sufficient to yield a reasonable return on the investment. The government should have free access to the records, besides power to prevent discrimination among individuals and to approve extensions and curtailments of service. The Interstate Commerce Commission at the present time has jurisdiction over wireless communication, but it has thus far remained inactive in this field.

Under this system there will naturally be competition between the cables, on the one hand, and the radio, on the other. In our general governmental attitude toward public utilities, we have inconsistently attempted both to regulate public utilities and to encourage competition. Through the principle of substitution, the radio and the cable will tend to check each other's monopoly power. Any attempt at collusion between the two should be summarily dealt with under our anti-trust laws. Since the radio and the cable are two separate agencies of communication rendering different types of service, it does not appear inconsistent to both propose competition between them and to uphold the principle that public utilities should be regarded as monopolies.

INTERNATIONAL PROBLEMS IN REGULATION

The United States, however, can regulate only one end of the international radio circuit. It has no direct control over the other end. To make the regulations effective, some kind of international agreement seems to be necessary. Federal control as opposed to that of the state has been necessary in the case of our internal common carriers. State and local prohibition, too, have required a comprehensive federal law. In like manner radio communication calls for concerted action among the nations of the world.

Radio waves know no national bounds, and the development of wireless communication has already raised numerous questions in international law. For instance, let us suppose, the United States says to the Radio Corporation of America: "You shall not charge more than 18 cents per word for any message which you send to England." The traffic agreement between the Radio Corporation and the British Marconi Company stipulates that "all tolls and receipts from communication between said stations—shall be added together and the sum be divided equally between the parties hereto." The limitation of the rates by the United States Government would affect the gross earnings of both ends. But in this case the Marconi Company could argue with great force that its earnings had been decreased by the action of a foreign government.[1] New international agreements will therefore be necessary. The fact that the waves from broadcasting stations in Canada, Mexico, and Cuba may interfere with American stations (or vice versa) may also necessitate additional international regulations. This will become more and more pressing as nations adopt broadcasting as a permanent policy.

There are a number of precedents for such international legislation. Stimulated by the inconveniences and delays which messages encountered in passing from one country to another, nations early entered into the Telegraphic Union. Persuaded that the expeditious handling of mail is necessary, they formed the Postal Union. They have likewise taken concerted action for preventing the spread of disease.

So also action was very early taken in the wireless field. At first because of the fear of monopoly, later because of the close connection of the wireless with naval and military operations and maritime intercourse in general, involving the need of preventing interference and insuring safety at sea, three world-wide Radio Telegraphic Conventions have been held. The first two of these met in Berlin in 1903 and 1906, the agreement drawn up in the latter year being signed by most of the important nations of the world. The third and most wide-reaching of all met in London in 1912. The agreement there made, which has been accepted by practi-

---

[1] It is, of course, possible that lower rates will result in increased earnings, especially if the circuits were not operating at full capacity.

cally the entire world, provided for the facilitation of ship-to-shore and international communication, for improving safety at sea, for the prevention of interference, and for the exchange of messages, and the settlement of accounts among the stations of the signatory powers.[1]

Recent developments in long-distance radio have now given it a significance which in 1912 the powers did not consider or anticipate. The forthcoming international convention should consider the settlement of policies in connection with the problem of monopoly and regulation. The nations ought to agree upon some uniform methods for control of rates, and their regulations should, as far as practicable, be made to apply to cables, so as to maintain these two important agencies of international communication upon the same basis. It may also be necessary to take up the question of preventing interference among the broadcasting stations of adjoining nations. An international allocation or zoning of telegraphic or telephonic wave lengths may be feasible.

COMPETITION DESIRABLE IN MAKING AND SELLING OF RADIO

Since the peculiar international complications outlined above do not enter directly into ship-to-shore and domestic radio, a state of competition may be fostered in these fields. A state of competition should exist in the making and selling of radio apparatus, and the Federal Government through its proper commissions should frown upon any attempt at monopoly. Except where public expediency may justify any restriction, such as the cross-licensing agreements, the corporation holding the monopoly in the field of external

---

[1]The convention provided for the allocation of wave lengths among the various uses. For example, 300 and 600 meters were authorized for general public service. It required that ships should communicate with the nearest coastal station, that the waves sent out should be as pure as possible, that emergency equipment should be carried. Provision was made as to the forms of radiograms, tolls charged, and the settlement of accounts. The words SOS were picked out as the distress signal. A uniform system of calling, and the so-called "Q" or abbreviated signals were adopted. The convention also stipulated duties of operators and the time of listening in. It also provides for intercommunication among different systems of wireless.

communication and the concerns engaged in ship-to-shore and domestic traffic, as well as the broadcasters and broadcast listeners, should be allowed to purchase their supplies from any source. In an intricate field like radio, strategic inventions are likely to be acquired by a large number of individuals. The mutual use of these should be permitted.

It will be interesting to note the situation in regard to the audion. The Fleming patent, having been granted in the year 1905, expired in 1922. DeForest, who had been restrained by the American Marconi Company from manufacturing tubes, was thus at liberty to make and sell them. Since 1922, therefore, this company has been manufacturing this device, though the proportion of the total produced and sold by it has been very small. But the patents which were assigned by DeForest to the Bell System were granted in 1906, 1907, and 1908; the audion patents being taken out in the latter two years. Thus, the DeForest audion and tube patents expire in 1924 and 1925. After those dates competition will exist even in the making and selling of this piece of apparatus known as the soul of radio. In the summer of 1924 several radio manufacturers announced that they were about to begin the making of vacuum tubes.

Several modifying facts should be considered. It is true that after 1924 and 1925 the manufacture of the DeForest audion will be free to all. But this pertains to the original invention, which is today almost obsolete. DeForest's audion tube contained a certain amount of air. Later it was determined that an absolute vacuum gives the best results. On the problem of creating the vacuum, two men, Langmuir and Arnold, as indicated in Chapter III, had successfully worked. Since both could not take out a patent on the same invention, interference proceedings resulted. The patent will undoubtedly be granted to one of these men. Therefore, since Arnold represents the Western Electric Company and Langmuir the General Electric Company, the patent, when granted, will belong to the one or the other of these companies, between which and with other com-

panies the cross-licensing agreements are in force. Furthermore, certain patented processes for the production and the
coating of the filament are available only to members of the
Big Four. Hence the competition will be between the old,
inefficient, partly evacuated tube and the present improved,
totally evacuated audion.[1]

PROPERTY IN AIR

Another problem, which has certain international aspects,
may be touched upon in this connection, though it concerns
the aeroplane as well as the radio. This is the question of
property in air. Some of the early law writers as well as
practically all modern economists (in defining "land")
adhere to the maxim *Cuius est solum, eius est usque ad
coelum.* Under this rule and the extension *et ad inferos,* if
I buy a piece of land, and there is nothing said about sub-
surface or air rights,[2] I acquire the legal title to everything
to the center of the earth and to the heavens above. Applying this maxim, it would seem to follow that an individual
state has sovereignty over the air above its territory as well
as the earth below.

Before the advent of the balloon, the aeroplane, and the
radio, this problem was purely academic. Now it is in-
tensely practical, especially in the law of Torts because of
the danger to property or life on the surface. Is an aeroplane passing over a farmer's land a legal trespasser?
Does a radio transmitting station, whose waves pass through
and over the property of millions of people, constitute a
nuisance? If the owner of an experimental laboratory finds
that his delicate apparatus is dislocated by radio waves, is
this an actionable interference with his property rights?

There are three views as to the ownership of the airspace.
One group of authorities, pointing to the fact that the shoot-

[1]For a detailed and technical discussion of the vacuum tube situation see
an article of this title by D. C. Wilkerson in *Radio News,* April, 1925, p. 1874.

[2]Occasionally the law or the sales contract stipulates that mineral rights,
if any, are reserved to the state or by the vendor.

ing of a gun, or the stringing of a wire, or the projecting of the eaves, or the growing of the apple tree, or the placing of the hand, over another's land is regarded by the courts as trespass, adhere strictly to the rule, *Cuius est solum, eius est usque ad coelum,* and argue that a land owner has exclusive proprietary rights in all the airspace above his head, and that anybody who passes, or sends his agents or agencies, over another's land at whatever height, commits an actionable trespass. These writers, who may be termed the strict constructionists, maintain that statutory legislation is necessary to give the aviator a right of way.

This view is not sound. The common law maxim was formulated at a time when land was the important form of wealth and when neither the aeroplane nor the radio was known. Its purpose was to protect the landowner in the enjoyment of what he owned rather than to extend his proprietary rights. An owned object must be capable of possession and use. This rule, it has been argued, should not be extended to conditions which did not exist at the time it originated, especially when the effect of such extension would be to hamper the aeroplane and radio traffic.[1]

The second group of writers hold that passing over another's land is not trespass. These authorities state that balloonists, smoke, carrier pigeons, wireless waves, fowl, and the like, have always or for a long time passed over private property and never yet has the subjacent owner recovered damages for their mere passage with no resultant damage. This group regards the air as common property. This is the doctrine of the Roman Law.

---

[1]Blackstone, who quotes this maxim approvingly, says: " .... so that the word 'land' includes not only the face of the earth, but everything under it, or over it. And therefore if a man grants all his lands, he grants thereby all his mines of metals and other fossils, his woods, his waters, and his houses, as well as his fields and meadows." In another connection he says: "*Cuius est solum, eius est usque ad coelum,* is the maxim of the law, upwards; therefore, no man may erect any building, or the like, to overhang another's land." 2 *Commentaries* 19 (Oxford edition).

It is significant that as careful a writer as Blackstone does not mention, in his specific enumeration, the airspace or anything pertaining thereto. In the second quotation he refers to "buildings, or the *like*."

The third group takes a position between the above extremes. They argue that, though the landowner has in theory full proprietary rights to the airspace, he holds it subject to a servitude or easement of passage by aviators, wireless waves, or other agencies of commerce as they take their place in our advancing civilization. Aircraft have a legal right to pass through the air at a reasonable height, which depends on the nature of the buildings and obstructions, as long as the owner's enjoyment of his life or property is not violated. If the machine should land, or fly so near to the ground as to damage property, or terrify or sicken individuals, or inconvenience or imperil them, or actually injure them, the person affected would have the right to damages.[1]

The opinion of the third group seems to be the best and the prevalent view. Accordingly, it must follow that an aviator is absolutely, or at least presumptively, liable for all direct and indirect damages due to his flying over or landing on private property. The right to fly does not include the right to land. The owner of the aircraft should be absolutely and conclusively liable for any damage caused by the passage, fall, or descent of his machine, or for the dropping of articles carried therein, for the following reasons: (1) since the fall of the plane often results in the death of the pilot and passengers, it is impossible for the person injured to prove negligence; (2) persons on land are powerless to ensure their own safety against damages from aircraft; (3) since the landowner has a full proprietary right to the

---

[1] This doctrine has taken form in the laws of several European nations. According to the German law "the owner cannot prevent interferences which take place at such height or depth that he has no interest in their exclusion." One authority has suggested a "statutory condemnation by act of Congress, of all the airspace over privately owned property, giving the owners a right of action against the United States for any damage they might be able to prove.... As it would be impossible to prove actual damages, the net result would be that the right would be acquired without expense to the government." Under this view, the landowner would have the right to damages if the alleged trespass actually interfered with the enjoyment of his property. Plan of Judge Lamb, described by William R. McCracken in 57 *American Law Review* 99, quoted by Edmund F. Trabue, in 58 *American Law Review* 65.

land, he should be compensated at least to the extent that his property and person be insured against damage; (4) the aeroplane owner will be able to shift the burden to a liability insurance company. In addition may be mentioned the argument that, since the aeroplane is an inherently dangerous thing, the driver or owner should handle it at his own risk. With the increasing safety of aircraft this argument becomes less potent. Even under this view it may be necessary, with the growing traffic, for states to establish regular airways.

As to the demand of the laboratory owner who finds that the wireless waves are interfering with his experiments, we may mention merely the fact that courts take into consideration only damages to ordinary individuals of ordinary sensibilities. To grant recourse to the laboratory owner would harm the public welfare due to the startling and disastrous effects on our broadcasting and communication system. He would have no more claim against the radio station than against a street-car company or the proprietor of a distant quarry.

What jurisdiction, if any, has the nation in the airspace over its territory? First, it may be stated that the air above the sea is governed by the same principles of international law as the sea itself. As to the airspace above a nation the early law writers liked to regard it also as being free to all nations, but the period from 1910 to the present time has witnessed the ascendancy of the sovereignty theory, which in turn may be subdivided into zone and absolute sovereignty. The advocates of the former, who are few in number, argue that, inasmuch as a nation has sovereignty over only a narrow strip of sea along the shore, the remainder being free, so a state should be regarded as supreme in a designated lower portion of the air, everything above this zone to be open to all countries. But this comparison of the air with the sea is not valid on account of the difficulty of determining and identifying the zone of sovereignty and the fact that the law of gravitation operates 5 miles above the earth as well as on the surface. An individual 10 miles from New York can do comparatively little damage, while if he were the same altitude above New York, he could probably wreck more havoc than one near the ground. The absolute sovereignty theory is, therefore, the logical view. Neutral nations during the war announced their adherence to the sovereignty theory and attempted to capture and interne all passing belligerent aircraft. The justice of their action was generally admitted even by the warring nations concerned.[1]

The Convention relating to International Air Navigation signed at Paris in 1919, stipulated that the "contracting states recognize that every state has complete and exclusive sovereignty in the airspace over its territory and territorial waters." Each nation, however, promises to allow freedom of innocent passage to the aircraft of the other signatory powers. Any nation may provide for so-called "prohibited areas" for public safety or for military purposes. The greater portion of the coast of England lies in the prohibited area, which includes harbors, forts, and populous areas.[2]

[1] J. M. Spaight enumerates about 80 internments by Holland, 9 by Switzerland, 13 by Denmark, 2 by Roumania, 2 by Bulgaria, and 1 each by Norway, Sweden, and China. *Aircraft in Peace and the Law.*

[2] The convention adopted the apparently inconsistent view that the legal relations between persons on board are governed by the law of the nationality of the aircraft and that jurisdiction as to crimes committed en route shall belong to the state of the aircraft's registry, unless the machine lands. Here the convention applies the law of the sea (which is free) to the airspace, over which it gives each nation exclusive sovereignty.

Though there are very few judicial opinions in the field of aerial navigation and wireless telegraphy, a rather extensive literature is available on the subject. The reader is first referred to 2 *Corpus Juris* 299 and to Bouvier's *Law Dictionary.* The outstanding books on the subject are Hazeltine, *Law of the Air,* 1911, University of London Press, and the treatises of J. M. Spaight, among which are *Aircraft in Peace and the Law,* 1919, The MacMillan Company, and *Air Power and War Rights,* 1924, Longmans, Greene and Company. Practically all books on the law of torts and on international law contain short sketches of radio and aeroplane law. A large number of references are found in the *Index to Legal Periodicals* under the heading "aerial navigation." Frequent articles have appeared in the *American Law Review, Case and Comment, Canada Law Journal, (now Canadian Bar Review), Cornell Law Quarterly, Green Bag, Harvard Law Review, Juridical Review, Law Notes,* and *Law Times.*

For a discussion of radio in time of war, see John Bassett Moore's *International Law and Some Current Illusions,* 1923, Macmillan, 1924, pp. 182-288, and F. Meili, *Die draftlose Telegraphie im internen Richt und Volkerecht,* 1908.

ECONOMICS OF THE RADIO INDUSTRY

PART IV

THE FUTURE OF RADIO

XIII

ORGANIZING BROADCASTING FOR SERVICE

Issues involved. The situation in Canada. Australia and broadcasting service. British policy and control. Public policy in the United States. Justification for limitation of stations. The "who shall pay" problem. Tax on gross sales economically and legally sound. Burden of tax on radio audiences. Advantages of a tax on gross sales. Has Congress power over radio?

WE may well be proud of this wonderful development [radio broadcasting], but in our self-congratulation let us not forget that the value of this great system does not lie primarily in its extent or even in its efficiency. Its worth depends on the use that is made of it. It is not the ability to transmit but the character of what is transmitted that really counts. Our telephone and telegraph systems are valuable only in so far as the messages sent from them contribute to the business and social intercourse of our people. For the first time in history we have available to us the ability to communicate simultaneously with millions of our fellow men, to furnish entertainment, instruction, widening vision of national problems, and national events. An obligation rests upon us to see that it is devoted to real service and to develop the material that is transmitted into that which is really worth while. For it is only by this that the mission of this latest blessing of science to humanity may be rightfully fulfilled.—

HERBERT HOOVER.

From the point of view of public policy and broadcasting, the two fundamental issues affecting the quality of radio service are: Who shall control and how? and Who shall pay and how? These are not isolated problems, but are closely connected. If the broadcasting stations are to continue making enormous expenditures with little or no material return, either of two things is likely to happen. If the stations stay in business, they will attempt to cut down their expenses by eliminating portions of their service. The other alternative is that the expenses will finally become so burdensome that a large number of the smaller stations will discontinue their operations and leave the field to their more powerful competitors. In other words, we should have a system of stations in the hands of a few favorably situated private individuals with inadequate public regulation. These stations would acquire the authority to dictate what shall and what shall not be placed on the electromagnetic waves. Unregulated private individuals would tend to possess too great an influence over the press and over our political life.[1]

Before proposing a solution of the difficulties in the United States, let us make a brief survey as to the attitude of a few foreign nations on this question of control and pay.

THE SITUATION IN CANADA

Canada has approximately 60 broadcasters, besides a large number of amateur, commercial, coastal, and ship stations. About one-half of the broadcasting stations are operated by companies interested in the manufacture or sale of wireless apparatus, and about one-half by newspapers, stores, and others. As in the United States, the main purpose is advertising and the building up of good-will. Owing to the lack of a direct revenue, the Canadian stations are, like the American, confronted with the problem of balancing their budgets.[2]

Under the Canadian law, no person is permitted to "establish any radiotelegraph station or install or work any radiotelegraph apparatus . . . except under and in accordance with a license granted in that behalf by the Minister [of Marine and Fisheries]." The minister has the power to lay down regulations governing each set or station.

It will be noted that this differs from our law in two important respects:

In the first place, it applies to "any radiotelegraph

[1] It is significant that the large broadcasters permitted the indiscriminate use of their stations during the 1924 presidential campaign by the three major candidates.

[2] The Canadian regulations specify that "no tolls shall be levied or collected on account of any service performed" by the private commercial broadcasting stations.

apparatus or station." Thus, receiving sets are subject to
this restriction. The United States statute of 1912 applies
only to transmitting apparatus.[1] Furthermore, it gives the
Minister a discretion as to whether he will grant the license
or not. The United States Secretary of Commerce is compelled to grant the permit if the applicant has fulfilled certain requirements.

Licenses for the operation of private commercial broadcasting stations are issued by the Department at Ottawa
only. The fee is $50 per annum. Permits for private
receiving stations may be procured upon the payment of
$1 per year at the offices of the Department, from radio
inspectors, and from the postmasters of the larger towns and
cities in the Dominion. The number of receiving licenses
issued in 1922 was about 10,000. It has been estimated
that about 50,000 were issued in 1923. The cost of the
inspection service and of the issuance of the licenses
absorbed, during the early years of broadcasting, more than
the amount of the fees.

The Dominion Government does not own or operate any
broadcasting station.[2] The Provincial Government of Manitoba, however, operates a broadcasting station at Winnipeg,
and has practically a monopoly of this service for the
province. Section 10 of the law permits the central government to pay to a provincial government, private company,
or other prescribed party a portion of the license fees collected, keeping the other portion itself. At the present time
the Manitoba Government is being given one-half the fees
collected for receiving licenses in that province.

AUSTRALIA AND BROADCASTING SERVICE

For a time Australia had a system of sealed receiving sets,
whereby, at the time of purchase, the buyer would specify
which broadcaster he wished to hear, the set being then

[1]For account of our federal law, see Chapter IX.

[2]Unless one can refer to the station of the Canadian National Railway as
belonging to this class.

sealed at the wave length of this station. The fees (paid to the dealer as collector) were turned over to the designated broadcaster. If the purchaser wished to patronize two or more stations, the set would be sealed accordingly, but the fees paid would then be higher. The government had the right of inspection at any time to see whether the seal had been broken. In the summer of 1924 the restrictions regarding sealed sets were removed. Open sets are now sold, and the importation of receiving sets is permitted.

The present regulations in Australia have separate provisions regarding broadcasting and receiving stations. Two classes of broadcasting licenses are issued: Class "A" and Class "B." The holders of the former type of license are to receive a certain proportion of the revenue collected by the government from the users of receiving sets. The holders of the latter type are those who broadcast without such compensation, but rely on their own resources and indirect returns.

For the purpose of administering the license tax on receiving sets, each state has been divided into three zones. The first includes the territory within 250 miles of the broadcasting station; the second, the area within 400 miles; and the third class includes the remainder. The owners of private receiving sets are taxed 35 shillings, if located in the first zone, 30 in the second zone, and 25 in the third zone. Hotel receiving licenses are sold for £10, £9, £7 10 shillings, respectively, for the three zones. The dealers' licenses are bought at the rate of £5, £3, and £2 for the three zones, respectively. The revenue collected is apportioned between the government and the owners of the class "A" broadcasting stations.[1]

BRITISH POLICY AND CONTROL

The policy of Great Britain avoids many of the evils of the American system. The power to license and regulate

[1] *Commerce Reports*, August 18, 1924. Electrical Section.

wireless stations was given to the Postmaster-General under the Act of 1904. When the great clamor for broadcasting facilities arose, this official foresaw difficulties. Accordingly, in May, 1922, he called a conference of firms who had applied for the broadcasting privilege. It was made plain to the conference that if all applicants were granted licenses, there would be too many stations, resulting in interference and duplication of service. Consequently, two principles of regulation were put into effect: (1) the number of broadcasters must be limited, and (2) the licensed stations must be so located as to serve the whole country efficiently and without discrimination.

The result of this policy was the formation of the British Broadcasting Company which any radio manufacturer or dealer may join by subscribing for one or more one-pound shares and by depositing £50. In February, 1925, there were 20 broadcasting stations licensed and operated by the company. Thus in reality every radio manufacturer or dealer who is interested in broadcasting has an opportunity to enter into the business indirectly through stock ownership in the company. Some of the regulations imposed on the company are as follows: The company is not to broadcast any paid advertising, or any news except such as it obtains from the four authorized news agencies (no news is to be broadcast till after 7 p.m.); it will broadcast weather reports without compensation; the programs must be to the "reasonable satisfaction" of the Postmaster-General; the time of broadcasting is limited to specified hours and the wave lengths are limited to 350-435 (except the "blanket" station at Chelmsford, which has a wave length of 1,600 meters) and the power to 3 kilowatts; the company is to allow any British radio manufacturer or dealer to become a member; a license fee of £50 a year is paid to the government by each station; the profits of the company are limited to 7½% on the investment and a reasonable reserve, any surplus profits to accrue to the government; the company's license is revocable for cause. Other regulations that have been adopted are: All receivers pay a fee of 10 shillings a year, which is divided between the company and the government; manufacturers of radio sets pay to the company a royalty ranging from 1 shilling to 17 shillings 6 pence per set sold, depending on the type; the Postmaster-General may license any additional broadcasting service, where the company's service is not adequate and if it is not willing or able to provide it. The Postmaster-General made it a condition of all receiving licenses granted that any receiving set or certain parts used thereunder should be marked "BBC-Type approved by the P. M.-General." The purpose of this was to prevent those who do nothing to aid broadcasting from gaining by the sale of apparatus to the receiv-

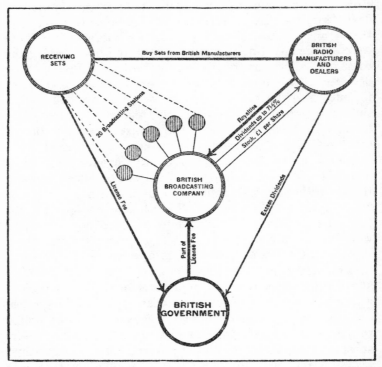

Figure 13: Organization of British broadcasting system.

ing public. On January 1, 1925, the restriction against the importation of radio apparatus was removed.

Up to the latter part of 1924 the number of receiving licenses sold was about 1,000,000. At 10 shillings a set, the revenue from this source is £500,000, of which the company receives three-fourths, or £375,000, the government retaining £125,000 for administrative expenses.

Owing to the even distribution of the stations throughout Great Britain, the receiving public is so near to the broadcasting facilities that crystal sets are in predominant use. The English people are apparently as a whole satisfied to regard a radio set as a means of entertainment and not as a method of competitively reaching out into space. There is no dividing of time among the stations, so that all work to the full capacity during the allotted hours. Each station has an orchestra. Artists', speakers', and copyright fees total £2,000 a week or £104,000 a year. The general policy is to pay for all entertainment.

Favorable reports are heard from all sides concerning the British system. Its advantages are: (1) provision for simultaneous broadcasting; (2) the reduction of social waste through the elimination of interference, the ability of stations to operate at full capacity, and the proper distribution of broadcasting facilities; and (3) the provision of an adequate system of payment so that satisfactory programs can be supplied.

PUBLIC POLICY IN THE UNITED STATES

What shall be the solution of the broadcasting problem in the United States? As to the question of control, four possible courses of action are open.

1. Continuance of the present system is the policy favored by those who believe that the situation will adjust itself. It is even contended that the need for the present restrictions will be eliminated when technical progress makes more wave lengths available. This laissez-faire attitude is

based on the suppositions that stations will be able to survive on the basis of indirect advertising, that if a station cannot survive, its existence is economically unjustifiable, and that telephonic broadcasting service is not affected with that degree of public interest which justifies stricter regulation. Essentially this is a "survival of the fittest" doctrine, based upon free competition and unrestricted private rights to use the air.

It should be pointed out, however, that the mortality rate has been highest among low-power stations and has resulted in an increasing number of high-power stations in the populous districts. This raises the question, which has not been conclusively determined as yet, whether sparsely settled areas will be adequately served—a question which interests farmers especially.

2. A second possibility is the amendment of our present radio laws so as to give the licensing authorities wider discretion in granting permits. This was one of the purposes of House Bill 7357, which was under consideration in March, 1924. Besides giving the Secretary of Commerce power to classify stations and to determine the nature (quality) of the service to be rendered, the bill stipulated that "The Secretary of Commerce, *if in his judgment public convenience, interest, or necessity will be served thereby*[1] and subject to the limitations of this act, *may*[1] grant any applicant therefor a station license—for a term not longer than ten years." The bill prohibited monopolies and provided for revoking licenses for cause.

Though this bill has obvious advantages, it was not enacted into law. Under it the Secretary would have had power to decide when and where stations may be erected. The anti-monopoly provision was also valuable, though possibly allowing the Secretary too much discretion, since he, and not a court, was to decide when and where monopoly or monopolistic intent existed. The term of the license was to be lengthened from 2 years (under the present law) to

[1]Italics the writer's.

10 years. The purpose of this extension was to protect the property rights of the licensee. He would have the right to operate at least 10 years before his license could be withdrawn except for cause. It will be noted that the Secretary might at the end of the term refuse to renew. He does not possess this power under the present law.

This bill, however, would not remedy the present maldistribution of broadcasting facilities. Private individuals would not, under it, be induced to erect stations in the sparsely populated areas, although the Secretary was apparently vested with power to minimize interference through the regulation of the number and location of stations.

3. A third alternative is the establishment under strict governmental regulation of a system of private high-power stations with a tentative maximum power of, say, 10 kilowatts.[1] Such a scheme would be analogous to our present policy of regulated private monopoly in the public utility field. The government could initiate this policy under the second possibility listed above. The 1924 Radio Conference suggested the provisional licensing of stations up to 5 kilowatts, and several have already increased their power.

Each high-power station in this plan might be granted an exclusive territory with a system of relaying and rebroadcasting so that one program could be broadcast throughout the country at one time.[2] The government might license low-power stations also (up to 100 watts), which could operate independently and serve as relaying agents for the larger concerns. Thus, private initiative would be preserved and stimulated. The low-power and the super-power stations would function together much as the metropolitan and the small-city newspapers, each performing its peculiar func-

[1]This power could, with experience, be increased until 50 or 100 kilowatts, or super-power status, were reached.

[2]There are, in general, two methods of rebroadcasting through a chain of stations. The one, perfected and used by the American Telephone and Telegraph Company, is the transmission of the material between the stations by means of wire telephone. The other, upon which progress has been made by the Westinghouse Company, is the use of a short wave length to distribute the material by wireless among the various members of the chain.

tion. In order to prevent the super-power stations from drowning out their smaller brothers, they should be assigned special wave lengths and should be located at least 25 miles from the great centers of population. Thus, as radio signals decrease in strength very rapidly as they leave their source, the radio audience could readily tune out these stronger stations, whenever they prefer. Still there might be the difficulty of inducing private individuals to erect stations in the thinly populated regions, because stations do not pay in these sections. In order to stimulate the construction of stations in the sparsely settled areas, as well as to provide adequate programs, including the payment of fees to the performers and royalties to copyright holders, provision might be made for subsidizing high-powered concerns by the United States Government. The low-power stations should receive compensation when they acted as relayers, but any one of them should be permitted to remain, if it desired, outside the system subject to government regulations.

It will readily be seen that the above policy is premised upon recognition of the public interest in good radio service —adequate quantity, quality, and continuity. As far as existing radio problems are concerned, the above policy may facilitate the elimination of interference and assure good quantity and continuity of service. But unless the license included provisions as to the quality of service, this phase of radio problems might remain unimproved under private initiative. It is well to remember that the type of broadcasting programs will be perhaps the major factor in determining whether radio service is sufficiently important to the public to justify regulation.

4. A fourth alternative is the establishment of a system of high-power stations (tentatively not more than 10 kilowatts) under public ownership and control. The main features of such a system might be as follows:

(a) The country would be zoned into districts according to area and atmospheric conditions.

(*b*) A Bureau of Communication would establish at an appropriate place within each zone one large public station with a maximum of 10 kilowatts.

(*c*) Private broadcasting stations might be authorized with a low power not exceeding 100 watts, since any system of government enterprise of this kind is apt to be deadening to private initiative. These private stations could be divided into two groups, A and B, the licensing of both classes to be within the discretion of the regulating authority.

(*d*) Group A stations might serve as government substations for the purpose of relaying programs within the zones, broadcasting special items of only local interest, and performing certain police duties such as the detection of interference from oscillating receivers. For these services the Bureau of Communication might make payment, although these stations might also be permitted to broadcast certain programs of their own.

(*e*) Group B stations would be those which do not desire to become government substations, and would be in practically the same position as the broadcasters of today.

(*f*) The Bureau of Communication would pay for talent, copyright royalties, patent rights, besides ordinary expenses. The right of private property in the copyright and the patent shall be protected.

(*g*) The central stations would sell a limited amount of advertising time.

(*h*) All the central stations would be so constructed as to make rebroadcasting possible.

(*i*) Government expenses might be met out of the proceeds of a gross sales tax on manufactures of radio apparatus. Such a tax would probably fall eventually on the users of radio service—the consumers—and would eliminate the necessity of licensing receivers and obtaining funds in that way. This tax should be relied upon also in the case of the third alternative above, in order to enable the government to subsidize private broadcasters.

(*j*) Army and navy wireless stations which at present are not subject to the civil authorities would be brought under sufficient control to prevent undue interference with other stations.

A policy either of regulated private monopoly or of public monopoly, as just outlined, would probably require a regulating commission with powers substantially like those now exercised by the Interstate Commerce Commission or various state public utility commissions. To such a board might also be delegated the power of regulating telephones, telegraphs, and cables—in fact all agencies of communication, present and prospective, the service of which is interstate in character.[1]

A public ownership and operation plan, like the one sketched above, is obviously open to the objections that private initiative will be stifled, that the government might attempt to dictate what the people may or may not hear, thus restricting the right of free speech, and that we already have too much centralization of authority in the Federal Government. Safeguards against the first two objection-

---

[1] As an instance of the working at loggerheads of various factors of our government, may again be mentioned the fact that the Navy Department suggested the cross-licensing agreements which were later assailed by the Federal Trade Commission. Both the navy and the Federal Trade Commission thought they were acting for the best interests of the people. Which was right? To prevent such inconsistency, it may be advocated that control of their own stations be taken from the army and navy, and that right of action for violation of the Federal Trade Commission and anti-trust acts be taken from the Federal Trade Commission, both to be given to the new communication body, on which the military interests should be represented. Thus unfair practices in the banking field would be cared for by the Federal Reserve Board, in railroads and allied fields by the Interstate Commerce Commission, in communication by the proposed bureau or board, and in industrial activity by the Federal Trade Commission. But military men will argue: We run our battleships and control the maneuvers of our army, why should we not have sole charge over our wireless? The answer is: Run the army and navy wireless as you please just as a private individual would, but if there is interference between your stations and others, the question of adjustment ought to be left to a body representing the people as a whole, on which you have representation. In case of war the exclusive control of their stations could, by proper decree of the President, revert to the army and navy. Under such proposed system the Radio Corporation would have known that the only body able to act as spokesman for the government in the matter of cross-licensing agreement was the Communication Bureau.

able features might be found in giving fairly liberal rights to low-power private stations. As for the last objection, if radio broadcasting is to be regulated at all, the interstate character of the service makes the Federal Government the only practicable regulating authority under our constitutional law.

The crux of the problem, in this as in all policies of stricter regulation, is the public importance of radio service. As long as the public looks upon the radio as one of many sources of entertainment, it is questionable whether the courts would construe favorably a law embodying more stringent regulation than now prevails. As more and more of the radio public, particularly farmers, come to regard the service as a necessary and non-reproducible utility of communication, more stringent regulation becomes both economically desirable and legally possible. And, if a prediction may be hazarded, the new public policy will in general follow the tendency of the third alternative listed above. The tendency toward super-power broadcasting is seen from the action of the United States Department of Commerce in provisionally licensing stations up to 5 kilowatts, and in the steps taken by private companies, such as the Westinghouse and the General Electric, in establishing chains which will enable them to "blanket" the greater portion of the country. The organization of a chain of stations to broadcast President Coolidge's inaugural address on March 4 is also of significance, in that it shows a natural tie-up and community of interest among some of the large private broadcasters. Such a prediction at least would follow the general lines of the development of public utility regulation.

JUSTIFICATION FOR LIMITATION OF STATIONS

An essential character of an adequate system of regulation is the limitation of the number of stations and the control over their location, so that interference and social waste resulting from the duplication of service and the necessity for dividing time among broadcasters may be reduced to a minimum. But, the reader will object, since you want to limit the stations, who is to do the choosing? Which applicants are to be granted the privilege of conducting high-powered stations? Who will be permitted to operate the smaller "A" and "B" stations? Let the new commission decide. Only a few broadcasters today render national programs. The commission will chose those which have shown themselves fit, provided they are properly located. If two already existing stations apply for a license to increase their power, and both cannot be accommodated, the commission will grant the license to the one, giving the other a choice between dismantling and selling to the government or of becoming either an "A" or "B" station. Is it not time that we abridge some of the private rights in the interest of the public welfare? The number of people concerned with the transmitting of wireless, though large absolutely, is small in proportion to the multitudes who look upon radio sets not as a subject of experimentation, but of entertainment and utility. Should not the rights of the former, then, be curbed in the interest of the latter? If a small number of high-power and a large number of "A" and "B" stations can cover the country more efficiently than almost 600 badly located and struggling broadcasters, is not the former alternative desirable?

The problem ought to be settled on the basis of service. Broadcasting is probably to a large extent vested with a peculiar public interest, thus justifying a considerable amount of social control. The Federal Reserve Act provided that national banks must enter the system or give up their federal charters. This compulsion was in general regarded as justifiable. A group of men may apply for a corporation charter to run a grocery store. If all legal conditions are fulfilled, the state authorities *must* grant it. A group of men apply for a charter to run a national bank. The Comptroller of Currency has power to refuse the application. A grocery store may enlarge its plant with the mere ministerial permission of the building commissioner. An interstate railway company must, before extending (or curtailing) its system or service, receive special consent from the Interstate Commerce Commission. Why the difference? Because banking and railroading have such a peculiar bearing on the public welfare that a large measure of government regulation is justified.

THE "WHO SHALL PAY" PROBLEM

As already suggested, the small stations would be divided into groups A and B. Group A broadcasters would act as a relay for the super-power stations in their respective zones, thus making the national programs available to a larger number of people; they would broadcast special local items, such as district weather reports and various advices of interest to small, compactly located groups of people; they would broadcast their own special programs in much the same way as a local newspaper today has its own clientele; they would perform various types of police duty; and finally they would pay for talent, news items, and copyright royalties.

This group would have the privilege of receiving payment for the performance of these special services. Group B stations would continue in much the same way as the ordinary broadcaster of today. Except for certain government restrictions, both classes would be independent.

The high-power stations, be they privately or government owned, would have available only a few sources of income, such as paid advertising, the stations being empowered to enforce a reasonable classification; fees from owners of new song copyrights, who wish to take this method of introducing their products; building up of good-will to the owner, if a private individual.

The expenses of the super-power stations would include: installation and ordinary operating expenses; payment of royalties to owners of patented radio apparatus; payment of talent; payment of royalties to owners of copyright, whether broadcasting helps advertise music or not; payment to news agencies; and compensation to Class A stations for services rendered.

TAX ON GROSS SALES ECONOMICALLY AND LEGALLY SOUND

Plainly the expenditures will be larger than the receipts. How make up the balance? A license tax on receiving sets would not be advisable or practicable. It would be a flat tax, and hence, in effect, regressive; it would be difficult and expensive to administer and collect; it would encourage secret evasion and cause much dissatisfaction. In short, on account of its directness, it would be difficult to enforce.[1] Neither should the expenses of broadcasting be borne by the public through general taxation.

The expenses of the broadcaster could be defrayed by a federal tax on the gross sales of radio manufacturers. As suggested, the government would subsidize the high-power and the Class A stations. The subsidy would roughly equal the annual deficit plus the amount paid to "A" stations.

The annual tax levy could be computed by dividing the sum of the operating deficit and the costs of administration by the gross sales.

Example:

Costs during year.....................$	900,000
Revenues during year...................	130,000
Operating deficit.......................$	770,000
Government cost of administration........	100,000
Total deficit ....$	870,000
Gross sales of manufacturers ....$	43,500,000

Tax $870,000 divided by $43,500,000 equals 2%.

[1]In favor of this tax may be mentioned: (1) It would enable the government to force the listener to promise not to make unauthorized use of any point-to-point messages, which he may happen to intercept. The back of the English receiving license contains a "secrecy" clause. This argument rests on the doubtful efficacy of the oath. (2) It would enable the authorities more readily to trace interference caused by oscillating receiving sets (since the location of all sets would be known). (3) The enrolment, as it were, of all operators, would be valuable in case of war. It is significant that 1,000,-000 people in the British Isles are annually buying receiving licenses at $2.50 each, and that there is very little evasion of the law.

If a temporary deficit should arise, treasury certificates could be used to bridge over the period until the next collection. If a surplus should result, it would be turned into the general fund. In case of a constant surplus or deficit, adjustments can be made in the next tax rates. This is similar to the practice of the American states and local communities in the collection of the general property tax. They divide the base into the amount of revenue needed. The result is the tax percentage. Though the computation has been made on the annual basis, there is no practical reason why monthly figures could not be used.

Such a levy and subsidy would probably be constitutional. The government would be legally justified in singling out the radio manufactures for taxation. They are a definite, distinct group inherently different from other industries. Such a classification seems reasonable. Today, under the internal revenue laws, manufacturers are classified and made to pay varying rates. Uniformity of taxation, as used in the Federal Constitution, means uniformity among states. Due process of law in taxation permits a reasonable classification founded on basic, inherent differences.

Likewise, the subsidy would probably be legally valid. It is a fundamental principle in the law of taxation that the revenues must be used for a public purpose. It has been held that the government may subsidize a railroad or a canal company or merchant marine, because all these businesses are essentially for a public purpose—closely related to the public welfare. The validity of this argument depends upon the public utility status of radio broadcasting.

BURDEN OF TAX ON RADIO AUDIENCES

This tax would fall upon *all* the manufacturers of radio, since they all have gross sales. It is not an income tax, which would fall only on the supermarginal firms. The proposed levy would be imposed upon marginal, as well as upon supermarginal and submarginal, manufacturers.

Therefore, this tax could be shifted in the form of higher prices to the purchaser of radio sets. Hence, every owner of a receiving set would help pay the cost of broadcasting.

The shifting process is illustrated in Tables 17 and 18, using examples of income tax and the proposed tax:

TABLE 17

INCOME TAX—NOT SHIFTED

	Gross Sales	Expenses	Net Profit
A	$100,000	$ 75,000	$ 25,000
B	500,000	300,000	200,000
C	50,000	50,000	000

If the Federal Government levied a tax of 10% on the net income, only "A" and "B" would pay. This 10% tax does not enter into expenses and, hence, cannot be shifted. Suppose "A" and "B" raised their prices in order to reimburse themselves. This new and higher market price would now give "C" a net profit and thus tend to encourage him to produce more, as well as beckon "D," a potential producer, into the scene. Thus, the *supply* would increase and the price *fall*, to a point near or at the original.

TABLE 18

WITH TAX OF 1% ON GROSS SALES—SHIFTED

	Gross Sales	Expenses	Net Profit
A	$100,000	$ 75,000 plus $1,000 tax	$ 24,000
B	500,000	300,000 plus 5,000 tax	195,000
C	50,000	50,000 plus 500 tax	*500

*Deficit.

"C," operating at a loss, would tend to decrease his production or drop out of business. Thus, the supply would be decreased and the market price raised.[1]

With the initiation of this plan, the Federal Tariff Commission should be asked to investigate the comparative costs of radio apparatus in the United States and other countries.

[1] In a state of competition the prices could not be raised much more than the amount of the tax. In so far, however, as the radio industry is one of decreasing costs, and if the increased price results in decreased production, there may be an increase over and above the amount of the tax.

If the findings justified, there may be a need of a compensating tariff.

The arguments for this plan can be summarized:

1. This tax could be easily administered. It would fall in the first instance on the relatively small number (3,000) of manufacturers. The *United States Census of Manufactures* listed 298 radio manufacturers as producing about $43,000,000 worth of radio apparatus (not including vacuum tubes) in 1923. Gross sales are relatively easily computed and checked.

2. The purchaser of radio apparatus would eventually, through the shifting process, pay the tax and, thus, the costs of broadcasting. This is just: the persons benefiting by broadcasting should pay. An icebox, kodak, victrola, or a player piano are valuable only so long as the owner possesses ice, films, records, or rolls to use with them. The purchaser of a victrola does not expect to be furnished the records free of charge. Likewise, a radio receiving set is worth while only so long as there is material in the air to be intercepted. The owner should pay for this entertainment. Under the proposed tax he would do so automatically with the purchase of a set or parts. He should not complain of a hardship any more than does the owner of a kodak complain when he is required to buy the necessary films.

3. The owner of an elaborate and expensive receiving set would pay a larger tax than the purchaser of a cheap set. Since he gets better service, it is just that he pay more.

4. Even the constructor of a simple receiving set would need to buy headphones and audions. If he makes a simple crystal set, he would buy fewer and less expensive articles, hence, pay a smaller tax, but he would hear and benefit less.

5. Delicate parts, such as audions, wear out. The listener, desiring to lengthen his range, buys a better set. The tax, then, becomes an ever-recurring levy. This is just,

because the expenditures of the broadcaster are continuous.

6. The plan is fair to the manufacturer, since he shifts the tax. The burden should not fall on him, since he is already, as a manufacturer, paying non-shiftable income and property taxes on his business. The tax, it must be recognized, may result in decreased profits, if the rise in prices causes a fall in demand.

7. Since the broadcaster also buys radio apparatus, this tax would fall partly on him. Since he may profit to some extent in an indirect way, it is just that he also bear part of the burden.

HAS CONGRESS POWER OVER RADIO?

Some question may arise as to the right of the Federal Government to regulate or to own a system of telephonic broadcasting, whichever of these two policies we adopt. When a bill providing for an increased appropriation for radio administration and inspection was introduced into the last congress, the opponents succeeded in defeating the measure by the use of the states' rights argument. Individuals may argue that no express or implied power over radio has been delegated to Congress. Is this a valid objection? It is undoubtedly true that the United States may use radio to carry on its own proprietary functions, such as the army, navy, and the post-office. Congress, having been given the power to establish these agencies, has the right to choose any reasonable means necessary for their operation and protection. But the jurisdiction of Congress over private radio is not so clear. The question may be approached from two angles. In the first place, Congress has power to control and regulate interstate commerce. The term "interstate commerce" is broad, general, and ever-changing. It applies to the carrying of ideas and intelligence, as well as of persons and commodities. Radio would seem to come under this category, and is so regarded. But suppose a station is so weak that its waves cannot extend beyond state lines?[1] Has the Federal Government control over this? In the case of *Chicago, Burlington and Quincy Railroad Company* v. *Wisconsin Railroad Commission*,[2] it was held that the authority of the central government extends over intrastate commerce, when the effect of the state regulation may radically affect interstate commerce. If the state of Wisconsin, the Supreme Court argued, has the power to enforce a 2-cent passenger rate on traffic between points within the state, then the railroad companies may be forced to petition the Interstate Commerce Commission for permission to increase their interstate rates so as to average a fair return on their investment. Following out the reasoning of the court by analogy, it seems that the propagation of intrastate wireless waves may interfere with interstate waves, and hence Congress should possess power over both.

But the strongest justification for the federal control over private wireless lies in the exercise of the treaty power. If a covenant is within the scope of the treaty-making power, it is valid law even though it apparently deprives the states of some of their reserved rights. A state presumably has the exclusive power to fix game and hunting regulations within its jurisdiction. But in 1916 the United States and Great Britain entered into a treaty stipulating that, whereas many species of birds in the annual migrations traversed many parts of Canada and the United States, they were in danger of extermination, and hence should be protected by certain closed seasons. Under the provisions of this treaty Congress passed an act prohibiting the killing, capturing, and selling of the migratory birds named in the treaty at certain specified seasons. In the case of *State of Missouri* v. *Holland*,[3] the Supreme Court, speaking through Justice Holmes, held that this was a proper exercise of the treaty-

---

[1] In reality there is no such thing as an intrastate transmitting station, as with a sufficiently sensitive receiving set, it can be noted that even the weakest waves may be intercepted across state borders.

[2] 42 Sup. Court 232 (1922). See also the Minnesota and the Shreveport Rate Cases, 230 U. S. 352 (1913), and 234 U. S. 342 (1914), respectively.

[3] 40 Sup. Ct. 382.

making power, and that the treaty may override the power of the state.

The United States, in 1912, signed the International Radiotelegraph Convention, and Congress passed an act giving effect to its provisions. Cannot wireless waves be regarded as "migratory birds," and thus a fit subject for treaty, and also for federal legislation? It must be noted that in the absence of further international conventions, the power of Congress under this argument is limited to the provisions of this treaty. Any further regulation of private radio must be justified under the interstate commerce clause or under a future international agreement.

XIV

RADIO AND OTHER SOCIAL AGENCIES

Early fear of wireless competition. Room for both cable and wireless. Competition has made for better service. Relative merits of cable and wireless. Costs in radio and cable. Law of increasing returns and radio. Wireless telephone versus wireless telegraph. The logical places of the various agencies of communication. The radio and newspapers. Radio in the schools. Prospects of a "Radio University." Radio in religion. The radio in photography. The radio in power transmission. The radio in hospitals. The radio as a medium for advertising. Radio and the talking machine. The radio and the farmer. Radio and real estate.

THAT the use of radio is extending is apparent. Hardly a day passes that the newspapers and the magazines do not report a new field for wireless. Radio is achieving things which formerly were regarded as impossible. It is also being used in fields which observers were wont to regard as belonging exclusively to some other agency. Thus two questions arise:

1. To what extent will radio supersede other mediums which formerly were essential to the performance of a certain function?

2. To what extent will radio be used for the accomplishment of previously unthought of functions?

If a city is considering the construction of a subway, there is often a large amount of opposition from the surface-car companies who believe that people will ride in the subway instead of the street-car. The experience of many cities, however, has indicated that in such a situation each of the two means of transportation will find its level and will supplement, not supplant, the other.

The same question arises in the problem of the truck and bus transportation versus the steam and electric railway. The best opinion seems to be that these two methods of transportation are supplementary: the truck and the bus serving as feeders and having the advantage in light local business; the railroad profiting through its adaptability to long-distance transportation. In communication there is a similar problem. The telegraph was firmly established before Bell developed the telephone, and the Western Union interests feared the innovation. But both have prospered.

EARLY FEAR OF WIRELESS COMPETITION

The first transatlantic cable was laid a quarter of a century before Marconi succeeded in establishing communication across the ocean. During the intervening period a network of cables had been stretched around the entire world, and even though they were strongly intrenched, the cable interests were very apprehensive of the innovation. When Marconi's transatlantic experiment on December 12, 1901, proved a success, there was a general fall in the prices of cable stocks. For example, in the period from December 12 to January 3 the quotations on Anglo-American stock fell from 52 to 48 (par 100), Direct United States from 10¾ to 9½ (par 20), and Eastern Telegraph from 140 to 130 (par 100).

The scare was only temporary. By the autumn of 1902, the prices of cable stocks were recovering and had soon exceeded their former long-time level. From that time on the cables held their own both in regard to their dividend records, the quotations on their stocks, and the amount of traffic handled. Marconi's early prophecy that "As soon as my wireless system succeeds, the vast network of cables and wires will become useless, and the money invested in the old system will be simply thrown away" has not been fulfilled.

ROOM FOR BOTH CABLE AND WIRELESS

Table 19 compares the dividend records of important cable companies for the years 1896 to 1900, when wireless was in its infancy, with the records for the 11 years ending in 1922. The dividends paid by the British and the International Marine Marconi companies also are indicated. It will be noted that the cables have continued their substantial payments to their stockholders.

TABLE 19

DIVIDEND RECORD OF CABLE AND WIRELESS COMPANIES—1912-1922, 1896-1900*

YEAR	Amazon	Anglo-American (Leased to Western Union)	Direct Spanish	Direct West India	Eastern Extension, Australasia, and China	Eastern Telegraph	Great Northern	Halifax and Bermuda	tional Marine Marconi	British Marconi
1912	4½%	3¾%	4 %	6 %	7 %	7%	20 %	5%	10 %	20 %
1913	4½	3¾	4	6	7	7	20	6	10	20
1914	3	3¾	6	6	7	7	22	13	10	10
1915	0	3¾	7	6†	8	8	22	13	12½	10
1916	3	3¾†	7	6	8	8	24	13	15	15
1917	4	3¾	7	6	8	8	22	13	15	20
1918	4½	3¾	7	6	8	8	22	13	15	25
1919	4½	3¾†	10	6	10	10	22	6	15	50
1920	4½	3¾†	10	6†	10	10	24	6	15	15
1921	0	3¾	10	6	10	10	22	6	10	15
1922	0	3 86/100	10	6	10	10	22	6	12½	15
1896	1910-11 was first dividend year		4		7	7	10	0	1910 was first dividend year on ordinary shares	1910 was first dividend year on ordinary shares
1897		3	4	2½	7	7	10	5		
1898		3 9-20	4	5	7	7	12½	5		
1899		3 27-40	4	6	7	7	12½	5		
1900		3⅛	4	6	7	7	15	5		

*Computed from data in *The Stock Exchange Official Intelligence*, London.
†Plus bonus.

COMPETITION HAS MADE FOR BETTER SERVICE

It must be admitted, however, that the introduction and the perfection of point-to-point long-distance telegraphy have in several senses tended to affect the cable business. The first influence has been in the matter of rates. The Radio Corporation of America made the following charges per word for its service to England which was begun in 1920:

1920	17 cents	1922	18 cents
1921	18 cents	1923	20 cents

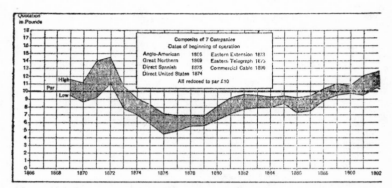

Figure 14a: Fluctuations in value of common stock of important cable companies, 1869 to 1919.

In 1923 the cable companies reduced their rates for the same service (A-ordinary) from 25 cents, which they had maintained for more than 35 years, to 20 cents, the radio rate. Likewise, the advent of wireless caused the New York–South African cable rates to be reduced in 1920, and again in 1922, until they reached the same level as the radio charges. If the reader will consult the volumes of the *Exporters Encyclopedia*, he will note that radio has reduced the cable rates to Poland, Germany, France, Italy, Norway, Sweden, Belgium, and Japan. To some of these points the cable and the wireless rates are equal, to others the cables are still above the radio. In regard to the messages sent from the inland United States via the Radio Corporation of America, the symbol "RCA" is counted as one word, while there is no corresponding charge if the message is to be sent via cable. If the radiogram is handed directly[1] to the Radio Corporation, there is of course, no need for the symbol "RCA."

The lower rates initiated by the wireless companies have diverted some of the traffic from the cables. The Radio Corporation today handles about 30% of our transatlantic and about 50% of our transpacific traffic. It seems that

[1] The corporation has established special offices for the accommodation of the public in the business sections of New York and several other cities.

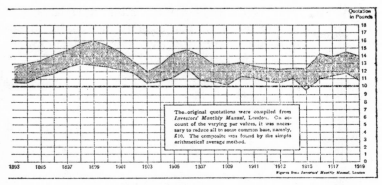

Figure 14b: Fluctuations in value of common stock of important cable companies, 1869 to 1919.

the proportion transmitted by the wireless companies is increasing. The traffic handled by the cable companies has grown absolutely, but has decreased proportionally. This is due to the fact that a large number of cables, especially the transpacific, were practically blocked with the vast amount of traffic immediately following the war, and to the fact that the cable companies in recent years have made very few extensions or additional investments. Moody's *Analyses of Investments*[1] reports that the plant and equipment value of the cable systems terminating in the United States had increased from 78 millions in 1912 to 80 millions in 1917—a growth of only a little more than 2%. The capital stock of the important cable companies increased by only a small percentage during the period 1901 to 1924, as is attested by Table 20. In 1923 the Commercial Cable Company completed its new cable to France via the Azores and Ireland. This was the first addition to the transatlantic cable system since 1910.[2] During the first quarter of the twentieth century there has been an unprecedented growth in communication both as an auxiliary to commerce and

---

[1] *Public Utilities*, 1924, p. 37.

[2] The construction of this new cable seems to show a "renewed faith in the permanence of the submarine cable as a channel of international communication." See *Commerce Year Book, 1923*. The year 1923 saw other improvements in the cable service.

for ordinary social contact.[1] Since the cables have not kept pace with the demand, is it not entirely reasonable that another agency should step in and engage in the same business? And is there not room for both?

TABLE 20

CAPITAL STOCK OF CABLE COMPANIES, 1901 AND 1924*

Name	1901		1924	
	Authorized	Issued	Authorized	Issued
Amazon..........................	250,000†	250,000	250,000	250,000
Anglo-American..................	7,000,000	7,000,000	7,000,000	7,000,000
Commercial Cable................	15,000,000	13,333,300	25,000,000	25,000,000
Compagnie Francaise des Cables Tele. (francs).......................	24,000,000	24,000,000	24,000,000	24,000,000
Direct Spanish..................	95,000	94,655	95,000	94,655
Direct West India..............	120,000	60,000	120,000	60,000
Eastern Extension, Australasia, and China......................	3,000,000	3,000,000	4,000,000	4,000,000
Eastern Tel. Co.................	6,000,000	5,930,807	7,000,000	7,000,000
Great Northern.................	1,500,000	1,500,000	2,000,000	1,500,000
Halifax and Bermuda............	50,000	50,000	50,000	50,000

*Sources: *Stock Exchange Official Intelligence* and *Stock Exchange Year-Book.*
†All figures pounds, unless otherwise specified.

RELATIVE MERITS OF CABLE AND WIRELESS

In spite of the fact that there is apparently room for both the submarine cable and the wireless as mediums for transoceanic communication, a bitter and futile controversy has been raging in regard to the relative merits of each. The advantages of the cable were well stated in 1912 by Sir Charles Bright[2] under the following headings:

[1] The wireless systems in the United States reported that they handled 285,091 messages in 1912 and only 122,224 in 1917, or less than one-half. But the total income of these same companies was, in 1912, $669,158, while in 1917 it was $1,385,060. In other words, in 1917 from one-half as many messages the companies received twice as much revenue as in 1912.

The cable statistics, though less striking, are, nevertheless, to the point. The systems terminating in the United States handled approximately the same number of messages in two years (2,845,168 in 1912, and 2,913,250 in 1917), but the total receipts were twice as great in 1917 as in 1912 ($16,749,058 in 1917). Figures compiled from Moody's *Analyses of Investments—Public Utilities,* 1924, p. xxxvii.

The reason for this difference in the case of the wireless, for example, is that in 1912 travelers used radio "Greetings from Mid-Ocean" messages, and that by 1917 people had learned the business value of the radio and, hence, were sending longer messages.

[2] A British cable engineer in "Cable Versus Wireless Telegraphy," *Nineteenth Century and After,* June, 1912, p. 1076.

1. *Sureness.* The cable has shown itself to be less prone to interruption than wireless. For example, Mr. Bright points out that the All-British Pacific Cable had suffered only one brief interruption after many years of steady work. When a cable has been broken, it is more rapidly repaired than a radio system. The German station at Nauen collapsed in 1912 during a gale and the work of repair required six months. It took upwards of a year to reinstate the Marconi transatlantic station at Glace Bay. Against these arguments we may mention the fact that within four days after Great Britain entered the World War the cable connections between Germany and the rest of the world were broken. Germany's only means of transoceanic communication thus became the wireless. During the Japanese earthquake of 1923, the cables were broken, and the full details of the disaster had to be transmitted to the world by radio. The internal troubles in Ireland caused an interruption of the transatlantic cables landing in Ireland, and the Radio Corporation of America assumed the extra burden.

2. *Secrecy.* Anybody possessing the required apparatus, says Mr. Bright, can listen in on a wireless message. This is not true of the cable. Though the lines can be tapped, it is apparent that the opportunity for so doing is not great. Though this is undoubtedly an advantage, great progress has been made in the direction of secrecy in radio. Here may be mentioned the beam system, the use of code messages, unusually high or low wave lengths, and great rapidity of sending.

3. *Speed.* Because of interference and static, wireless messages require more repetitions than the cable. The British Imperial Wireless Telegraphy Committee,[1] in its *Report* (1919-1920), concludes that the "repeats" in wireless range from 8% to 50%. This has always been a dis-

---

[1] This committee states (page 1) that on four different occasions studied in respect to transatlantic radio, of 7,557 words there were 945 repeats; of 6,883 words there were 568 repeats; of 5,444 words there were 1,544 repeats; and of 4,656 words there were 2,394 repeats. The tests were made at random. The repeats range from about 8% to 50%.

advantage of radio, but recent developments in the elimination of interference and static, and the invention of chemical and tape and mechanical and multiplex methods of receiving and sending tend to offset this disadvantage. With the rapid development of radio photography it is now possible to transmit pictures of printed matter at the rate of 1,000 words per minute.

4. *Accuracy.* This is another great advantage of the cable, argues Mr. Bright.

5. *Disturbance and interruption.* Though this is Mr. Bright's fifth and last argument in favor of the cable, it could readily be included under some of the earlier mentioned. Mr. Bright, it must be remembered, wrote in 1912. At that time the cable had behind it 40 years of development, while its 15-year-old competitor was still in a rather primitive stage. The comparison was not quite fair.

In addition to the above-mentioned points of comparison, the following may be mentioned:

6. *Rapidity of transmission.* Electromagnetic waves travel at the speed of light. A radio message would flash around the globe seven times in one second. Wire transmission is considerably slower. The Riverhead receiving station of the Radio Corporation of America is connected with New York by 18 wires, a distance of 80 miles. It takes a message one-sixtieth of a second to cross the Atlantic, and one one-hundredth of a second to travel the 80 miles from Riverhead to New York. In 1924 the letters *S* and *C* were radioed around the world in opposite directions by relays in five and six seconds respectively. The *Radio Service Bulletin,* for March, 1924, records the fact that on "September 22, 1918, wireless messages transmitted from Carnarvon were received in Sydney, 12,000 miles away. Cable confirmations of these messages were sent forward at the same time, but were received some hours later than the corresponding radiotelegrams."

COSTS IN RADIO AND CABLE

7. *Comparative costs of radio and cable.* In wireless the rate of energy radiated to energy received is "in fair trans-oceanic communication, one hundred trillions to one." That is, for every one hundred trillion units radiated from the antenna, only one is absorbed by the receiving set. Furthermore, not all the energy is radiated. "The efficiency of the mere act of radiation may be from 50% to 1% or 2%."

In striking contrast, comparatively little energy is lost in the transmission of messages over wires. But where the wireless has free use of its medium of transmission, the telegraph companies must stretch their wires and lay their submarine cables. Thus, "there is an approximate balance between the high cost of the long cable and its comparatively inexpensive terminal stations and the high cost of radio transmitting stations, the low cost of the radio receiving stations, and the zero cost of the medium."[1] The beam system has tended to lower the costs, on account of the fact that less of the radiated energy is wasted. A 500 to 1,000 kilowatt beam station is able to transmit as far and as efficiently as a 20,000 kilowatt high wave length station. Thus, the energy costs of the beam system are probably less than 5% as large as those of the present type of high-power transoceanic stations.

LAW OF INCREASING RETURNS AND RADIO

Certain authorities, as, for instance, Mr. Marconi, have argued that the 2-cent rate for both the cable and the radio is possible. This statement rests upon the assumption that the law of increasing returns applies to these fields. In other words, it is argued that since the big expense of the cable is in its laying, the fixed costs or overhead, if a sufficient amount of traffic is carried, will be distributed over a

---

[1] Facts on costs are from a serial article entitled "World Communication" beginning in the January, 1924, number of the *Telegraph and Telephone Age*, by Dr. Alfred Goldsmith (pp. 4 and 5 of January number).

wider area with a smaller proportion being assigned to each unit. The operating costs will increase with the amount of traffic, but the decrease of the fixed charges will finally cause a 2-cent rate to be possible.

Does the doctrine of increasing returns apply to the cable and radio communication fields? To a certain extent, yes. But it must be remembered that when a customer places a message on the wire, he expects it to be transmitted immediately. This prevents a company from distributing its work and keeping the wires full 24 hours of the day. Furthermore, in spite of the development of mechanical and multiplex sending and receiving, the time must come with the increasing traffic, when the laying of new lines, or the enlarging or construction of new stations is inevitable, thus necessitating a considerable increase in fixed charges, and, therefore, an increase in total costs per word. The communication business may be termed as an industry of alternately increasing and decreasing returns. Many of the cables were overloaded with traffic in 1919. It would appear that if the diminishing costs theory were absolutely true in the communication field, the rates would have been lowered long since. But when the post-war period saw the cables overworked, three courses of action were possible: the laying of new cables, which requires two years at least, or the authorizing of naval stations to handle commercial traffic, or the organization of new private radio facilities. The latter two expedients were adopted.

Both the cable and the radio telegraph seem to have a logical function in overseas communication. The two will supplement each other. The coordination and fair competition as to service and rates should work to the advantage of each and ought to make for an improved public service.

WIRELESS TELEPHONE VERSUS WIRELESS TELEGRAPH

The problem of the place of radio is also closely related to the question of the relative merits and place of the wireless telephone and telegraph. One often hears the prophecy that in the not very distant future one will be able to sit in his residence in a remote American town and communicate by wireless with a friend in London; then, the very next moment he will be able to call a business man in Paris. The writer ventures the opinion that this can be done. Already great strides have been made in the transmission of the human voice without wires. But the fundamental problem is: Will this be a commercial possibility? A German scientist has announced that he has discovered the secret of alchemy and has succeeded in the production of gold from the baser metals at the cost of $60,000 per ounce. The process may be *possible*. But the costs will have to be lowered enormously before we need to search for a new monetary standard. The wireless telephone will probably not be extensively used for point-to-point communication for the following reasons:

1. The wireless telephone requires a greater power than the wireless telegraph. This has been estimated to be from 3 to 20 times as large.[1]

2. The chances for interference will be greater on account of the greater power required.

3. Atmospheric disturbances are more serious in the case of radio telephony than radio telegraphy. On account of the distinctness of the signals, telegraphic dots and dashes can be copied through static. Even though in telegraphy there is interference among stations, the operator often can distinguish the pitch and thus follow the signals. A listener at a band concert can follow the melody of any group of instruments to the exclusion of the others. But if two voices are heard at the same time, it is almost impossible to distinguish and understand the one to the exclusion of the other. There would be a danger of a babel of voices.

4. Users of the telephone like to get immediate connection and to have their wishes instantly understood. Many otherwise gentle men and women are metamorphosed at the

[1]Report of the British Radio Research Board, 1922.

taking down of the telephone receiver. A wireless telephone subscriber would not be more patient at delay. Under a general system of radio telephony, the static and the interference from other parties would be as steadily and as vainly abused as is the present-day central operator. On the other hand, a telegram could be delayed for brief intervals without harm being done.

5. Only a small percentage of the people possess a "radio voice." Broadcasting stations inform us that it is exceedingly difficult to secure a good announcer. He must have good articulation and the proper pitch and loudness of voice. His lips must be in a certain position before the mouthpiece. Let the reader test himself by his own experience in carrying on an ordinary wire telephone conversation.

6. A universal point-to-point telephone service would be so expensive that it could be used only by a few, although the perfection of the beam system would tend to decrease the cost on account of the lower power required and the smaller amount of interference.

7. As to the comparative slowness of radio telegraphy, all witnesses before the subcommittee on Radio Telephony of the British Radio Research Board agreed that it is necessary to repeat or spell unusual words or proper names and to repeat figures (page 3 of *Report*, 1922).

THE LOGICAL PLACES OF THE VARIOUS AGENCIES OF COMMUNICATION

The radio telephone and the radio telegraph, the land lines, and the cables each have their peculiar characteristics and their individual fields for which they are especially well adapted. What, then, are these uses?

1. In the first place, the wireless telephone should be used for the dissemination of material which is of interest to a large group of people. To attempt an extensive point-to-point communication would be an economic waste, as well as the source of wide-spread public irritation and impa-

tience. The matter broadcast must be of importance to a large group of individuals.

2. The wireless telephone should not be used when other methods of communication are available.

3. Either the wireless telephone or the telegraph may be used for extending service to ships at sea.

4. Either system may be used for the air service and in general communication between or to moving bodies.

5. Radio telegraphy and telephony are especially adapted for communication in undeveloped and sparsely settled countries, where extensive construction of land lines would be unduly expensive in proportion to the population served. Then, too, natural barriers, such as mountains or swamps, may obstruct the placing of land wires.

6. Radio telegraphy is also adapted for transoceanic communication and between islands and continents widely separated. As already pointed out, there seems to be room for both the cable and the radio.[1]

We have thus far in this chapter discussed the extent to which radio will supersede other agents which formerly were regarded as monopolies. That is, the cable early possessed a monopoly of transoceanic communication; the wire telephone, of the transmission of the human voice; the wire telegraph, of the sending of telegrams. Radio has invaded all these fields. We will now discuss new lines of endeavor which have been opened up by the development of wireless.

THE RADIO AND THE NEWSPAPERS

Will the radio supplant the newspaper? Some say yes, and point to the fact that events of national importance like the death of President Harding are heralded throughout the land long before the newspapers print extras. When the extras do appear, the people, especially in the more thickly

---

[1]For the views of various authorities and government officials as to the proper fields of cable, land lines, wireless telephone and telegraph, see Appendix.

settled districts, buy them merely for the purpose of getting the details. Numerous people heard the proceedings at the Democratic Convention in 1924 even before the audience seated in the back part of Madison Square Garden in New York, was aware of what was happening. Extras were old before they reached the newsstand. Fight fans no longer call up their newspapers for the latest news. They listen in at their own or their friends' radio sets.

Another line of thought is that illustrated in the *Radio Times*, the official organ of the British Broadcasting Company, for August 15, 1924, in an article entitled the "Return of the Ear." The writer here argues that the invention of the wireless has increased the access of knowledge to the mind by means of the ear. Before the invention of printing and the popularizing of education, information was spread mostly by the spoken word. Proclamations were read in public; itinerant peddlers commended their wares and made themselves welcome by bringing to their prospective customers the news of the day.

Then, both by the cheapening of its cost and the lifting of the barriers of illiteracy, the newspaper was made available to the masses. Except in the schools and the public platform, almost all the impressions received by the twentieth-century man have been conveyed by means of printed matter and the eye.

With the advent of broadcasting and the radio, the situation has been largely reversed. As in times of old, we again hear the calling of the time of day and the condition of the weather, not by the old town crier, but by the radio announcer. We again hear the latest news told on the street, not by the traveler and the peddler, but by the radio loudspeaker. We again hear verses recited, not as in days of old in order that the unlettered might learn, but because they are transmitted to us, literate or illiterate, by means of the wireless waves.

Will the return of the ear be so extensive and pronounced that the radio ultimately will replace the printed matter and,

especially the newspaper? To this query we may venture
a negative answer for the following reasons:

1. Getting news of the day by radio goes contrary to
human nature. People are willing to listen to a report of
the proceedings of a convention or a prize fight, or to an
account of any other occurrence of the day, if *they are able
to get it immediately.* But would they be willing to wait
through an hour's account of political, social, and economic
news, until the turn came for the broadcasting of the type
of news in which they happen to be interested? How can
the radio newspaper cater to individual preferences?

2. The newspaper, as taken by radio, cannot be filed, nor
can clippings be taken.

3. The reader of an ordinary newspaper can easily adapt
himself to the language used. If it contains an unknown
word or phrase, he can consult a dictionary. Or, if he wishes
to read certain parts more carefully than others, he can do
so. This would be impossible in the case of news by radio.

4. Radio is an imperious thing. The news must be taken
at a specified time, or not at all.

5. Owing to the slowness of the process of radio announc-
ing, a wireless newspaper can at best recount the outstanding items only, and merely in a very general way.
Getting news by radio is very similar to reading the head-
lines of the papers. Detail and color cannot be given.

6. The modern newspaper lives on its advertising. If the
radio news items should be interspersed with the same proportion of advertising matter as is found in a typical news
sheet, the radio audience would throw up its hands in disgust, and tune in for something more to its liking. Radio
would "go dead."

7. Reliance on the radio newspaper would tend to over-
crowd the air. The sending of extra items and news of
unusually great importance is justifiable, but the large-scale
use of the ether for this purpose is not necessary on account
of the satisfactory service rendered by our modern newspapers.

So it seems that the radio, instead of displacing the modern newspaper, will supplement it. It may eliminate the "extra." Conceivably, through the stimulation of interest, radio may aid the sale of newspapers.[1]

RADIO IN THE SCHOOLS

The radio has also invaded the school and is taking over some of its functions. One of the most interesting enterprises in this connection was the installation of the courses in Browning at Columbia University. The plan of the work was as follows: The Director of the Extension Home Study Department announced a series of short 10- to 20-minute talks on Browning. The lectures were gratuitous, but the director explained that a syllabus of the course would be sent to any applicant for the sum of $5. This outline would permit the radio student to follow the course more easily.

The response was instantaneous. The director announced after the first of the lectures that the cost of the experiment had already been paid for by the sale of the syllabus. The American Telephone and Telegraph Company gave the free use of its station WEAF.[2]

In February, 1924, the Board of Education of New York City inaugurated what was probably the first extensive educational radio program. Lectures were broadcast from 2 to 2:30 on every school day. Concerning this feature Superintendent of Schools Ettinger says:

I see through this radio service a wonderful opportunity to bring the actual work of the school system into closer relation with the home. . . . The nature of the entertainment offered

---

[1]It is to be noted that the British Broadcasting Company must use only the material furnished by the regular news agencies or associations. See Chapter XII. British broadcasting stations cannot broadcast news until after 7 p. m.

The Associated Press and the United Press have adopted diametrically opposite policies as to radio. The former is attempting to forbid its use by its newspapers; the latter is making wireless its ally. The United Press policy seems to be the most logical.

[2]Account in the *Radio Broadcast*, February, 1924, in article entitled "Broadcasting Browning," p. 271.

by the schools might very well include short talks on special phases of education: music lessons, recitations in reading, English, history, civics, geography, arithmetic, nature study, science, and the like, spelling lessons and various exercises for special holidays.[1]

One of the most comprehensive projects in agricultural education by means of the radio has been initiated by the Extension Division of the Kansas State Agricultural College at Manhattan, Kansas. During the school year 1923-1924 the college broadcast courses in poultry, dairying, crops, home economics, and agricultural economics, besides an interspersion of musical entertainment. The lectures were prepared chiefly by the resident faculty members. Sam Pickard, the extension editor of the College, describes the plan as follows:[2]

This fall we are changing our plans in this respect: four 8-week courses will be offered on a subject. For instance, 15 minutes will be devoted to poultry one night each week for 8 weeks. First courses will be on egg production, which will be of primary interests for September to November. This will be followed with a course in marketing, another in the early spring on breeding, and a two months' course on baby chick production will terminate the year's work.

Our idea is to offer a more diversified program this fall and one which will lend itself to the timely element, a factor on which we place considerable emphasis. There will be no music or entertainment on our program this winter. The two 15-minute lectures which will be cataloged under the order of courses for which enrolment will be solicited will be followed by a timely lecture. Specialists will be scheduled for timely topics. Announcements will complete the program each evening. We feel that the instruction and meaty information is the back-bone of our program; that the air is full of entertainment and only in exceptional cases will the college leave the field of instruction. We believe that it is advisable again to offer certificates as a stimulus to secure enrolments and keep the interest of students to the end of the course. Our plan last fall was entirely successful and we are placing great emphasis on radio as a modern means of doing effective extension work.

[1] *School and Society,* February 23, 1924, p. 218.
[2] Letter to the writer dated June 27, 1924.

PROSPECTS OF A "RADIO UNIVERSITY"

Will the "radio university" tend to displace the modern resident school? It is believed that radio will have very little influence on the school and college. It may be used to give lectures leading up to formal certificates, but it is to be doubted whether the radio school, if we may dignify it by that name, will ever offer work leading up to a degree.

In the first place, students. and people generally, are inclined to be lazy. We all have the tendency to choose the path of least resistance. Pressure is needed. The student must be given a stimulus to work. This could not be supplied in a radio school.

Furthermore, the radio school would be deprived of the use of the blackboard, chart, and the atlas, as well as the laboratory and an adequate library. The personality of the teacher cannot radiate over the ether waves. Let the reader seat himself in a lecture room in such a position that he cannot see the speaker. He will, then, realize the importance of visual as well as auditory contact. No course even in a resident college is 100% solid instruction. The radio course would need to approach 100% entertainment. An interesting subject matter is essential in a successful radio program. From the behavior of his class and from the nature of the questions asked, the resident instructor learns to understand his students. He can reiterate and explain the hazy points in detail. The radio lecturer has no such contact with his audience.

A radio school does not provide for social contact among the students, such as fellowship meetings and athletic games. To the small boy, as well as to the collegian, these human relationships are an essential part of life. Indeed, far from superseding, the radio may stimulate interest in the resident college.

The radio has, however, an important field in education. It is used by the agricultural departments of the states and the Federal Government for the dissemination of market news and weather reports and for the spreading of information to aid the farmer in his battle against his many insect and animal enemies, and for combating epidemics. The radio also has its place in the broadcasting of information regarding the problems confronting the housewife in her daily tasks. But for the conduct of a systematic and prolonged course of study, the wireless is not expedient.

THE RADIO IN RELIGION

Many broad statements have been made regarding the use of radio in religion. A writer in the *Universalist Leader*, after making a well-justified criticism of the method of conducting some of our rural churches, prophesies a speedy revolution in our system of religious worship. "Instead of the ordinary barn-like meeting-house, there will be a chapel good to look at and with an interior suggestive of worship, meditation, and prayer. Instead of an organ, there will be a well-equipped radio. Instead of a choir making day hideous, songs will be caught out in the air, in which the congregation may join, led by some one who knows enough to beat time. Instead of a preacher who cannot preach but makes up for his defect by noise and bluster, the people will listen to some one who has something to say and knows how to say it. The radio, when a little further perfected, as Marconi assures us it soon will be, will supplant the pitiful and painful service of the ordinary country church."

To the country parson this writer would assign the role of "organizing the social life of the rural community, and superintending the Sunday radio services."[1]

But he ignores the fact that to most people religion is a matter of the heart and the soul. It is hard to conceive of any one's being inspired by a human voice from afar. The friendly greeting, the warm handshake, the words of sympathy and of encouragement—these are some necessary

[1] Quoted in *Literary Digest* for August 23, 1924, p. 31, "Religion by Radio."

parts of a church service. A matter-of-fact prayer from some silver-tongued orator a thousand miles away invoking divine blessing upon "all those who are afflicted and grieved" can have little cheer for the bereaved widow. She likes to feel that the words of sympathy are meant for her individually. It is difficult to think of religious fervor as being inspired by the impersonal voice of the phonograph or the radio receiving set.

In other aspects it must be noted that the radio will have important religious and social effects. Many pulpits are today inadequately filled, either on account of the congregation's lack of funds or numbers or because of the desire of ministers to locate in the urban districts. These are either supplied by itinerant preachers or have services conducted by one of the foremost citizens. Then, also, the opportunity of radio lies in bringing messages to isolated individuals. Pastors report letters from sailors who have heard their services at sea. Wireless can connect these people with the opportunities in the outside world. "I am told," says a Columbus pastor, "that in our County Infirmary and Columbus Hospital for Tuberculosis about 600 people listen in for each service. Within the last month three letters reported gatherings of people in private homes, ranging in numbers from 21 to 63." This pastor's regular church attendance has not decreased. Thus, the gospel is spread to people who, otherwise, would not have heard it.

A great amount of discussion has arisen as to the effect of radio upon church attendance. Since people can hear the sermons lying in bed or while in their own homes, why bother about the inconvenience of going to church? With the view of procuring some first-hand information on this question, the writer inquired of a number of ministers as to the effect of the broadcasting of religious services upon their attendance. The inquiries were sent only to those churches which were operating broadcasting stations.

A total of 19 responses were received. They reported as follows:

Tendency of radio to increase church attendance.... 15
Tendency both to increase and decrease; that is,
    cause a shift in attendance................. 1
No noticeable effect........................... 2
Tendency to diminish.......................... 1

Dr. A. W. Beaven, of Lake Avenue Baptist Church, Rochester, New York, cited a few satistics, which may be classified as follows:

TABLE 21

EFFECT OF THE BROADCASTING OF RELIGIOUS SERVICES UPON
CHURCH ATTENDANCE

	Sept., Oct., and Half of Nov., 1924	Sept., Oct., and Half of Nov., 1923
Total attendance at morning service......	11,975	10,815
Total attendance at evening service......	6,677	5,481

During the 1924 period the church's broadcasting station was working steadily, while at the beginning of the 1923 period, the station had just been installed. Thus, the experience of this congregation indicates that the broadcasting of its services, probably, tended to increase attendance. In a comprehensive study of this problem it would be necessary, of course, not only to compare church attendance from year to year, but also to ascertain whether the increase would have occurred regardless of the broadcasting.

As reasons why broadcasting by a church tends to increase its regular attendance may be cited the following:[1]

(1) Many who tune in to hear out of curiosity, come to church to pray in sincerity; (2) indifferent church members are stimulated to church attendance by hearing over the radio; (3) no instrument, however wonderful, can ever take the place of'the human voice and the human touch; (4) the radio does for the church what the victrola does for music —it stimulates interest. A large number of the pastors report that individuals who have heard the services by radio come to church to know the pastor and congregation at first-

[1]The first three of these points are extracts from a letter from Dr. M. E. Dodd, Shreveport, Louisiana.

hand; (5) people who misjudge the church and its messages are helped to a fairer estimate and in this way may be induced to attend services.

The resident church need not fear the radio. Pessimists apparently assume that the saturation point in religion has been reached, but just as the broadcasting of opera stimulates an interest in good music, so the broadcasting of sermons, far from eliminating the local church, will spread the message to a greater number of people.

The ultimate value of church broadcasting is likely to depend, however, upon the judicious selection of programs and the avoidance of unduly controversial issues.

THE RADIO IN PHOTOGRAPHY

As photographs have been successfully transmitted and copied by means of wire, so considerable progress has been made in the development of radio photography. The American Telephone and Telegraph Company has made the greatest progress in the transmission of photographs by wire, while one of the foremost inventors in the wireless field in this connection is C. Francis Jenkins, of Washington, D. C., who maintains a private laboratory for the "development of photographs by radio, radio movies, and radio vision; that is, seeing in one's home by radio what is happening in a distant place."[1]   In the latter part of 1924 some very successful tests were made by the Radio Corporation of America in sending photographs by wireless across the Atlantic.

THE RADIO IN POWER TRANSMISSION

As early as 1901 mention was made of the transmission of electrical power by means of wireless; for example, the exploding of a mine at a distance.[2]   In the year 1912 Mr.

---

[1] For a brief, popular discussion of the methods of radio photography, see the testimony of Mr. Jenkins before the House Committee on Merchant Marine and Fisheries on H. R. 7357, a bill to regulate radio communication.

[2] *Pictorial Magazine*, September, 1901.

Marconi predicted that, "Within the next two generations we shall have not only wireless telegraphy and telephony, but also wireless transmission of all power for individual and corporate use, wireless heating and light, and wireless fertilizing of fields."[1]

Large-scale radio transmission of power is as yet impracticable. Experiments have proved that energy can be so transmitted and that it can be guided definitely, but for the present at any rate, the inevitable question "Does it pay?" must be answered in the negative. Power transmission over wires is practicable only for a limited number of miles. Radio transmission can never be economical unless scientists succeed in reducing enormously the attendant wastes and losses.

THE RADIO IN HOSPITALS

To the bedridden and the disabled, radio has been a godsend. The United States Government has especially recognized this fact, and has taken steps for the installation of radio apparatus in all the army and navy hospitals, including those for disabled veterans. At Walter Reed General Hospital in Washington, D. C., the government has installed 1,500 headsets and loudspeakers. The services of one man are required for the operation of the apparatus. About 40 of the United States veterans hospitals have already been provided with such equipment.

Many other uses of the radio will occur to the reader: For example, to report location of schools of fish, to guide aircraft, to control the motions of vehicles and ships from a distance, to dispatch trains, and, in time of war, to paralyze the apparatus of the enemy, especially aeroplanes.

THE RADIO AS A MEDIUM FOR ADVERTISING

The value of radio as a means of advertising is approximately proportional to its novelty. An individual who is

---

[1]*Technical World Magazine*, October, 1912, pp. 145-150, "Marconi's Plans for the Future."

still mystified by the "wonders of it all" will very willingly listen to some political speeches or announcement of would-be buyers or sellers of merchandise and services. Even a screech will give him satisfaction. But he early becomes sophisticated and develops a mind of his own. If he is to listen, he wishes to choose the entertainment. The radio fan is a person of great authority. He says, "Come" and the entertainment of the world is marshaled before him. He says, "Go" and the well-chosen words of the political speaker and the advertiser are relegated to oblivion.

Such being the case, ordinary and extensive advertising by radio is either futile or wasteful. If the radio listener notes a bit of advertising is coming through the air, he can easily tune it out and turn to something else. Or if he has already developed an interest in what is coming, the radio cannot be given credit for stimulating it. In either case the advertisement would be ineffective.

How many of the readers of this paragraph note the gist of the advertisements which are flashed on the screen immediately before the movie? How many do not turn away in disgust? If you could get some other sort of diversion during these moments of imposition, would you not resort to it with a feeling of thankfulness? The radio audience has such an opportunity.

But, some will object, the newspaper or magazine reader can, likewise, disregard the advertisement; yet such advertising pays. But the publisher often sandwiches in the advertisements with the news matter or articles. Moreover, the reader is accustomed to finding them there and is not annoyed, but is often even gratified by their presence. If he consults them, he does so voluntarily; if he disregards them, as he reads, they are still on the side-lines, beckoning to his subconscious mind. He thinks he reads only the news, but the extraneous material also makes an appeal which is occasionally so strong that he turns to it. This is the reason advertisers pay at varying rates for different positions in the paper.

The radio advertiser cannot thus appeal to the subconscious. His advertising, if direct, is obnoxious; if indirect, it must be cleverly subterfuged. It cannot be kept in the margin of the field of consciousness. At any rate the direct or indirect display of his wares occupies valuable space in the ether.

A very limited amount of advertising can, and should, be done by wireless. Crucial and keynote political speeches could be successfully broadcast.[1] Indirect advertising may be done, provided the material is of such a nature as to command a wide public interest and has great educational value. Just as in the case of newspapers and magazines, the federal law should require that all radio advertising be so labeled. The self-interest of the unseen audience will also prevent the abuse of the advertising privilege.

Unrestricted advertising done by private broadcasting, even though it should be successful, would preempt such a vast proportion of the ether that there would not be room for other legitimate traffic. Services that can be better, or equally well, performed through other agencies, should not be carried out by means of the radio.

RADIO AND THE TALKING MACHINE

The popularization of radio broadcasting occurred during a period when the talking machine, like practically every other industry, was suffering from depression. It is difficult to determine to what extent, if any, the fall in phonograph production was due to the interest in radio and to what extent it was the result of general business conditions. At any rate, some phonograph manufacturers have sought to ally themselves with the newly popularized industry. Radio manufactures were increasing by leaps and bounds. The

---

[1] In the last presidential campaign it seems to be the opinion of many that Coolidge had a better radio voice than Davis, and that this is one of the reasons for the Democratic defeat. Others point to the fact that in 1924 millions of people attended a political convention for the first time, and that the prompt action at Cleveland as contrasted with the indecision and numerous ballots at New York had an impressive effect upon the voters.

talking machine output was falling behind. Why could not
the talking machine industry bolster up its sales by entering into the production of the radio supplies for which it
is fitted, such as cabinets, combination radio and phonographs, and loudspeakers? The Sonora Phonograph Company did enter the new field, with the result that its plant
began to run at full capacity and later took on a night shift.[1]
The Radio Corporation of America is selling Radiolas to the
Brunswick-Balke-Collendar Company to be used in combination radio-phonograph sets. Brunswick artists also broadcast from the former's stations. A trade body, formerly
including only the talking machine interests, extended its
membership, and is now known as the Talking Machine and
Radio Men, Incorporated.

The alliance between the industries is, it seems, economically justifiable. Radio sets today are to a large extent
made in cabinet style, so as to be an ornament in the home,
as well as a source of entertainment. "The radio manufacturer is not at home with cabinet design and production,
and would be just as unlikely to consider cabinet manufacturing as the phonograph factory would consider radio
production."[2] Thus, each performing its own peculiar function, there may tend to be a natural combination of these
industries.

In the long run radio should not have adverse effects on
the sale of talking machines and supplies. The act of
broadcasting, indeed, may tend to popularize a certain
selection, thus increasing the demand for it in permanent
form in records and in sheet music.[3] The Victor Company,
which at first opposed the radio, in January, 1925, also allied
itself with the new industry. After permitting Alda, Bori,
and McCormack to sing to the radio audience, the Victor

[1] As to the work to the Sonora Company, see the various issues of the
Sonora Bell and a speech by its president, S. O. Martin, before the Talking
Machine and Radio Men, Inc., December 3, 1924.

[2] Quotation from "The Phonograph and Radio," by Charles C. Henry,
Radio Dealer, August, 1924, p. 34.

[3] See Chapter X.

Company ran full-page advertisements in the popular magazines stating that:

It is one thing to hear a beautiful singer by radio, another to be able to hear that singer sing to you when you want to be sung to.

It should be noted that this company proceeds upon the sound business principle of limiting the amount of broadcasting done by its artists.[1]

THE RADIO AND THE FARMER

The value of broadcasting service to farmers is perhaps best indicated by the results of the radio conference sponsored by the Department of Agriculture in December, 1924. The superintendent of radio operations of the Westinghouse Company stated to the conference that "radio broadcasting's greatest mission in this country would probably be the serving of American agriculture." As reported by the official in charge of the forecast division of the Weather Bureau, "Hundreds of thousands of dollars' worth of live stock and other property have been saved by a knowledge of weather conditions made possible by radio broadcasting." To illustrate the farmers' appreciation of the educational value of radio, reference may again be made to the experience of the Kansas State Agricultural College, which has inaugurated the "college of the air." In 1923 this college broadcast courses on various subjects to an enrolment of 967 people; and of this number 311 took the examination scheduled at the end of the short course. Radio will supplement present agencies in bringing technical education to millions of farm men and women, and will assist in delivering the farmer from his state of comparative isolation. The market reports will enable him to ship grain and cattle at the most advantageous time. The agricultural colleges will announce the dates for spraying trees and for the taking of other precautions against disease. As Secretary of Agri-

---

[1] See page 200.

culture Jardine has said, radio's greatest contribution may lie in this service to the farmer.[1]

If the farmer is to derive full benefit from the radio, however, his use of it must be stimulated. As pointed out in Chapter VI, most of the advantages of radio are received today by the urban populations. County agents, agricultural colleges, and, above all, the radio dealer himself, through appropriate advertising, should attempt to stimulate a continued and greater use of radio by the farmer, and should render aid in the choice of the proper kind of set; or if the farmer wishes to construct one of his own, in the details of construction. Of 1,166 farmers from which the Federal Bureau of Agricultural Economics received data, 45% reported that they had made their own sets, and that the average cost of the parts employed in construction was $83. More than 75 different makes were reported by the 55% that bought their equipment. The average price of the complete sets was $175, but many farmers paid $400 to $500.[2]

The public importance of radio broadcasting was recognized by the radio conference sponsored by the Department of Agriculture in December, 1924, when it unanimously adopted a resolution which included the following recommendations:

1. That agricultural radio broadcasting be extended as rapidly as the evidences of need justify, and reliable broadcasting facilities become available until all parts of the agricultural community are reached with a satisfactory and regular service.

2. That the attention of all broadcasting station operators be called to the vital importance of using only accurate and dependable information and to the dangers of broadcasting unauthentic information and propaganda, and that we urge that every means

---

[1] Radio telephone broadcasts of weather reports were first begun at the University of Wisconsin in January, 1921, and by July of the same year 12 stations had made arrangements to broadcast daily weather forecasts. Today about 117 stations are supplying daily weather forecasts. In December, 1920, the first market report was broadcast by radio telegraph from the laboratory of the United States Bureau of Standards. *Wireless Age*, March, 1925, "Rural Life Modernized," by J. C. Gibbert, of Bureau of Agriculture Economics.

[2] Gibbert, J. C., *Wireless Age, supra.*

be employed to protect the listener from deception of all kinds.

3. That, in addition to the character of the material, especial attention be given to the timeliness and continuity of broadcasting periods, and that all governmental agencies responsible for the direction of radio recognize the farmer's interest in timely information.

4. That we recognize the great importance of weather reports and storm warnings to all on land and sea and lake.

5. That the present cooperative supervision of the broadcasting of market reports by federal and state marketing agencies be continued, to the end that the farmer be not confused by conflicting reports.

6. That the consumer's interest in agriculture be recognized, and that broadcasting stations in populous centers be urged to give consideration to the use of suitable material on agriculture which will promote a better understanding of the farm situation, and also aid the consumer to buy farm products in season and to the best advantage.[1]

RADIO AND REAL ESTATE

The popularity of radio broadcasting may have important effects on the urban real estate business. Prospective home owners, in selecting their sites, have a regard for the radio conditions in the community. In the large cities there are occasional dead spots in which the nearest broadcasting station can be heard only with difficulty. Close proximity to a powerful broadcasting station or to elevated railroads and to power lines may result in interference and a tendency toward lower land values.[2] Home owners object alike to extreme noise and extreme solitude: in the future they may likewise object more and more to radio interference as well as to lack of opportunity to listen to radio programs. As a protection to urban property values, the 1924 radio conference called by Herbert Hoover recommended that future high-power stations be located at least 25 miles from the populous districts of cities.

---

[1] *Official Record of Department of Agriculture*, December 17, 1924.

[2] See quotation from *Radio Press Service* in *Literary Digest*, February 14, 1925, "Radio and Real Estate."

The popularization of radio may tend to cause a shift in our urban populations. The interurban train has made the suburbs desirable. May not the radio, by enabling the commuters to take a part of their entertainment and instruction into their homes, cause more migration from the centrally located sections to the suburban districts?

XV

THE SATURATION POINT

Peculiar characteristics of radio. One radio set per family? Future of radio exports. Lundquist on radio exports. The Radio Corporation and the future. World wireless by and for Americans. The "Big Four" and broadcasting. Service plans of the Marconi Company. Radio and the future.

WILL radio continue its phenomenal growth? On this question, which is of tremendous practical importance from the point of view of the public and also of the investor, there is a difference of opinion. The radio magnates are very optimistic. Bankers, who are rightly conservative in all their judgments, have a tendency to be pessimistic. Certain business forecasters, such as Roger Babson, promise a good future for this new industry.

Who is right?

The growth of radio during the last half-decade has been abnormal. In predicting the future one cannot extend the line of growth in the past and forecast that such will be the proportional progress in the days to come. A few qualifying facts must be noted.

1. One of the forces which have produced this surprising increase is the novelty of radio and its innate appeal to human curiosity. No invention or discovery has ever created such enthusiasm and awe as has wireless. People have always seen birds soar through the air. Thus, though admiring the art, they could readily understand the reality of the aeroplane. People have ridden in stage coaches and on horseback, and so it was not long before they accepted the train and the automobile. Even in the case of wire telephone and telegraph, the existence of the wires added a note of reality. But ever since Marconi's first successful experiment wireless has gripped the imagination of the world.

But this rapid growth will probably not continue, for people are beginning to take radio for granted. The strangeness of it is gradually being replaced by a critical matter-of-fact attitude. The same thing, but to a less extent, happened in the field of the wire telephone. The writer remembers how, when the first farmer telephone system—a party line—was installed in his home community in the northern part of Wisconsin, so much "business" was at first transacted that at a community prayer meeting held at one of the farm houses the wires had to be disconnected in order that the worshippers might hear. Today in that neighborhood a prayer meeting can easily be held in peace.

2. To most people radio will continue to be a source of pleasure and entertainment and not of livelihood. Unlike the automobile, it is not used for business or for a combination of business and pleasure.[1]

3. Unlike the automobile, the radio receiving set is a family or a community affair. There will not be much tendency for several members of the family to own sets.

4. The cost of installing a good radio receiving set is comparatively low, and on account of standardization and large-scale production it is decreasing. This holds true both of ready-made sets and of parts.

5. Today the owners of receiving sets are competing as to who can receive messages from the greatest distance. Magazines are conducting long-distance contests. When people learn that it is very easy to pick up signals from afar, the fascination of distance will tend to disappear. The audiences may then be satisfied with simple sets and even with crystal detectors. This fact would tend to decrease the average cost of installation, and would also make for stabilization in styles.

Has the saturation point been reached?

By the saturation point is meant that point at which the

---

[1] Radio has made the greatest appeal to the people through the practice of broadcasting. The above remark holds especially for this and not for point-to-point wireless communication or telegraphic broadcasting.

annual demand for goods becomes equal to that amount necessary to replace the number of units worn out or destroyed plus the quantity demanded by the increases in the population. Consider an analogy. If one pours sugar into a tumbler of water, a point will be reached at which it will be wasteful to add extra sugar, and the only way in which more sugar could be dissolved is through the addition of more water.

To arrive at any conclusion as to the saturation point in the radio industry, it is necessary to determine three things:

1. How many radio sets are in operation today?
2. What is the full theoretical market?
3. What are the opportunities (for American manufacturers) in foreign trade?

The number of radio receiving sets in operation in the United States today is impossible of accurate estimation. Since no formalities at all are necessary for the installation of a receiving set, we have as yet no official figures. The amount of sales is not a good indicator, because of the prevalence of home-made apparatus. The estimates run all the way from three millions to five millions.[1]

---

[1]Colonel J. F. Dillon, radio supervisor for the Pacific Coast Radio District, states that there are 500,000 receiving sets in California. The population of this state was, in 1920, 3,426,861. Counting the average family as 4.4 members, there are almost 800,000 families in that state. In other words, according to Mr. Dillon's estimate, there are five sets for every eight families in California. The Ohio Federal Crop Reporter has estimated that 1 farm in every 17 in Ohio is equipped with radio. (*Radio Broadcast*, August, 1924, p. 306.)

The Radio Manufacturers' Association estimates that "at the present time less than 10% of the farmers have radio apparatus and less than 40% of the city families are using receiving sets." (Letter from Chas. H. Porter, executive secretary, under date of October 3, 1924.)

Secretary Hoover of the Department of Commerce says that "There are certainly three to five million telephone receiving sets." (Testimony before House Committee on Merchant Marine and Fisheries on Bill H. R. 7357, March 11, 1924.)

The Federal Bureau of Agricultural Economics estimates that in 1924 there were 364,800 radio sets on American farms, as compared with 145,350 in 1923. Some "estimates" are merely guesses. For instance, one observer writing in a radio magazine noted that there were antennae on 9/10 of the tenement buildings in New York. Therefore, he concluded 9/10 of the tenants own radio receiving sets!

ONE RECEIVING SET PER FAMILY?

There being about twenty-four millions of families in the United States, it appears that at the most not more than one out of six is equipped with a radio. What is the full theoretical market? Can we anticipate placing one radio set in every family? Advocates of the one radio set per family idea point to the fact that there are 15,000,000 automobiles in the United States, or three for every five families. The average price per car is much higher than the average price per radio set. Hence, they ask, why is not the theoretical market for radio much greater than that for motor cars? But in this connection it must be noted that the automobile is used for business as well as recreation. Many cars serve this double purpose; some are used for business only; others, for pleasure. Some families have no cars at all; many boast machines belonging to individual members.

The situation with radio is different. It can at the best (as far as broadcasting is concerned) serve as a means of indirect gain. Its general purpose in the present state of development is pleasure, though increasing numbers of our population, especially farmers and housewives, are regarding it as a necessity. Just as families who feel able to spend $500 for a car hesitate in buying a hundred-dollar victrola, so will they, when the novelty has worn off, pause before purchasing a radiola. Today for every dollar spent in the purchase of musical instruments, including pianos and phonographs, 19 cents is spent for radio. There is no particular reason why the market for radio telephone apparatus should be more active than that for musical instruments, of which about $230,000,000 worth was manufactured in the United States in 1923. According to this calculation, the extent of the possible annual radio market is about $230,000,000, manufacturers' value, or possibly $450,000,000, price to the consumer. It, then, becomes very necessary as a precaution for the future that American manufacturers scour the foreign fields for radio possibilities.

FUTURE OF RADIO EXPORTS

Outside of the question of providing an adequate future market for our radio manfacturers, the encouragement of exports will tend to eliminate the seasonal aspects of the business. Radio is more popular in the winter than in the summer. The effect of this fact on labor turnover and on the general stability of the industry is apparent. We ship much radio apparatus to sections of the world whose seasons are the opposite of ours. Thus, during the late spring and summer, the slack in the trade will be taken out by the demand in foreign countries; and at the end of the year when the foreign consumption falls off, the market will be maintained by the increased domestic demand.

The future of American exports of radio supplies is, in general, bright. The figures for the last six years follow:[1]

TABLE 22

AMOUNT OF AMERICAN EXPORTS OF RADIO SUPPLIES, BY YEARS, 1919-24

Year	Value of Exports
1919	$ 830,887
1920	713,798
1921	1,010,891
1922	2,897,799
1923	3,448,112
1924	6,030,914

The imports of radio have been practically nil and are not classified by the Census Bureau.

Table 23 shows the value in dollars of radio exports to selected countries during the years 1918 to 1924.[2] The unusually large exports to Poland in 1922 and to Sweden in 1923 are due to the fact that in these years transoceanic

[1] For the years 1919 to 1921, inclusive, the figures are for the official class "Telegraphy Apparatus, including Wireless," while for the last two years cited the class is "Radio and Wireless Apparatus." From data furnished by the Bureau of Foreign and Domestic Commerce.

[2] Compiled from *Special Circular* No. 345 of the Electrical Division of the Bureau of Foreign and Domestic Commerce.

stations were constructed to communicate with the Radio
Corporation of America.

TABLE 23

EXPORTS OF RADIO APPARATUS FROM THE UNITED STATES TO
SELECTED COUNTRIES DURING 1918-1924

Year	1918	1919	1920	1921	1922	1923	1924
DESTINATION							
Austria..............	0	0	0	0	0	185	11,700
France..............	18,770	23,845	7,184	9,723	2,968	57,487	30,467
Germany............	0	0	0	0	1,388	10,508	9,378
Italy...............	5,242	2,030	0	0	425	7,061	28,952
Netherlands.........	0	9,601	4,587	19,401	4,418	23,859	53,665
Norway.............	0	5,918	1,157	95	10,049	15,114	27,639
Poland and Danzig...	0	0	0	0	572,284	10,730	5,684
Sweden.............	0	3,548	230	440,687	1,746	458,886	131,938
England............	101,255	183,407	52,627	62,587	319,543	199,541	140,479
Canada.............	106,355	197,874	84,430	71,199	816,685	797,006	2,413,687
Mexico.............	8,779	20,339	32,386	29,792	89,246	281,275	393,517
Cuba...............	16,965	29,974	47,326	21,203	119,852	212,288	103,486
Argentina..........	100	2,129	9,964	12,891	650,572	646,993	291,740
Chile...............	2,861	8,522	12,132	14,682	7,095	51,502	182,356
Japan..............	63,068	97,299	73,004	59,523	41,638	45,761	358,222
Australia...........	2,021	21,686	8,513	12,855	25,293	213,214	1,052,707
New Zealand........	201	174	343	4,576	28,901	83,426	88,191
British So. Africa...	0	0	15,870	3,451	1,263	9,207	27,898
China..............	352	5,855	14,160	2,404	6,904	20,656	4,864
British India.......	22	44	252	27	89	26,968	14,204

As the data in this table reveal, radio is continually receiving more and more attention in foreign countries. Certain nations, for example, China and India, have maintained
a strict control of the means of transmitting and receiving
messages and have forbidden the importation and private
use of wireless sets. Others, such as Argentina, though
maintaining radio as a government monopoly, have adopted
a liberal attitude or policy toward its use and enjoyment by
the people. Others, such as New Zealand, have been marking time and have adopted no particular policy. Still others,
such as Canada, have permitted broadcasting on a large
scale and have imposed slight restrictions on the use of
receiving sets. Thus, it can be readily understood why our
exports to China and India are comparatively small, while
to Canada and Argentina they are very large.

Foreign countries, however, are lifting their restrictions
and are liberalizing their policies. Thus, new potential markets are being opened to American manufacturers. Will the

United States be able to maintain the advantage of her early start?

LUNDQUIST ON RADIO EXPORTS

Concerning this point R. A. Lundquist, Chief of the Electrical Equipment Division of the Bureau of Foreign and Domestic Commerce, says:[1]

A growing interest in radio is evidenced in many foreign countries, by revision of laws and removal of restrictions on broadcasting. While the activity in amateur radio work and in broadcasting is greatest in the United States, marked advancement has been made abroad in the last year.

The development abroad has had its greatest growth in Europe. The broadcasting of programs of entertainment and news is on a rather regular basis in the British Isles, France, Germany, Sweden, Switzerland, Holland, Belgium, Denmark, and Czechoslovakia; while in Italy, Finland, Spain, and Austria programs are sent out at irregular periods with a decided likelihood of regular schedules being adopted later. Some sales of long-range sets to pick up British and French stations have been made in other countries of Europe.

In South America, Argentina stands out as having made the greatest progress in the dissemination of music and other entertainment by radio telephony, with Chile also maintaining regular broadcasting service. Regular services were also maintained in Brazil, for a time, and will, undoubtedly, be reestablished eventually. Uruguay, as a result of broadcasting from Buenos Aires, has shown considerable interest in radio, and in Peru arrangements are going forward toward the establishment of regular service.

Australia and New Zealand have each displayed much interest in the new art, and in view of the recent lifting of hampering regulations in Australia, a marked expansion in radio interest in that country may be looked for. In the Orient little has as yet taken place, though intermittent broadcasting is being provided in India and Ceylon. In Japan adequate legislation has been enacted, making provision for the establishment of broadcasting stations. In China radio is technically barred under an embargo, forbidding the entry of anything usable as war material, but in the British port of Hongkong and in the international settlement of Shanghai some broadcasting has been done.

[1]"World-Wide Interest in Radio," *Commerce Reports,* September 22, 1924.

In no foreign country is the use of radio receiving sets as free and unrestricted as in the United States. Even in Canada users of receiving sets must pay a nominal license fee, while in some countries the restrictions imposed and the license fees assessed are onerous. In Canada the charge is only $1 per annum, but in England it is 10s (about $2.45 at par); in South Africa, £2 (about $9.75); in Germany, 24 gold marks (about $5.85); in Japan, an annual license fee of 2 yen ($1) is provided for; in the Irish Free State, 20s (about $4.85); in Sweden, 3.50 crowns ($0.95); in India, 10 rupees ($3.25); in Australia, 25 to 35s ($6.10 to $8.50), depending upon the zone in which the receiving set is installed.

While most of the countries that have enacted legislation on radio telephony during the past year or two have established a certain wave band, not varying widely from that in the United States, which must be used for private broadcasting, a number of European stations are at wave lengths greater than those in use in this country and for which American sets are designed. The Eiffel Tower, for instance, uses 2,600 meters, while the Radiola Station in France uses 1,780 meters. Certain other well-known European stations broadcast at wave lengths of from 1,000 to 3,000 meters. The English stations of the British Broadcasting Company, however, operate at wave lengths between 350 and 450 meters, while new German stations, Belgian stations, Swedish stations, and others being promoted in Europe, also appear to be adopting wave lengths more in accordance with American practice. An exception to the European tendency is found in Australia, where the recent regulations provide for a broadcasting wave band between 250 and 2,000 meters, and where the principal existing broadcasting station operates at 1,100 meters.

The home market situation and research in the development of equipment for the reception of radio broadcasting have given the United States almost a preeminent position in the radio telephone field, when due consideration is given to quality, reliability, and simplicity of product. American manufacturers are undersold by German and French manufacturers in many markets, but as a rule it is found that the quality of such sets is not equal to that of ours and that the price margin enjoyed by them is not commensurate with this difference of quality. Some business will always be done on a purely price basis, but the quality of American equipment will bring a steady and satisfactory volume of sales from practically all markets. American manufacturers are able to meet the demands of foreign buyers of radio equipment as efficiently and economically as the manufacturers of any other nation.

A potential field exists for the sale of high-class radio receiving sets to people living in remote regions who are cut off from regular and frequent mail service. The interest shown by plantation owners, mine operators, and ranchers in the interior of India, Ceylon, Central America, South America, Australia, and parts of the East Indies is sufficient to indicate that the field is there. While the potentialities of these fields cannot be developed until better broadcasting is provided at points within a distance that can be regularly and reliably covered by a good modern set, even now in Central America, northern South America, the West Indies, and many of the island groups of the South Seas the high-class American set will enable the isolated planter or mine operator to reach some of the more powerful American stations.

Manufacturers and exporters, it would seem, have become so accustomed to having the merits and possibilities of radio well understood by the potential buying public, as a result of the publicity given radio by the press of this country, that they lose sight of the fact that people in outlying regions do not appreciate fully the possibilities of radio. To develop the use of radio in these outlying sections some method must be developed whereby effective demonstrations can be given. It should not be difficult to arrange for such demonstrations, and it is believed that they will be amply justified by the returns that will be received.

THE RADIO CORPORATION AND THE FUTURE

As mentioned in Chapter III, the Radio Corporation of America made arrangements with British, French, and German radio companies for the development of South America through the so-called A.E.F.G. Trusteeship of nine members. This board, organized for the purpose of carrying on external radio communication from South America later formed the Radio Sud America which was to act for the four companies as the sole and common distributor of radio apparatus in that continent. The latter arrangement (the Radio Sud America) "did not prove sufficiently flexible to enable the participating members to conduct their individual business on a basis best suited to the technical and commercial development of the art and industry in South America."

So it has been canceled. The American Company (as well as the other companies) is now free to carry on its South American selling as it sees fit. There is now a "system giving direct contact with the South American Radio Market from New York, thus eliminating the expense incidental to carrying on operations through intermediate distributing centers. With newly organized outlets forming a part of the distributing circuits, terminating at Buenos Aires, Montevideo, Sao Paulo, Rio de Janeiro, Valparaiso, and other leading cities, every new development in broadcasting apparatus will be made immediately available to South Americans simultaneously with their introduction in the United States."[1] It must be noted that the trusteeship is still in effect for external radio communication from South America.

WORLD WIRELESS BY AND FOR AMERICANS

This is one step in the fulfilment of the Radio Corporation's motto "World-Wide Wireless." Its plan is to develop a cosmopolitan system, owned and operated by Americans. By means of its high-power transmitting stations on the Atlantic Coast and its receiving station at Riverhead, Long Island, this company is now in continuous communication through one centralized control with Poland, Great Britain, France, Norway, Italy, Sweden, Germany, and points in South America. From Bolinas and San Francisco on the Pacific, this same company sends out messages to Hawaii, the Philippines, and Japan, and will soon, through its connections with the Federal Telegraph Company, extend its range to China. It has encircled the world. Through the vastness of its service, it hopes to provide cheap and efficient communication. Except for the navy high-power stations, this corporation has a monopoly of transatlantic and transpacific radio. Thus, it appears that the competition of the future will not be between the various wireless companies or between the various cable companies, but between the

[1]Statement of President J. G. Harbord of the Radio Corporation of America in New York *Times*, July 24, 1924.

radio as one system and the cable as another. There will be room for both. They will supplement, not supplant, each other.

The Radio Corporation of America has also developed an extensive marine service. By virtue of their control of the vacuum tube through the cross-licensing agreements, it and its associated companies are a powerful factor in the marine field.[1] They have made for the great efficiency of the ship-to-shore wireless. The expiration of the patents on the vacuum bulb may facilitate future competition in marine traffic. Thus, to a certain extent independent companies will be able to equip ships with this device.[2]

THE "BIG FOUR" AND BROADCASTING

In broadcasting, also, the Radio Corporation of America will take an important part, unless a system of government-owned, super-power stations is installed. This corporation and its associated companies conduct a system of broadcasting stations which blanket the entire territory east of the Mississippi River. The General Electric Company has also established large stations at Denver, Colorado, and Oakland, California. Through their control of the essential patents, these companies will probably maintain their important position.

In the radio manufacturing field a state of competition should continue to exist. There are upwards of 3,000 radio manufacturers in the United States. More than 200 con-

---

[1] The Radio Corporation of America has shore stations on both Atlantic and Pacific Coasts. The Independent Wireless Telegraph Company maintains such (shore-to-ship) stations on the Atlantic Coast, while the Kilbourne and Clarke Mfg. Co., a subsidiary of the Ship Owners' Radio Service Co., maintains stations on the Pacific Coast. On November 10, 1923, the R. C. A. furnished the radio service on 122 ships of the Emergency Fleet Corporation; the Ship Owners' Radio Service (Inc.), 156; and the Independent Wireless Telegraph Co., 123 ships; the last named maintaining a radio service in 1923 on a total of 750 vessels. See *Report of Federal Trade Commission on Radio Industry*, p. 34, and *Commerce Yearbook*, 1923, p. 418. The Radio Corporation furnished the service on more than 700 vessels during 1924.

[2] See Chapter XII.

cerns are engaged in the manufacture and sale of complete
sets without tubes, and about 500 are manufacturing parts
and devices necessary and useful in radio. "Replies received
in answer to a questionnaire sent to a number of manufacturers of radio apparatus indicate that their business has
increased in the first half of 1923 anywhere from 25% to
100% over the business done for the same period in 1922."[1]

The situation in the Orient, especially China, is confusing.
British, French, American, Japanese, and Danish companies
hold concessions in that nation for international wireless
communication. Here there is apt to be a great deal of
duplication, unless some combination among these competing companies is effected. Mr. Marconi reported in 1923
that the British, French, and Japanese had combined to
build a high-power station at Peking, which by the end of
that year was practically complete.

SERVICE PLANS OF THE MARCONI COMPANY

The British Marconi Company has also for a long time
had world-wide wireless as its ideal and ambition. This
plan bids fair to be realized. At the twenty-seventh annual
meeting, Senatore Marconi stated (August 15, 1924): "It
is not too much to say that the prospects are brighter today
than they have been at any previous period in the history
of the company. For the last 14 years, at least, your directors have realized that this company's main objective must
be the creation of a world-wide wireless telegraph service.
Today your directors are able to say with some confidence
that there is every probability of that ideal being realized."[2]

The reasons for Marconi's optimism may be summarized
as follows:

1. The consummation of a new agreement with the English Post-Office Department, whereby it was provided that
the Marconi Company should erect for the government the

---

[1] Quotation, *Federal Trade Commission Report*, p. 38.
[2] London *Times*, August 16, 1924.

necessary stations in Great Britain at a profit of 10%, plus 5% overhead charges—a sort of a cost-plus system. In addition, the company is to receive a royalty of 6¼% on the total wireless receipts of the government stations. The reader will remember that a 10% royalty was provided for in the ill-fated agreement of 1912. This new agreement deals only with the wireless telegraph services between Great Britain and the rest of the Empire.

These stations are to be erected for the operation of the so-called "beam" system, on which Mr. Marconi has done a large amount of experimental work. While the government, through the company, will be erecting the necessary stations at home, the company, through its associates, will be erecting reciprocal stations in Canada, India, South Africa, and Australia. These stations will be operated by the appropriate associated companies, in which the original company has a substantial interest. The Canadian Marconi is well advanced with work on the beam station at Montreal, which will communicate with England and Australia. The beam station near Cape Town is expected to be ready for trials in September, 1925. The Melbourne station will be completed in September, 1926, and the one in India will be ready for business about the middle of the year 1926.[1]

2. The recent securing of concessions from a large number of foreign governments. An agreement was made in 1922 between the Australian Government and the Amalgamated Wireless, Limited, a company which has an exclusive license for the use of all Marconi patents in the Australian territory, and in which the British company has a substantial interest. The Amalgamated Company agreed to establish direct communication between Australia and other British territory. In order to meet the wishes of those who say that wireless shall remain under government control, the Australian Government holds more than one-half of

[1]Annual statement of British Postmaster-General to the House of Commons July 20, 1925, quoted in the 1924 *Report of the Directors* of Marconi's Wireless Telegraph Company, Limited, as presented at the annual meeting on July 31, 1925.

the shares.   During the year 1923, the Marconi Company
secured concessions from Austria, Portugal, Greece, South
Africa, Canada, India, Ireland, and other countries.[1]

3. Decreased cost of wireless service, whereby it is hoped
that rates will be able to be further lowered. This, it is
predicted by Mr. Marconi, will come about through the
adoption of the beam system, some of the advantages of
which are comparative freedom from atmospheric interference, reduced capital costs, and lower costs of operation.
By means of this system, day and night communication is
maintained between England and Australia at less than 5%
of the cost of the high wave length stations.

RADIO AND THE FUTURE

Considering the world situation, it is probable that the
radio industry has not reached the saturation point, for it
has not yet fulfilled the promise of its possibilities.   The
very existence of commerce and civilization is dependent on
the means of communication.   Take away the telegraph and
the telephone, the cable and the wireless, the steamship, the
train, and the automobile, the trolley, and the aeroplane,
and civilization and commerce would be set back by more
than a hundred years.

Radio will facilitate a closer and more accurate adjustment of prices between markets.   The more rapid and efficient the means of communication, the greater will be the
velocity of commerce and the smaller the margin of profit
on each transaction.   The practice of arbitrage or profit on
foreign exchange exists in spite of, and because of, our rapid
cable and wireless systems.   With the development of better
and cheaper world communication, this profit may tend to
become smaller and smaller.   Good systems of wireless will
permit the owners of cargoes in transit to deflect their ships
from points where prices are low to points where they are
high.   Thus, in non-perishable and standardized commodi-

[1]See London *Times*, December 4, 1923.

ties there will be a close adjustment of prices the world over. Wireless is permitting the efficient functioning of industries which would otherwise be seriously handicapped. Forced into it by the unfavorable conditions in the tropics for land line communication, the United Fruit Company has built up an extensive and efficient radio service.

Radio is one of the greatest educational forces the world has ever seen. Through the broadcasting of lectures on subjects of popular importance and interest, through the dissemination of reports, instruction, and entertainment to the housewife and the farmer, through the popularization of opera and music, through the spreading of the gospel, and through the performance of many other services, radio is becoming a potent socializing factor.

One hundred and ten years ago several thousand British soldiers died in vain at the battle of New Orleans three months after the signing of the treaty of peace. Today Japan is stricken with an earthquake, and within a few hours messages of sympathy and material expression of good-will are pouring in from all parts of the world. A president and an ex-president of the United States pass away, and within a few hours messages of condolence from all sections are received by the bereaved family and nation.

Too much international and internal strife is the result of "active ignorance." Efficient means of communication by encouraging commercial intercourse, by dispelling the smug complacencies and pharisaical self-righteousness of isolated people and nations, and by spreading the gospel of sympathy and mutuality of interests, should, if properly utilized, make for that tolerance which, in the final analysis, is the basis of a permanent world peace.

APPENDIX

APPENDIX

VIEWS OF PROMINENT EXPERTS AS TO PLACE AND FUTURE OF RADIO

HERBERT HOOVER
Secretary of Commerce

Telegraphic [wireless] communication may be conducted from individual to individual and is highly adapted for personal communication parallel with and competing with our other forms of electrical communication.....

Telephonic [wireless] communication, however, is impossible between individuals from the point of view of public interest, as there are a very limited number of wave lengths which can be applied for this purpose and the greater usefulness of the available wave bands for broadcasting communication inhibits their use for personal communication.[1]

DR. J. H. DELLINGER
United States Bureau of Standards

Since there is not room for all of the radio transmissions desired, it is recognized that those uses of radio must be given precedence which give service that can be obtained through no other means of communication. Thus, advertising need not be done by radio, inasmuch as that kind of service is covered by the newspapers and the mail; and, generally speaking, no communication between two individuals on land should be carried on by radio, inasmuch as they can use the ordinary telephone for that.[2]

DR. ALFRED GOLDSMITH
Director of Research of Radio Corporation of America

The great bulk of communication is now carried on by wire methods. There is no question but that wire transmission must always carry the bulk of the communication, particularly in the well settled and highly developed parts of the world, where its

[1]Hearings before Merchant Marine and Fisheries on H. R. 7357, p. 8.

[2]*Lefax,* March, 1923, p. 22, quoted in *Amrad Radio Products,* 1923, pp. 80-82.

methods permit the setting up of reliable and economical paths for carrying a tremendous number of messages without mutual interference.

In another connection he says:

So far as economic and service possibilities are concerned, the guided systems of wire communication promise the more important future developments in the field of normal overland communication, although there is no doubt that a valuable service of increasing magnitude will be furnished by radio communication. In the field of overseas communication, it is believed that for some time there will be very helpful coordination of cable and radio communication to the advantage of each and with a resultant improved service to the public. There is probably no field where cooperation between the various agencies is more important than in the field of universal communication.[1]

BRITISH RADIO BOARD
Subcommittee on Radio Telegraphy

All the witnesses that we have examined agree that for the transmission of a specific message over any distance—long or short—the radio telephone is greatly inferior to the radio telegraph in accuracy, speed, and cost; and is likely to remain so.... We consider, therefore, that the spheres of utility of the two systems are as separate and clearly defined as those of land line telephony and telegraphy.[2]

CHARLES BRIGHT
The Famous Cable Engineer

My own view is that cable and wireless telegraphy each has its independent uses. While we require more cables, I am also in favor of wireless telegraphy as an auxiliary service. I would indeed supplement every inter-imperial cable by some wireless system, thereby affording a convenient test for the relative merits of cables and of different wireless systems.[3]

DEPARTMENT OF COMMERCE
Conference on Radio Telephony, 1922

In view of the demand for broadcast service by the general

[1] Serial article, "World Communication," in *Telegraph and Telephone Age,* January-February, 1922.

[2] *Report,* 1922, p. 3.

[3] "Cable versus Wireless Telegraphy," *Nineteenth Century and After,* June, 1912, p. 1088.

public, it is not desirable to disseminate information over wide areas for the purposes of point-to-point communication, except where that communication cannot be effectively maintained otherwise.

The conference is of the opinion that the use of radio communication for point-to-point communication over land in most cases constitutes an uneconomic use of the available wave bands and it is recommended that at the present state of the art such communication should be carried on by some other means, in so far as possible.[1]

J. J. CARTY
Vice-President of the American Telephone and Telegraph Company

As a result of exhaustive researches too extensive to describe here, it has been ascertained that the function of the wireless telephone is not to do away with the use of wires, but rather to be employed in situations where wires are not available or practicable, such as between ship and ship, ship and shore, and across large bodies of water. The ether is a universal conductor for wireless telephone and telegraph impulses and must be used in common by all who wish to employ those agencies of communication. In the case of the wireless telegraph, the number of messages which may be sent simultaneously is much restricted. In the case of the wireless telephone, owing to the thousands of separate wave lengths required for the transmission of speech, the number of telephone conversations which may be carried on at the same time is still further restricted and is so small that all who can employ wires will find it necessary to do so, leaving the ether available for those who have no other means of communication.[2]

THEODORE N. VAIL
Late President of the American Telephone and Telegraph Company

Wireless telephony can be compared to an attempt to carry on all telephone exchange business over one great conductor connecting every one, and over which all telegraph, all artificial electrical disturbances caused by transmission of power lines, and all the natural electrical disturbances are in free play at the same time. These are the conditions which govern radiograph activity and limit its possibilities.[3]

[1]From *Radio Service Bulletin*, May, 1922.

[2]Speech delivered in Philadelphia on May 17, 1916, shortly after the first transcontinental radio telephone conversation had been carried on from Washington, quoted in Appendix of Towers, *Masters of Space*.

[3]*Scientific American Supplement*, March 4, 1916, p. 155.

David Sarnoff
Vice-President and General Manager of the Radio Corporation of America

The practical vision of the future of radio does not include the scrapping of undersea cable systems; radio will supplement, rather than supplant, the cables. In the first place, experience has shown that new inventions usually result in the improvement of previously existing methods. In the second place, communication facilities have always been inadequate—just as new subways never quite relieve congestion. . . .

In some measure, the same considerations apply to the future prospects of radio telephony over land. In the mobile services, in connecting up isolated communities, and the shore with the sea, there is a rich field for development. That radio will supplant the wire telephone is not to be contemplated. Wire telephone communication, as we know it today, has the greatest utility for the type of service rendered. It is a wonderfully developed and complete system for seeking out for the user, through a wire network and the central exchange personnel, the particular individual wanted. This entire system would have to be duplicated to establish radio telephony on a parity in usefulness; and even if this were technically practicable with radio telephony—which it is not—there is no economic justification for such duplication. The radio telephone, on the other hand, has a large sphere reserved for it in reaching locations where wires cannot be placed or maintained, in spanning inland waters or connecting up islands off the coast. As a supplement to wire telephony alone, radio is assured of a great future.[1]

Newcomb Carlton
President of the Western Union Telegraph Company

The radio is not yet an equal rival of the cables and probably never will be. It is, and probably will continue to be, a valuable adjunct to the cables.[2]

[1]New York *Sunday Herald*, May 14, 1922.
[2]*Radio Broadcast*, September, 1922, p. 376.

IMPORTANT EVENTS IN RADIO[1]

1827—Savary found that a steel needle could be magnetized by the discharge from a Leyden jar.

1831—Farady discovered electromagnetic induction between two entirely separate circuits.

1837—The first patent for an electric telegraph was taken out by Cooke and Wheatstone (London) and by Morse (United States).

1838—Steinheil discovered the use of the earth return.

1840—Henry first produced high frequency electric oscillations and pointed out that the discharge of a condenser is oscillatory.

1842—Morse made wireless experiments by electric conduction through water.

1843—Lindsay suggested that if it were possible to provide stations not more than 20 miles apart all the way across the Atlantic there would be no need of laying a cable.

1845—Lindsay made experiments in transmitting messages across the River Tay by means of electricity or magnetism without submerging wires, using the water as a conductor.

1849—Wilkins revived the same suggestions for wireless telegraphy.
Dr. O'Shaughnessy succeeded in passing intelligible signals without metallic conduction across a river 4,200 feet wide.

1862—Heyworth patented a method of conveying electric signals without the intervention of any continuous artificial conductor.

1867—Maxwell read a paper before the Royal Society in which he laid down the theory of electromagnetism, which he developed more fully in 1873 in his great treatise on electricity and magnetism. He predicted the existence of the electric waves that are now used in wireless telegraphy.

1870—Von Bezold discovered that oscillations set up by a condenser discharge in a conductor give rise to interference phenomena.

1872—Highton made various experiments across the River Thames with Morse's method.

1879—Hughes discovered the phenomena on which depends the action of the coherer. The coherer was later used practically by Marconi.

1880—Trowbridge found that signaling might be carried on over

---

[1] *Radio Service Bulletin,* March, 1924. The reader will also find chronologies in the various editions of the *Yearbook of Wireless Telegraphy and Telephony.*

considerable distances by electric conduction through the earth or water between places not metallically connected.

1882—Bell's experiments with Trowbridge method on the Potomac River resulted in the detection of signals at a distance of 1½ miles.

Professor Dolbear was awarded a United States patent in March, 1882, for wireless apparatus in connection with which he made the statement that "electrical communication, using this apparatus, might be established between points certainly more than one-half mile apart, but how much farther I cannot say." It appeared that Professor Dolbear made an approach to the method that was, subsequently in the hands of Marconi, to be crowned with success.

1883—Fitzgerald suggested a method of producing electromagnetic waves in space by the discharge of a conductor.

1885—Edison, assisted by Gillilaud, Phelps, and Smith, worked out a system of communication between railway stations and moving trains by means of induction and without the use of conducting wires. Edison took out only one patent on long-distance telegraphy without wires. The application was filed May 23, 1885, at the time he was working on induction telegraphy, but the patent (No. 465,971) was not issued until December 29, 1891. In 1903 it was purchased from him by the Marconi Wireless Telegraph Co.

Preece made experiments at Newcastle-on-Tyne which showed that in two completely insulated circuits of square form, each side being 440 yards, placed a quarter of a mile apart, telephonic speech was conveyed from one to the other by induction.

1886—Dolbear patented a plan for establishing wireless communication by means of two insulated elevated plates, but there is no evidence that the method proposed by him did, or could, effect the transmission of signals between stations separated by any distance.

1887—Hertz showed that electromagnetic waves are in complete accordance with the waves of light and heat, and founded the theory upon which all modern radio signaling devices are based.

Heaviside established communication by telephonic speech between the surface of the earth and the subterranean galleries of the Broom-hill Collieries, 350 feet deep, by laying above and below ground two complete metallic circuits, each about 2¼ miles in length, and parallel to each other.

1889—Thompson suggested that electric waves were particularly suitable for the transmission of signals through fogs and material objects.

1891—Trowbridge suggested that by means of magnetic induction between two separate and completely insulated circuits communication could be effected between distances.

1892—Preece adopted a method which united both conduction and induction as the means of affecting one circuit by the current in another. In this way he established communication between two points on the Bristol Channel and at Lochness in Scotland.

Stevenson, of the Northern Lighthouse Board, Edinburgh, advocated the use of an inductive system for communication between the mainland and isolated lighthouses.

Branly devised an appliance for detecting electromagnetic waves, which was known as a coherer.

1894—Rathenau experimented with a conductive system of wireless telegraphy and signaled through 3 miles of water.

1895—Smith established communication by conduction with the lighthouse on the Fastnet.

Marconi's investigations led him to the conclusion that Hertzian waves could be used for telegraphing without wires.

1896—Marconi lodged his application for the first British patent for wireless telegraphy. He conducted experiments in communicating over a distance of 1¾ miles successfully.

The first demonstration of directional wireless using reflectors was given in England. Experiments were conducted to determine the relative speed of propagation of light waves and the electric vibrations which actuated a receiver at a distance of 1½ miles between reflectors.

1897—March: Marconi demonstrated communication being established over a distance of 4 miles.

March 17: Balloons were first used for the suspension of wireless aerials.

July 10-18: Marconi maintained communication between the shore and a ship at sea at distances up to 10 miles.

September and October: Apparatus was erected at Bath, England, and signals received from Salisbury, 34 miles distant.

November 1: First Marconi station erected at the Needles, Alum Bay, Isle of Wight. Experiments were conducted covering a range of 14½ miles.

December 6: Signals transmitted from shore to a ship at sea, 18 miles distant.

December 7: First floating wireless station was completed.

1898—June 3: The first paid radiogram was transmitted from the Needles (Isle of Wight) station.

July 20-22: Events of the Kingstown regatta in Dublin reported by wireless for Dublin newspaper from steamer *Flying Huntress*.

1899—April 22: The first French gunboat was fitted with wireless telegraph apparatus at Boulogne.

July: During the naval manœuvres three British warships equipped with Marconi apparatus interchanged messages at distances up to 74 nautical miles (about 85 land miles).

The international yacht races which took place in September and October were reported by wireless telegraphy for the New York *Herald*. At the conclusion of the races series of trials were made between the United States cruiser *New York* and the battleship *Massachusetts*, signals being exchanged between the vessels at distances up to 36 miles. On the return journey from America Marconi fitted the steamship *St. Paul* with his apparatus, and on November 15 established communication with the Needles station when 36 miles away. Reports of the progress of the war in South Africa were telegraphed to the vessel and published in a leaflet entitled *The Transatlantic Times*, printed on board.

1900—February 18: The first German commercial wireless station was opened on Borkum Island.

February 28: The first German liner fitted with wireless apparatus communicated with Borkum Island over a range of 60 miles.

November 2: The first wireless land station in Belgium was finished at Lapanne.

Between 1900 and 1905 Dr. DeForest was granted numerous patents in the United States and other countries for inventions connected with wireless telegraphy.

1901—January 1: The bark *Medora* was reported by wireless as waterlogged on Ratel Bank. Assistance was immediately sent.

January 19: The *Princesse Clementine* ran ashore, and news of the accident was telegraphed to Ostend by wireless.

February 11: Communication was established between Niton Station, Isle of Wight, and the Lizard Station, a distance of 196 miles.

March 1: A public wireless telegraph service was inaugurated between the five principal islands of the Hawaiian group; namely Oahu, Kauai, Molaki, Maui, and Hawaii.

October 15: The first fan aerials were erected for experiments between Poldhu and Newfoundland.

December 12: The letter "S" was received by Marconi from Poldhu, England, at St. Johns, Newfoundland, a distance of 1,800 miles.

Professor R. A. Fessenden applied for United States patent on September 28 for "Improvements in apparatus for the wireless transmission of electromagnetic wave, said improvements relating more especially to the transmission and reproduction of words or other audible signals." It appears that in connection with this apparatus there was contemplated the use of an alternating-current generator having a frequency of 50,000 cycles per second. Professor Fessenden was granted a number of United States patents between 1899 and 1905 covering devices used in connection with radiotelegraphy.

1901-1904—During this period Dr. John Stone was granted more than 70 United States patents covering radiotelegraphy.

1901-1905—More than 40 United States patents were granted to Harry Shoemaker covering certain apparatus used for radio communication.

1902—February: Steamship *Philadelphia*, American Line, received messages a distance of 1,551½ statute miles and received Morse signals up to a distance of 2,099 statute miles from Poldhu Station, Cornwall, England.

June 25: The first moving wire magnetic detector actuated by clockwork was installed on the Italian cruiser *Carlo Alberto*.

July 14-16: Marconi received messages from Poldhu on the Italian cruiser *Carlo Alberto*, lying at Cape Skagen, a distance of 800 miles; and at Kronstadt, 1,600 miles.

December: On the seventeenth the first wireless message was transmitted across the Atlantic. On the eighteenth wireless messages were despatched from Cape Breton Station to King Edward VII.

1903—January 19: President Roosevelt sent a transatlantic radiogram to King Edward via Cape Cod and Poldhu stations.

March 30: First transoceanic radiogram was published in the London Times.

August 4: First International Radiotelegraphic Conference was held at Berlin.

Poulsen patented the improved arc oscillation generator, using a hydrocarbon atmosphere and a magnetic field.

1904—January 20: The first press message was transmitted across the Atlantic.

August 15: The wireless telegraph act of Great Britain was passed.

November 16: Dr. J. Ambrose Fleming took out his original patent No. 24,850 for thermionic valves.

1905—In October of this year erection of Clifden, Ireland, high-power radio station was commenced.

1906—Dr. DeForest was granted a patent on January 18 for a vacuum rectifier, commercially known as the audion.

Second International Radiotelegraphic Convention was held at Berlin, and a convention was signed by a majority of the principal countries of the world.

Dunwoody discovered the rectifying properties of carborundum crystals and Pickard discovered the similar properties of silicon crystals. These discoveries formed the basis of the widely used crystal detectors.

1907—October 17: Transatlantic stations at Clifden and Glace Bay were opened for limited public service.

1908—February 3: Transatlantic radio stations were opened to the general public for the transmission between the United Kingdom and the principal towns in Canada.

In carrying out his invention Professor Fessenden constructed a high-frequency alternator with an output of 2.5 kilowatts at 225 volts and with a frequency of 70,000 cycles per second. Later Professor Fessenden reported successful wireless telephonic communication between his station located at Brant Rock, Massachusetts, and Washington, D. C., a distance of about 600 miles.

1909—The steamship *Republic,* after colliding with the steamship *Florida* off the coast of the United States on January 23, succeeded in calling assistance by wireless, with the result that all her passengers and crew were saved before the vessel sank.

1910—The steamship *Principessa Mafalda* received messages from Clifden at a distance of 4,000 miles by day and 6,735 miles by night. On April 23 the Marconi transatlantic (Europe-America) service was opened.

June 24: Act approved by the United States Government requiring radio equipment and operators on certain passenger-carrying vessels.

1911—July 1: Radio service organized in Department of Commerce and Labor to enforce the act of June 24, 1910.

1912—F. A. Kolster, of the Bureau of Standards, invented and developed the Kolster decremeter, which is used to make direct measurements of wave length and logarithmic decrement. This instrument has been used by the radio service of the Department of Commerce since it was invented.

Early in the year the Marconi Company absorbed the United Wireless Company, of the United States.

In February the Marconi Company procured the patents of Bellini and Tosi, including those for the wireless direction finder.

On February 9 the Australian Commonwealth station was opened.

On April 15 the steamship *Titanic,* on her maiden voyage, struck an iceberg and sank, but, owing to the prompt wireless call for assistance, the lives of more than 700 of her passengers were saved.

The International Radiotelegraphic Conference opened in London on June 4 and approved important regulations to have uniformity of practice in wireless telegraph services. On July 5 the International Radiotelegraphic Convention was signed at London.

July 23: Act approved by the United States Government extending act of June 24, 1910, to cover cargo vessels and requiring auxiliary source of power, efficient communications between the radio room and the bridge, and two or more skilled radio operators in charge of the apparatus on certain passenger-carrying vessels.

August 13: Act approved by the United States Government licensing radio operators and transmitting stations.

1913—F. A. Kolster submitted to the government a paper pointing out the advantages of certain applications of radio signaling for use at lighthouses, light-ships, and life-saving stations, especially in time of fog.

During this year the governments of France and the United States experimented between the Eiffel Tower and Washington by wireless to procure data for comparing the velocity of electromagnetic waves with that of light.

In June a wireless telegraph bill was presented to the Ottawa Parliament and passed under the title "Radiotelegraph Act of Canada."

On October 11 the *Volturno* was burned in mid-Atlantic, and in response to the wireless appeal 10 vessels came to the rescue, 521 lives being saved.

On November 24 the first practical trials with wireless apparatus on trains were made on a train belonging to the Delaware, Lackawanna and Western Railroad.

The station at Macquerie Island was the means of keeping Doctor Mauson, the Australian explorer, in touch with the outer world. Radio dispatches were published in a small journal which was established, called the *Adelle Blizzard*.

November 12: Safety at Sea Conference held in London. At this conference the use of radio received appropriate consideration.

November 24: The first practical trials with wireless apparatus on trains were made, messages having been received and transmitted on board trains.

1914—Experiments in wireless telephony were carried out between several vessels lying at anchor five-eighths of a mile apart, ordinary receivers being used with success. The wireless telegraph experiments were continued between two warships on the high seas, and the reception was consistently good over a distance of 18½ miles. Successful wireless telephone communications were effected later, using only very limited energy between vessels on the high seas 44 miles apart. These experiments were repeated where land intervened between the communicating vessels, and in this case again excellent results were obtained. On this day radiotelephonic communication was constantly maintained for 12 hours.

On April 15, at Godalming, a memorial was unveiled to the memory of Jack Philips, chief radio operator of the ill-fated *Titanic,* who died at his post when the vessel foundered in mid-Atlantic on April 15, 1912.

A new departure in the application of radiotelegraphy to the safety of life at sea was the equipment of the motor lifeboats of the steamship *Aquitania* with radio apparatus.

High-powered transoceanic stations were completed at Carnarvon, Wales, Belmar, Honolulu, and San Francisco during the autumn of

1914. The.Honolulu–San Francisco stations were opened to public service September 24. The Tuckerton-Eilvese and Sayville-Nauen stations were in operation about this time.

Most of these stations made use of the latest developments in the art, using undamped and long waves as produced by the Poulsen arc and the radio frequency alternator.

On October 6 E. H. Armstrong was issued a patent covering the regenerative circuit, also known as the feed-back and the self-heterodyne circuit.

1915—During this year F. A. Kolster, of the Bureau of Standards, developed a radiocompass said to be more effective than that which was being used.

On February 20 the Panama-Pacific Exhibition at San Francisco was officially opened by President Wilson at Washington, through the medium of wireless telegraphy.

On May 12, in Battery Park, New York City, the mayor unveiled the monument in memory of wireless operators who had lost their lives at the post of duty.

On July 27 wireless communication between the United States and Japan was effected. Two terminal stations were located at San Francisco and Funabashi, near Tokio, and the messages were relayed through Honolulu.

On July 28 the American Telephone and Telegraph Company, working in conjunction with the Western Electric Company, succeeded in telephoning the wireless across the American continent from Arlington to Hawaii, a distance of nearly 5,000 miles.

On October 26 the wireless telephone experiments were continued, communication being effected across the Atlantic from Arlington to the Eiffel Tower, Paris.

During this year ship service was greatly improved through the installation of new equipment, embodying features of great practical value, by various operating companies. Efficient emergency radio transmitters came into wider use, owing considerably to the efforts of the radio service of the Department of Commerce and its refusal to pass inefficient equipment. Such installations considered as essential are safeguards to shippers and the seagoing public.

1916—During the course of severe blizzards in the United States during February wireless telegraphy was extensively used for train dispatching, as the telegraph wires were down.

The determination of the difference in longitude between Paris and Washington with the aid of radio which had been in progress since October, 1913, was completed during May, the result, expressed in terms of time, being 5 hours 17 minutes 35.67 seconds, and has a probable accuracy of the order of 0.01 second.

The initiation of the newly established transpacific wireless service between the United States and Japan was celebrated on November 5, by an interchange of messages between the Mikado and President Wilson.

1917—June 2 marked the "coming of age" of wireless telegraphy in England, that is, that 21 years elapsed since the registration of patent 12,039 in 1896.

1918—The trend of progress toward the continuous-wave communication as distinct from that by damped waves was very marked during this year, a particular impetus being given by the continued development of the electron tube as an efficient receiver and generator of undamped oscillations. Steady improvement was also evident in the arc form of generator which was installed in many new high-power stations.

Wireless telephony also progressed to a marked extent, particularly in the direction of reliability and increase of range, due mainly to the development of valve generator and receivers.

In the equipment of aircraft with wireless great progress was made, both in radiotelegraphy and radiotelephony.

At the end of the year a high-power station, erected by the United States Government, was opened at Croix d'Hins, near Bordeaux.

In the Argentine the erection of a station destined for direct communication with the North American Continent was commenced in the vicinity of Buenos Aires.

The extension in the application of wireless telegraphy to merchant vessels continued, and at the close of the year some 2,500 to 3,000 vessels of the British Merchant Marine carried installations.

On July 31 the United States Government took over all wireless land stations in the United States, with the exception of certain high-power stations, which remained under the control of commercial companies.

On September 22 messages transmitted from Carnarvon were received in Sydney, 12,000 miles away. Cable confirmations of these messages were sent forward at the same time but were received some hours later than the corresponding radiotelegrams.

In April a high-power station was opened at Stavanger, Norway, for the use of the Norwegian Government. The station communicates with the United States.

1919—The successful transatlantic flights of Alcock and Brown, of the American *NC4*, and of the British dirigible *R34*, during the summer of the year focused attention upon the application of radio for aviation purposes and its great value for aerial navigation.

On June 30, 1919, there were 2,312 ship stations of the United States, having increased from 1,478 on June 30, 1918. At this time new ship stations were increasing at the rate of 100 a month. This increase was due to the great number of vessels built during the war period.

The temporary war measures relative to the installation of wireless telegraph apparatus on all merchant vessels of 1,600 tons or over under the British flag was made permanent by a bill passed by the British Parliament.

In February a Spanish decree was issued to the effect that all sailing vessels of 500 tons or over and carrying 50 or more passengers must be equipped with wireless apparatus.

During the year Radio Corporation took over the radio interests of the American Marconi Company.

The war-time ban on private and experimental wireless stations was removed.

1920—The steady development of continuous-wave wireless work was continued during the year and some further progress made in the commercial application of tube apparatus.

On January 14 a law was passed in Greece making the carrying of wireless apparatus obligatory on all Greek merchant ships of 1,600 tons gross and over, or having 50 or more persons aboard, including crew.

On January 25 a new high-power station was opened at Monte Grande, Argentine, call letters LPZ.

Ameteur radio work in this and other countries progressed steadily during the year with the gradual removal of war-time restrictions.

Bordeaux, France, high-power station opened.

1921—Experiments were carried out in France with successful results in the application of Baudot and similar high-speed telegraph apparatus to radio work.

The Nobel Prize for physics was awarded this year to Professor Edouard Branly for his researches in radio.

The progress made in amateur and experimental wireless is exemplified by the attempts made in February and December of this year to effect communication on short wave lengths between the wireless amateurs of the United States and Great Britain. The first attempt was unsuccessful, but during the second test signals from many American amateur stations were heard both by British radio amateurs and by the representative of the American Radio Relay League who was sent over for the tests. The signals were also heard in Holland.

The American Radio Relay League held its first annual convention in Chicago, August 30—September 3, at which many thousands of amateurs of the United States were present.

The first licenses for broadcasting stations were issued in September.

New York radio central station opened on Long Island.

1922—During this year broadcasting stations increased rapidly in keeping with the great interest taken in the art.

On June 7 E. H. Armstrong read a paper before the Institute of Radio Engineers on some recent developments by him of regenerative circuits. Professor Armstrong was granted a patent for the super-regenerative circuit.

Experiments in radiotelephoning from ship to shore were conducted during this year. In tests from the steamship *America* it was proved possible to communicate with land telephone stations more than 400 miles distant from the ship.

1923—On March 2 L. A. Hazeltine, of Stevens Institute of Technology, presented a paper before the Radio Club of America on tuned radio frequency amplification with neutralization of capacity coupling. Professor Hazeltine was granted a patent for the non-radiating netrodyne receiver.

Great progress was made during the year in the development of vacuum tubes.

Short wave lengths were used to greater advantage than heretofore. The McMillan expedition to the polar regions had radio for their only means of direct communication. Using low power and short wave lengths, their vessel, *Bowdoin,* communicated with several stations in the United States while they were frozen in thousands of miles away. Broadcasting concerts from United States stations were heard during the long dark nights of the artic zone.

During the year foreign countries became interested in radiotelephone broadcasting.

Broadcasting in United States heard in England, and vice versa.

1924—In January radio was used in the region of the Great Lakes during a blizzard for dispatching trains.

An expedition from the United States, under the leadership of Hamilton Rice, which explored the Amazon and Orinoco Rivers in Brazil and Venezuela in the interest of geographical science in general, had radio as their only means of communication.

On February 5 a radio program broadcast in the United States from Pittsburgh station of Westinghouse Electric and Manufacturing Company was received and rebroadcast in England for the benefit of English stations.

On February 23 a concert broadcast by the same station and relayed from London was heard clearly in Calcutta, India.

Roger Babson, economist, estimates that during this year the American people will spend approximately $350,000,000 for radio equipment. Sales of radio equipment are running nearly twice as large as all kinds of sporting goods.

A wireless lighthouse has been set up on an island in the Firth of Forth, Scotland. Wireless waves are concentrated by reflectors into a beam which can be sent 100 miles, giving ships their position in a fog.

INDEX

INDEX

HISTORY OF BROADCASTING:
Radio To Television
An Arno Press/New York Times Collection

Archer, Gleason L.
Big Business and Radio. 1939.

Archer, Gleason L.
History of Radio to 1926. 1938.

Arnheim, Rudolf.
Radio. 1936.

Blacklisting: Two Key Documents. 1952–1956.

Cantril, Hadley and Gordon W. Allport.
The Psychology of Radio. 1935.

Codel, Martin, editor.
Radio and Its Future. 1930.

Cooper, Isabella M.
Bibliography on Educational Broadcasting. 1942.

Dinsdale, Alfred.
First Principles of Television. 1932.

Dunlap, Orrin E., Jr.
Marconi: The Man and His Wireless. 1938.

Dunlap, Orrin E., Jr.
The Outlook for Television. 1932.

Fahie, J. J.
A History of Wireless Telegraphy. 1901.

Federal Communications Commission.
Annual Reports of the Federal Communications Commission.
1934/1935–1955.

Federal Radio Commission.
Annual Reports of the Federal Radio Commission. 1927–1933.

Frost, S. E., Jr.
Education's Own Stations. 1937.

Grandin, Thomas.
The Political Use of the Radio. 1939.

Harlow, Alvin.
Old Wires and New Waves. 1936.

Hettinger, Herman S.
A Decade of Radio Advertising. 1933.

Huth, Arno.
Radio Today: The Present State of Broadcasting. 1942.

Jome, Hiram L.
Economics of the Radio Industry. 1925.

Lazarsfeld, Paul F.
Radio and the Printed Page. 1940.

Lumley, Frederick H.
Measurement in Radio. 1934.

Maclaurin, W. Rupert.
Invention and Innovation in the Radio Industry. 1949.

Radio: Selected A.A.P.S.S. Surveys. 1929–1941.

Rose, Cornelia B., Jr.
National Policy for Radio Broadcasting. 1940.

Rothafel, Samuel L. and Raymond Francis Yates.
Broadcasting: Its New Day. 1925.

Schubert, Paul.
The Electric Word: The Rise of Radio. 1928.

Studies in the Control of Radio: Nos. 1–6. 1940–1948.

Summers, Harrison B., editor.
Radio Censorship. 1939.

Summers, Harrison B., editor.
A Thirty-Year History of Programs Carried on National Radio Networks in the United States, 1926–1956. 1958.

Waldrop, Frank C. and Joseph Borkin.
Television: A Struggle for Power. 1938.

White, Llewellyn.
The American Radio. 1947.

World Broadcast Advertising: Four Reports. 1930–1932.